VENOM
X-MEN
POISON-X

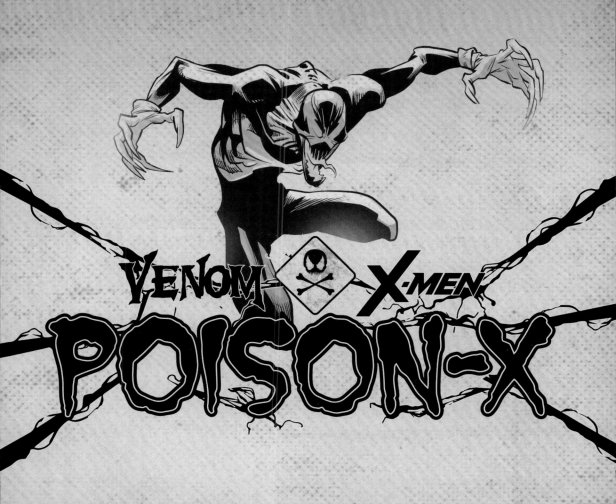

VENOM X-MEN
POISON-X

YEARS AGO, PETER PARKER (A.K.A. THE AMAZING SPIDER-MAN) ACCIDENTALLY BONDED WITH AN ALIEN BEING CALLED A SYMBIOTE. WHEN PETER REALIZED THE COSTUME WAS ACTUALLY AN AGGRESSIVE LIVING ORGANISM, HE REJECTED IT. BUT DURING THEIR TIME TOGETHER, THE SYMBIOTE HAD ACCESS TO SPIDER-MAN'S GENETIC CODE AND NOW GRANTS EDDIE BROCK SKILLS SIMILAR TO SPIDER-MAN'S — WALL-CRAWLING, THE POWER TO GENERATE BIO-ORGANIC WEBBING AND UNIQUE ABILITIES TO SHAPE-SHIFT AND BECOME INVISIBLE — TURNING EDDIE INTO VENOM.

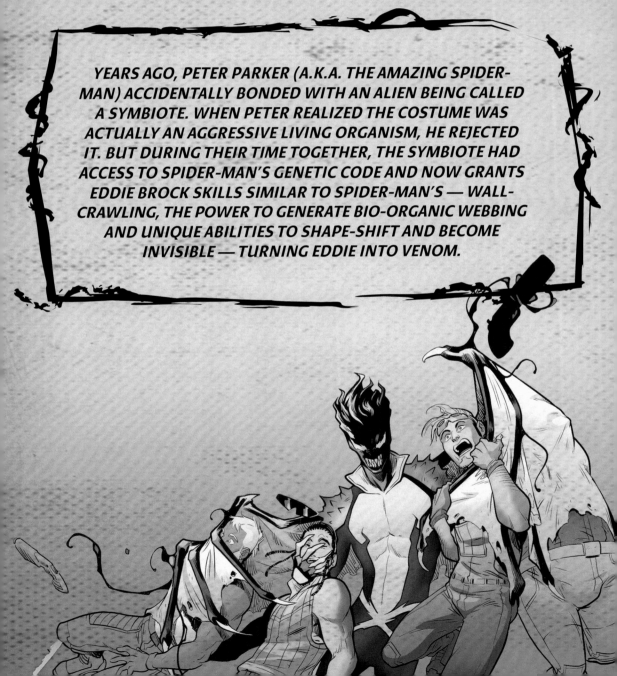

CULLEN BUNN
WRITER

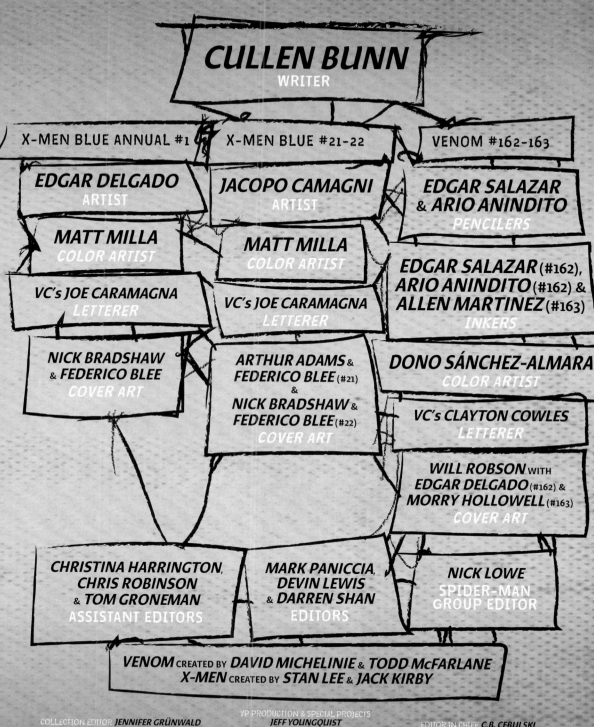

X-MEN BLUE ANNUAL #1

EDGAR DELGADO
ARTIST

MATT MILLA
COLOR ARTIST

VC's JOE CARAMAGNA
LETTERER

NICK BRADSHAW & FEDERICO BLEE
COVER ART

X-MEN BLUE #21-22

JACOPO CAMAGNI
ARTIST

MATT MILLA
COLOR ARTIST

VC's JOE CARAMAGNA
LETTERER

ARTHUR ADAMS & FEDERICO BLEE (#21)
&
NICK BRADSHAW & FEDERICO BLEE (#22)
COVER ART

VENOM #162-163

EDGAR SALAZAR & ARIO ANINDITO
PENCILERS

EDGAR SALAZAR (#162), **ARIO ANINDITO** (#162) & **ALLEN MARTINEZ** (#163)
INKERS

DONO SÁNCHEZ-ALMARA
COLOR ARTIST

VC's CLAYTON COWLES
LETTERER

WILL ROBSON WITH **EDGAR DELGADO** (#162) & **MORRY HOLLOWELL** (#163)
COVER ART

CHRISTINA HARRINGTON, CHRIS ROBINSON & TOM GRONEMAN
ASSISTANT EDITORS

MARK PANICCIA, DEVIN LEWIS & DARREN SHAN
EDITORS

NICK LOWE
SPIDER-MAN GROUP EDITOR

VENOM CREATED BY **DAVID MICHELINIE & TODD McFARLANE**
X-MEN CREATED BY **STAN LEE & JACK KIRBY**

COLLECTION EDITOR JENNIFER GRÜNWALD
ASSISTANT EDITOR CAITLIN O'CONNELL
ASSOCIATE MANAGING EDITOR KATERI WOODY
EDITOR, SPECIAL PROJECTS MARK D. BEAZLEY

VP PRODUCTION & SPECIAL PROJECTS
JEFF YOUNGQUIST
SVP PRINT, SALES & MARKETING
DAVID GABRIEL
BOOK DESIGN
JAY BOWEN WITH ADAM DEL RE

EDITOR IN CHIEF C.B. CEBULSKI
CHIEF CREATIVE OFFICER JOE QUESADA
PRESIDENT DAN BUCKLEY
EXECUTIVE PRODUCER ALAN FINE

VENOM & X-MEN: POISON-X. Contains material originally published in magazine form as X-MEN BLUE #21-22 and ANNUAL #1, and VENOM #162-163. First printing 2018. ISBN 978-1-302-91225-3. Published by MARVEL WORLDWIDE, INC., a subsidiary of MARVEL ENTERTAINMENT, LLC. OFFICE OF PUBLICATION: 135 West 50th Street, New York, NY 10020. Copyright © 2018 MARVEL No similarity between any of the names, characters, persons, and/or institutions in this magazine with those of any living or dead person or institution is intended, and any such similarity which may exist is purely coincidental. **Printed in Canada.** DAN BUCKLEY, President, Marvel Entertainment; JOHN NEE, Publisher; JOE QUESADA, Chief Creative Officer; TOM BREVOORT, SVP of Publishing; DAVID BOGART, SVP of Business Affairs & Operations, Publishing & Partnership; DAVID GABRIEL, SVP of Sales & Marketing, Publishing; JEFF YOUNGQUIST, VP of Production & Special Projects; DAN CARR, Executive Director of Publishing Technology; ALEX MORALES, Director of Publishing Operations; DAN EDINGTON, Managing Editor; SUSAN CRESPI, Production Manager; STAN LEE, Chairman Emeritus. For information regarding advertising in Marvel Comics or on Marvel.com, please contact Vit DeBellis, Custom Solutions & Integrated Advertising Manager, at vdebellis@marvel.com. For Marvel subscription inquiries, please call 888-511-5480. **Manufactured between 3/30/2018 and 5/1/2018 by SOLISCO PRINTERS, SCOTT, QC, CANADA.**

10 9 8 7 6 5 4 3 2 1

X-MEN BLUE ANNUAL 1

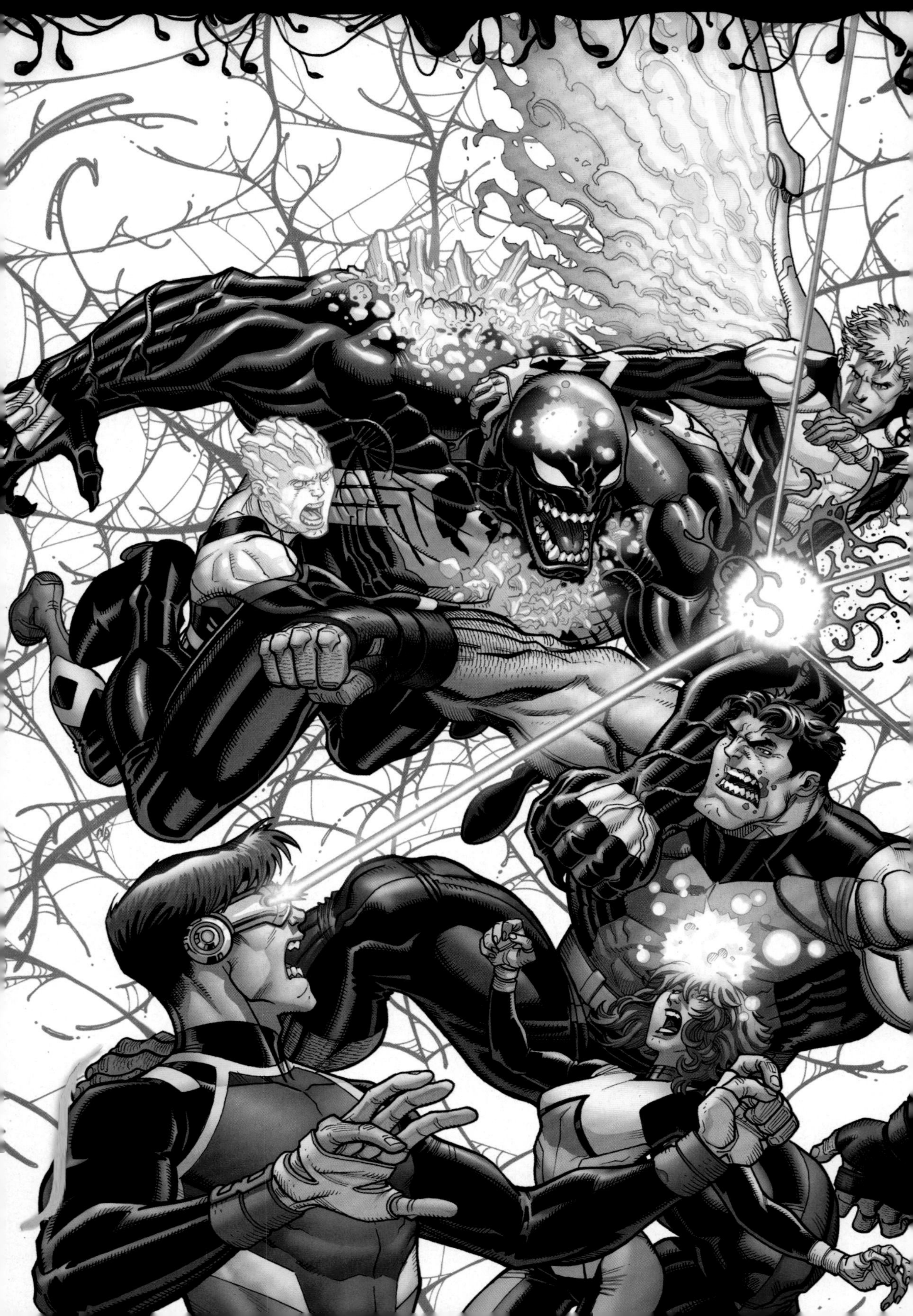

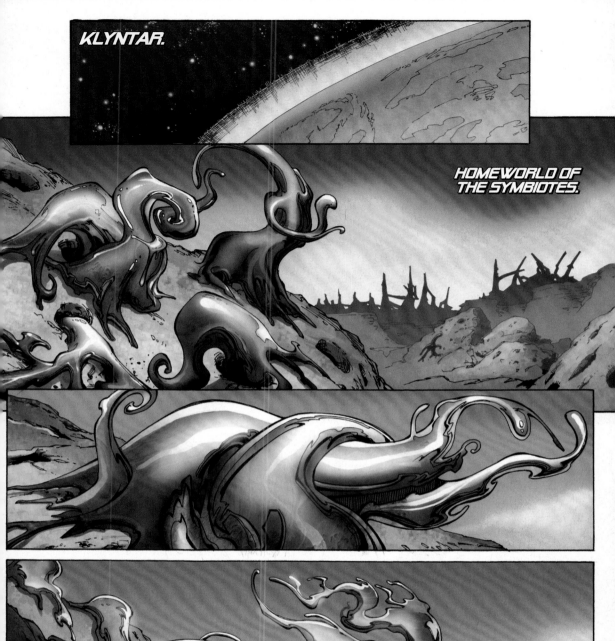

KLYNTAR.

HOMEWORLD OF THE SYMBIOTES.

WELL, WELL, WELL.

LOOKIT WHAT I'VE FOUND FER MESELF.

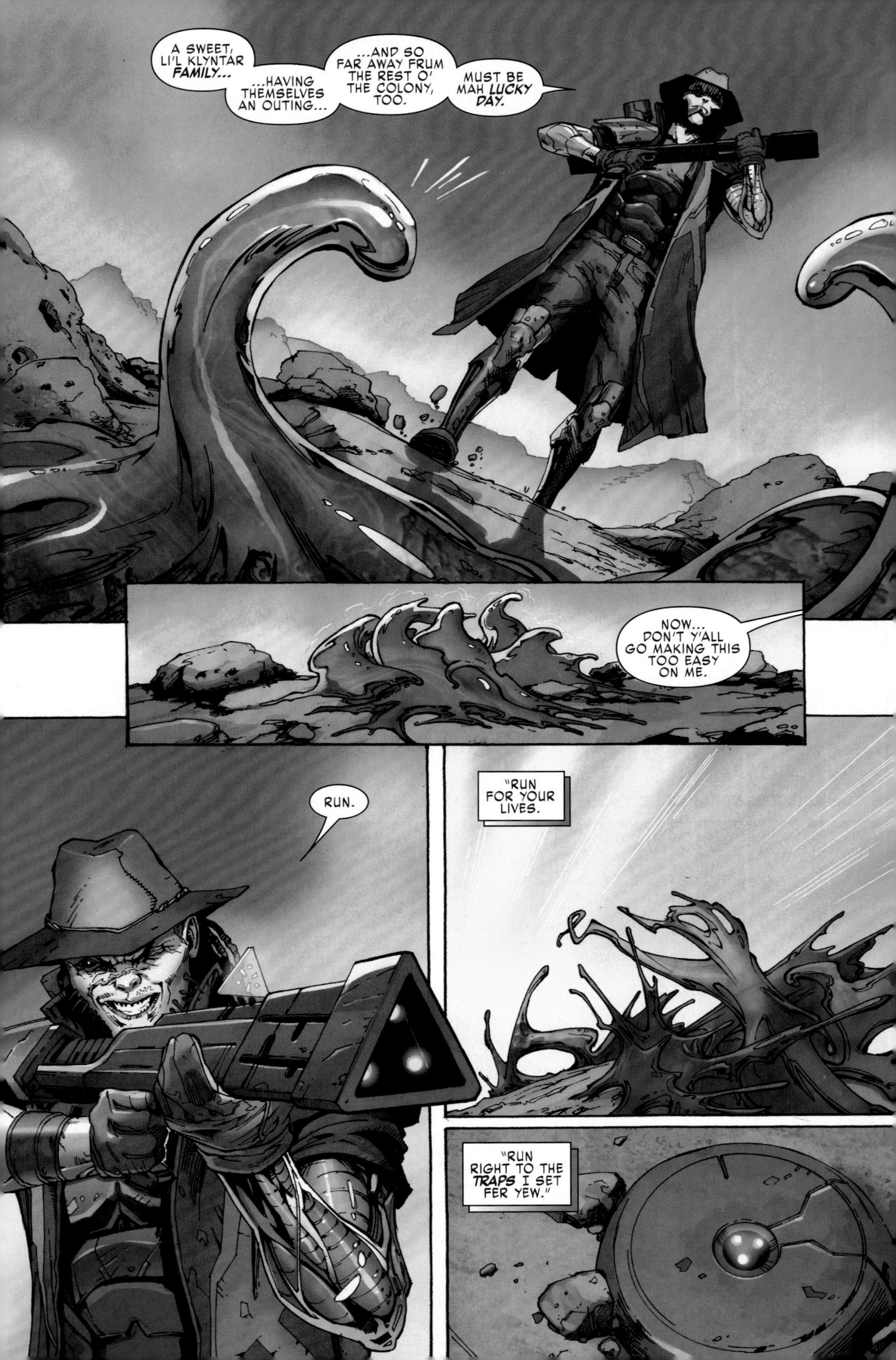
A SWEET, LI'L KLYNTAR FAMILY...
...HAVING THEMSELVES AN OUTING...
...AND SO FAR AWAY FRUM THE REST O' THE COLONY, TOO.
MUST BE MAH LUCKY DAY.
NOW... DON'T Y'ALL GO MAKING THIS TOO EASY ON ME.
RUN.
"RUN FOR YOUR LIVES.
"RUN RIGHT TO THE TRAPS I SET FER YEW."

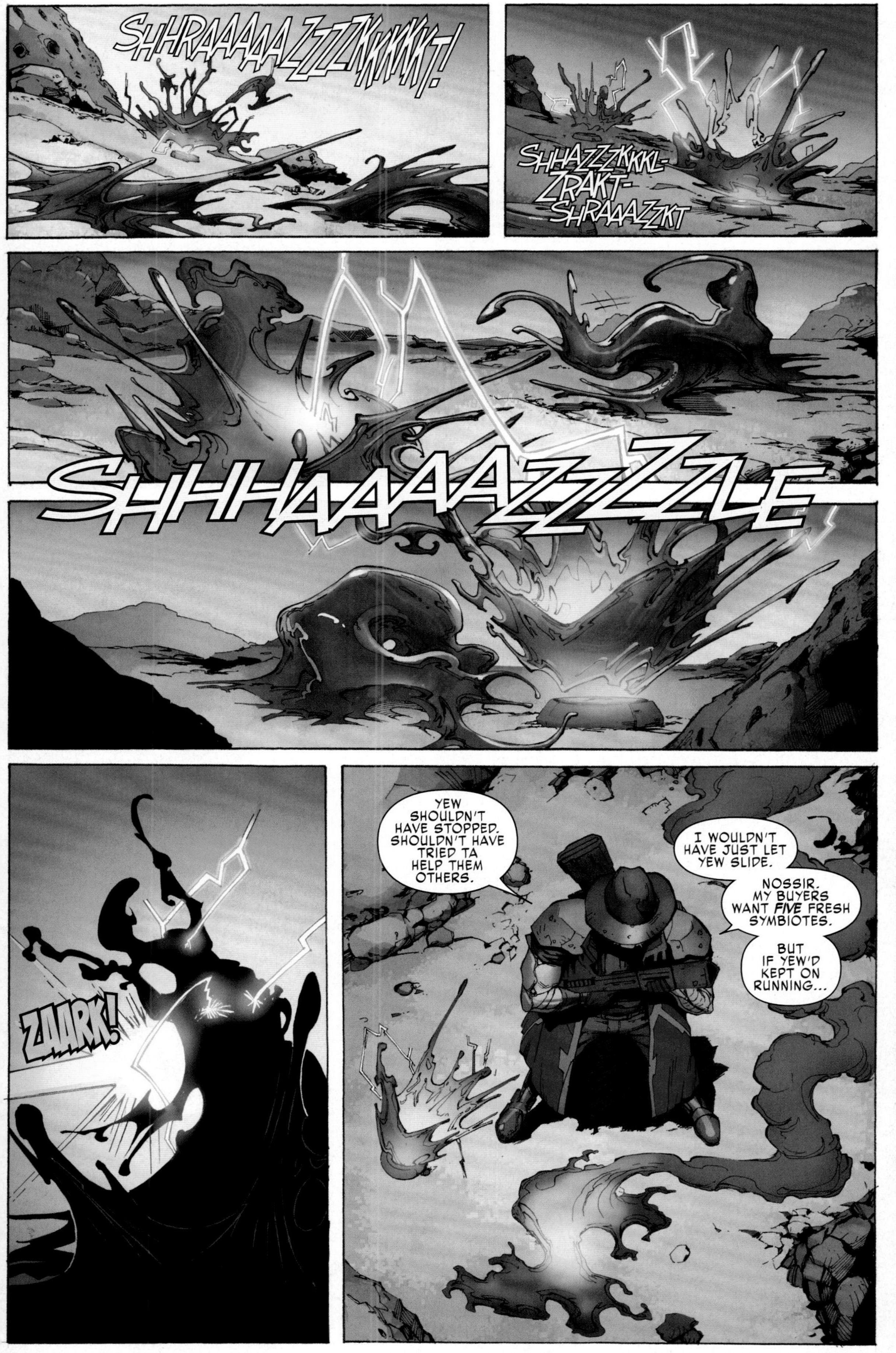
SHHRAAAAAZZZZKKKKKT!
SHHAZZZKKKL-ZRAKT-SHRAAAZZKT
SHHHAAAAAZZZZLE
ZAARK!
YEW SHOULDN'T HAVE STOPPED. SHOULDN'T HAVE TRIED TA HELP THEM OTHERS.
I WOULDN'T HAVE JUST LET YEW SLIDE.
NOSSIR. MY BUYERS WANT *FIVE* FRESH SYMBIOTES.
BUT IF YEW'D KEPT ON RUNNING...

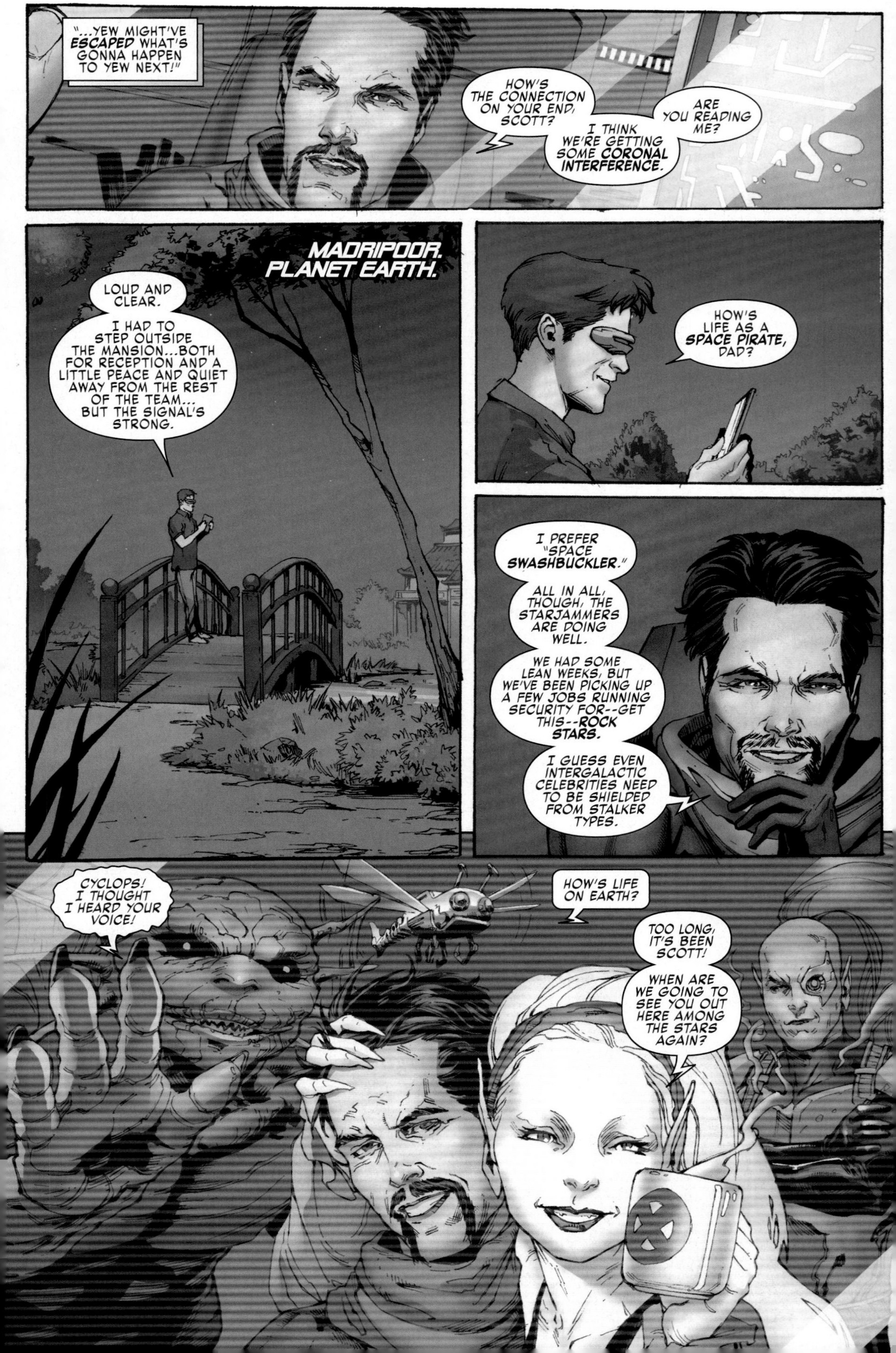
"...YEW MIGHT'VE ESCAPED WHAT'S GONNA HAPPEN TO YEW NEXT!"
HOW'S THE CONNECTION ON YOUR END, SCOTT?
I THINK WE'RE GETTING SOME CORONAL INTERFERENCE.
ARE YOU READING ME?
MADRIPOOR. PLANET EARTH.
LOUD AND CLEAR.
I HAD TO STEP OUTSIDE THE MANSION...BOTH FOR RECEPTION AND A LITTLE PEACE AND QUIET AWAY FROM THE REST OF THE TEAM... BUT THE SIGNAL'S STRONG.
HOW'S LIFE AS A SPACE PIRATE, DAD?
I PREFER "SPACE SWASHBUCKLER."
ALL IN ALL, THOUGH, THE STARJAMMERS ARE DOING WELL.
WE HAD SOME LEAN WEEKS, BUT WE'VE BEEN PICKING UP A FEW JOBS RUNNING SECURITY FOR--GET THIS--ROCK STARS.
I GUESS EVEN INTERGALACTIC CELEBRITIES NEED TO BE SHIELDED FROM STALKER TYPES.
CYCLOPS! I THOUGHT I HEARD YOUR VOICE!
HOW'S LIFE ON EARTH?
TOO LONG, IT'S BEEN SCOTT!
WHEN ARE WE GOING TO SEE YOU OUT HERE AMONG THE STARS AGAIN?

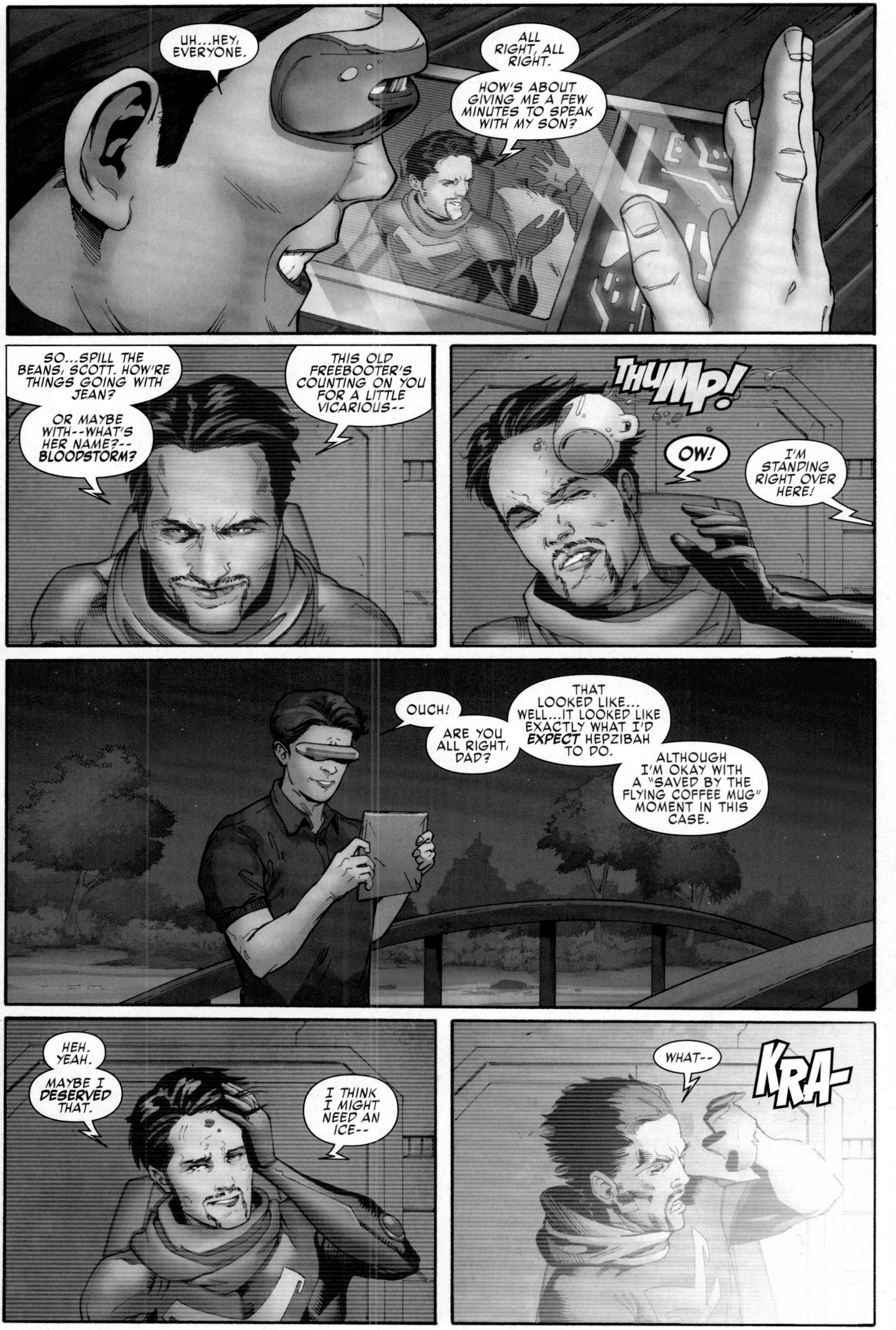
UH...HEY, EVERYONE.
ALL RIGHT, ALL RIGHT.
HOW'S ABOUT GIVING ME A FEW MINUTES TO SPEAK WITH MY SON?
SO...SPILL THE BEANS, SCOTT. HOW'RE THINGS GOING WITH JEAN?
OR MAYBE WITH--WHAT'S HER NAME?--BLOODSTORM?
THIS OLD FREEBOOTER'S COUNTING ON YOU FOR A LITTLE VICARIOUS--
THUMP!
OW!
I'M STANDING RIGHT OVER HERE!
OUCH!
ARE YOU ALL RIGHT, DAD?
THAT LOOKED LIKE... WELL...IT LOOKED LIKE EXACTLY WHAT I'D EXPECT HEPZIBAH TO DO.
ALTHOUGH I'M OKAY WITH A "SAVED BY THE FLYING COFFEE MUG" MOMENT IN THIS CASE.
HEH. YEAH.
MAYBE I DESERVED THAT.
I THINK I MIGHT NEED AN ICE--
WHAT--
KRA-

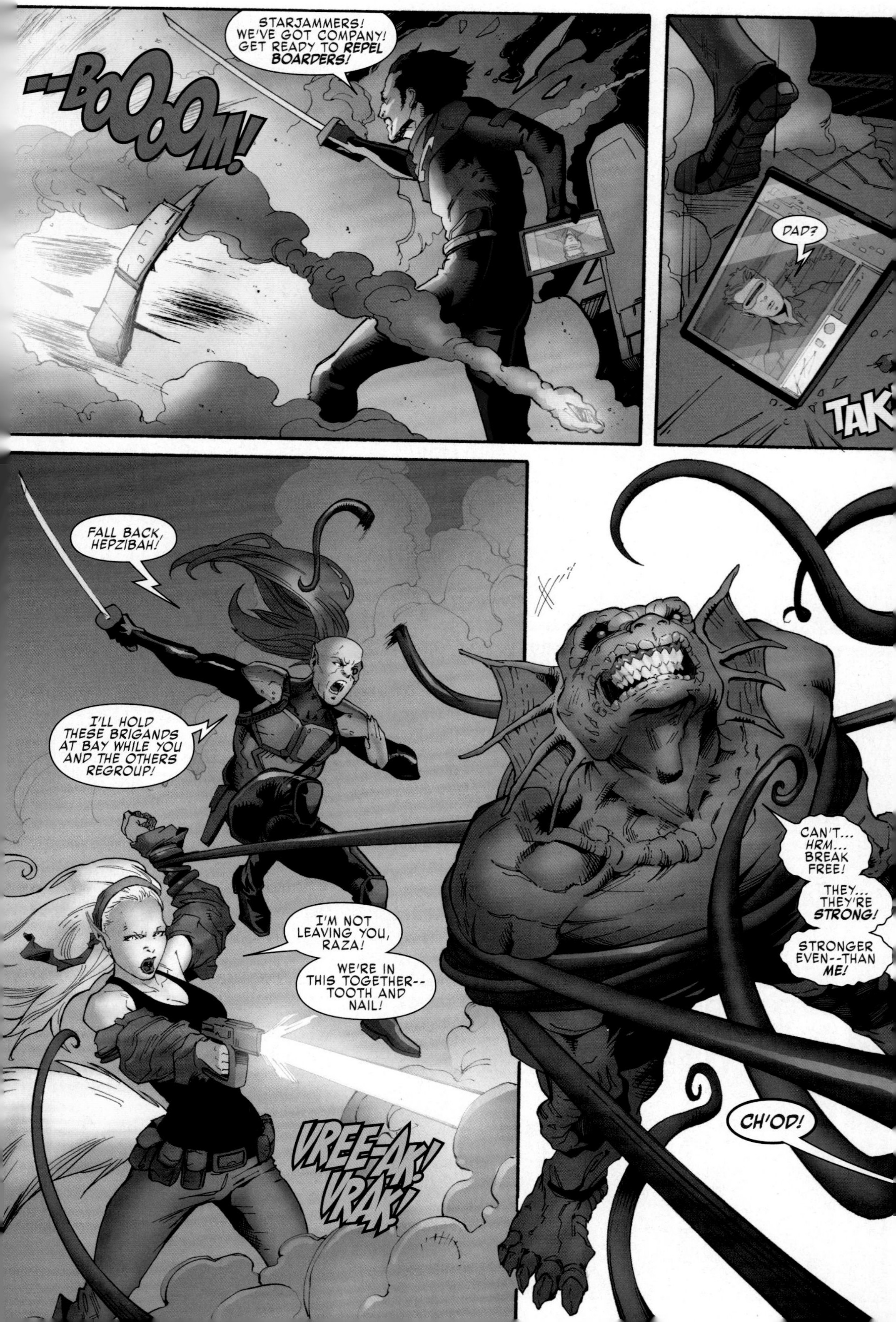
STARJAMMERS! WE'VE GOT COMPANY! GET READY TO REPEL BOARDERS!
--BOOOOM!
DAD?
TAK
FALL BACK, HEPZIBAH!
I'LL HOLD THESE BRIGANDS AT BAY WHILE YOU AND THE OTHERS REGROUP!
I'M NOT LEAVING YOU, RAZA!
WE'RE IN THIS TOGETHER-- TOOTH AND NAIL!
VREE-AK! VRAK!
CAN'T... HRM... BREAK FREE!
THEY... THEY'RE STRONG!
STRONGER EVEN--THAN ME!
CH'OD!

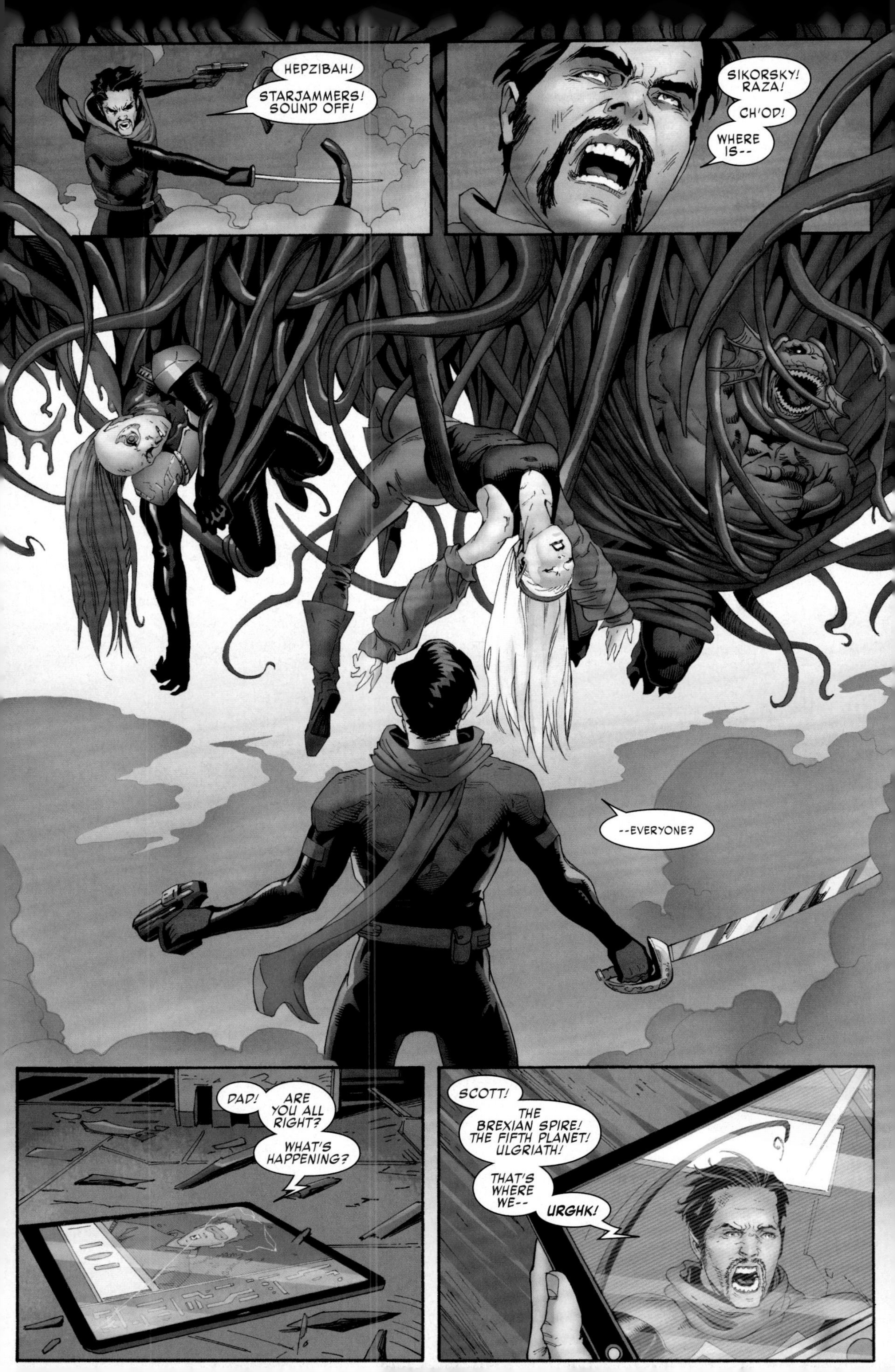
HEPZIBAH!
STARJAMMERS! SOUND OFF!
SIKORSKY! RAZA!
CH'OD!
WHERE IS--
--EVERYONE?
DAD!
ARE YOU ALL RIGHT?
WHAT'S HAPPENING?
SCOTT!
THE BREXIAN SPIRE! THE FIFTH PLANET! ULGRIATH!
THAT'S WHERE WE--
URGHK!

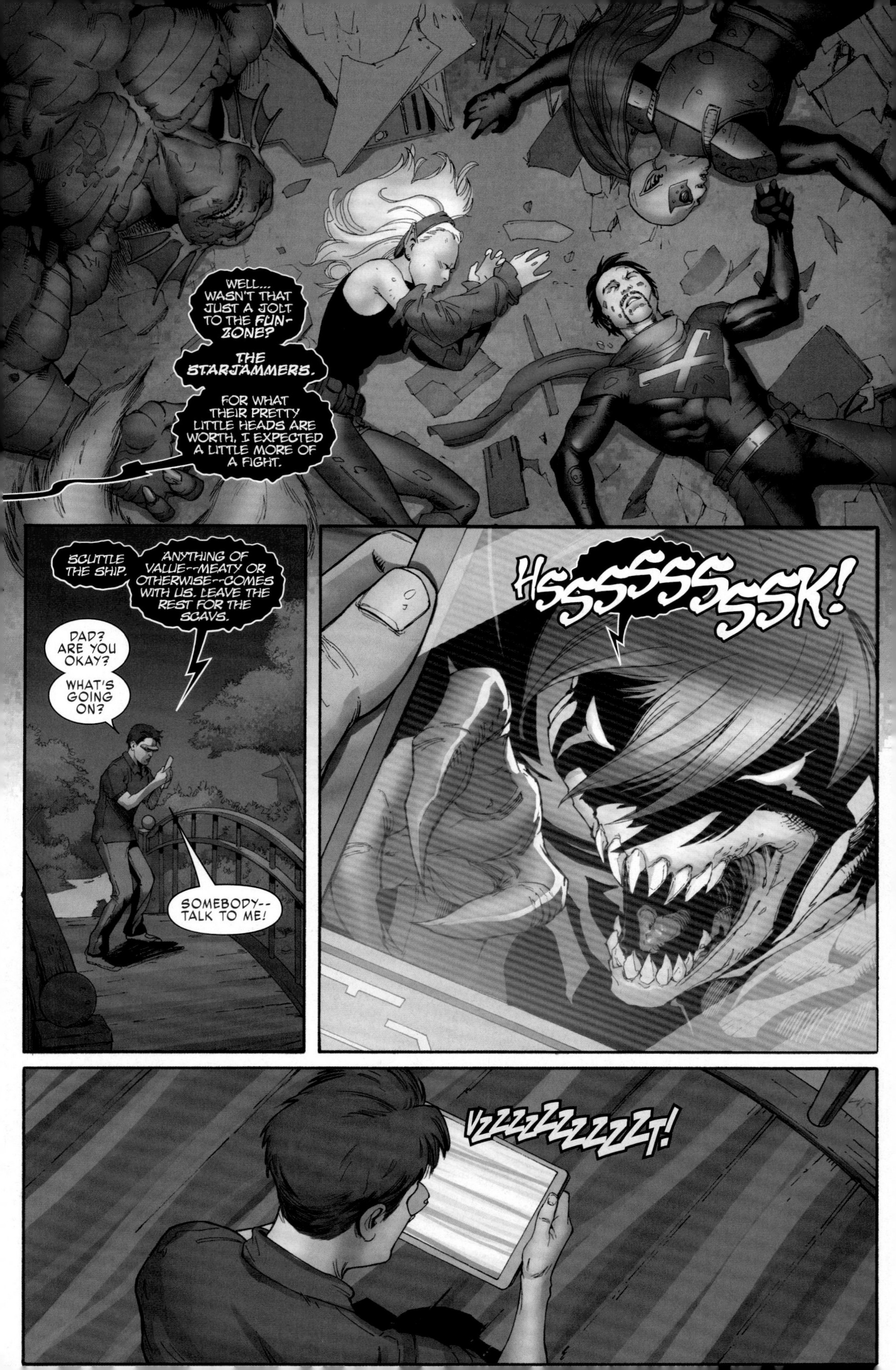

WELL... WASN'T THAT JUST A JOLT TO THE FUN-ZONE?
THE STARJAMMERS.
FOR WHAT THEIR PRETTY LITTLE HEADS ARE WORTH, I EXPECTED A LITTLE MORE OF A FIGHT.
SCUTTLE THE SHIP.
ANYTHING OF VALUE--MEATY OR OTHERWISE--COMES WITH US. LEAVE THE REST FOR THE SCAVS.
DAD? ARE YOU OKAY?
WHAT'S GOING ON?
SOMEBODY--TALK TO ME!
HSSSSSSSSK!
VZZZZZZZZZZZZT!

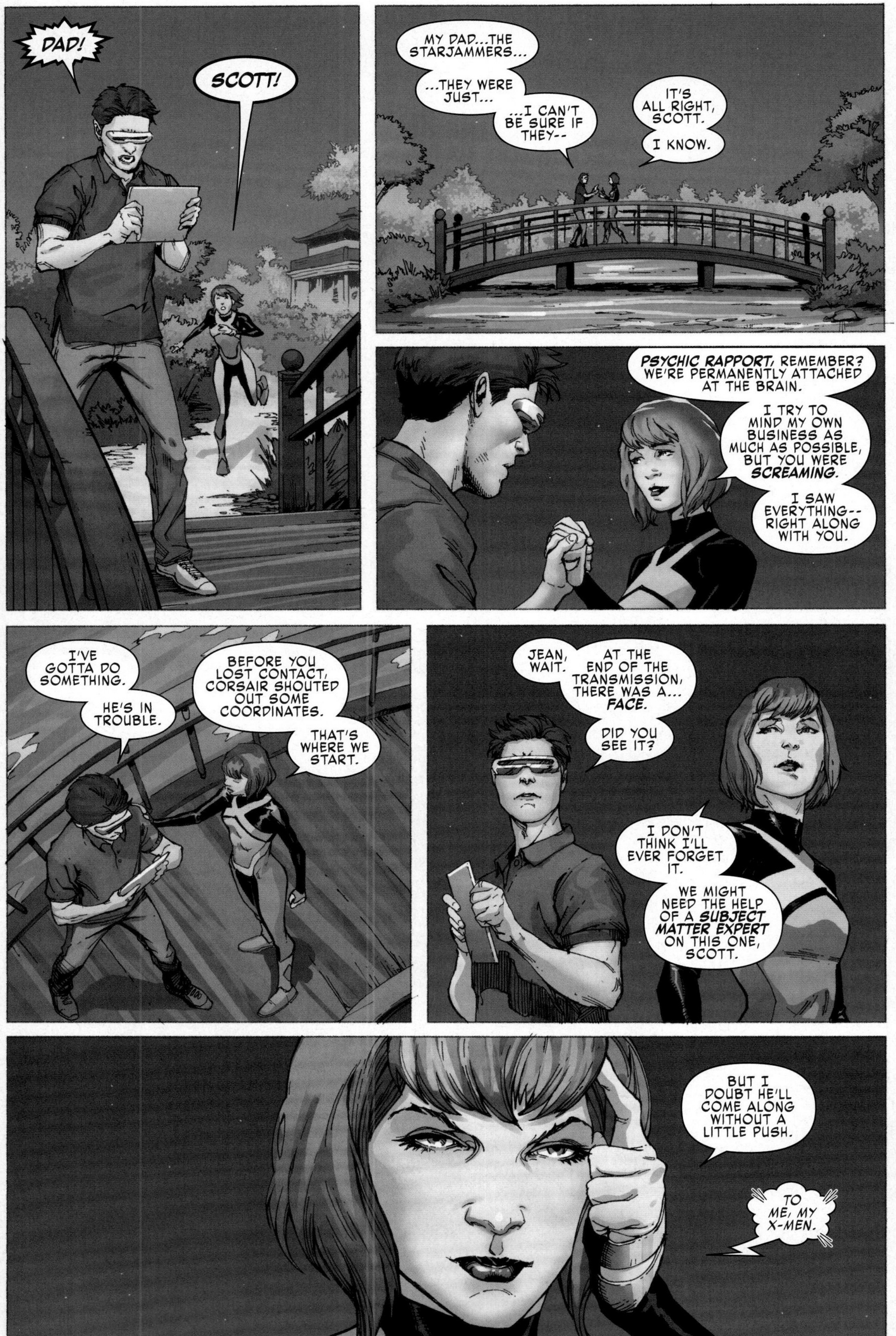
DAD!
SCOTT!
MY DAD...THE STARJAMMERS...
...THEY WERE JUST...
...I CAN'T BE SURE IF THEY--
IT'S ALL RIGHT, SCOTT.
I KNOW.
PSYCHIC RAPPORT, REMEMBER? WE'RE PERMANENTLY ATTACHED AT THE BRAIN.
I TRY TO MIND MY OWN BUSINESS AS MUCH AS POSSIBLE, BUT YOU WERE SCREAMING.
I SAW EVERYTHING-- RIGHT ALONG WITH YOU.
I'VE GOTTA DO SOMETHING.
HE'S IN TROUBLE.
BEFORE YOU LOST CONTACT, CORSAIR SHOUTED OUT SOME COORDINATES.
THAT'S WHERE WE START.
JEAN, WAIT.
AT THE END OF THE TRANSMISSION, THERE WAS A... FACE.
DID YOU SEE IT?
I DON'T THINK I'LL EVER FORGET IT.
WE MIGHT NEED THE HELP OF A SUBJECT MATTER EXPERT ON THIS ONE, SCOTT.
BUT I DOUBT HE'LL COME ALONG WITHOUT A LITTLE PUSH.
TO ME, MY X-MEN.

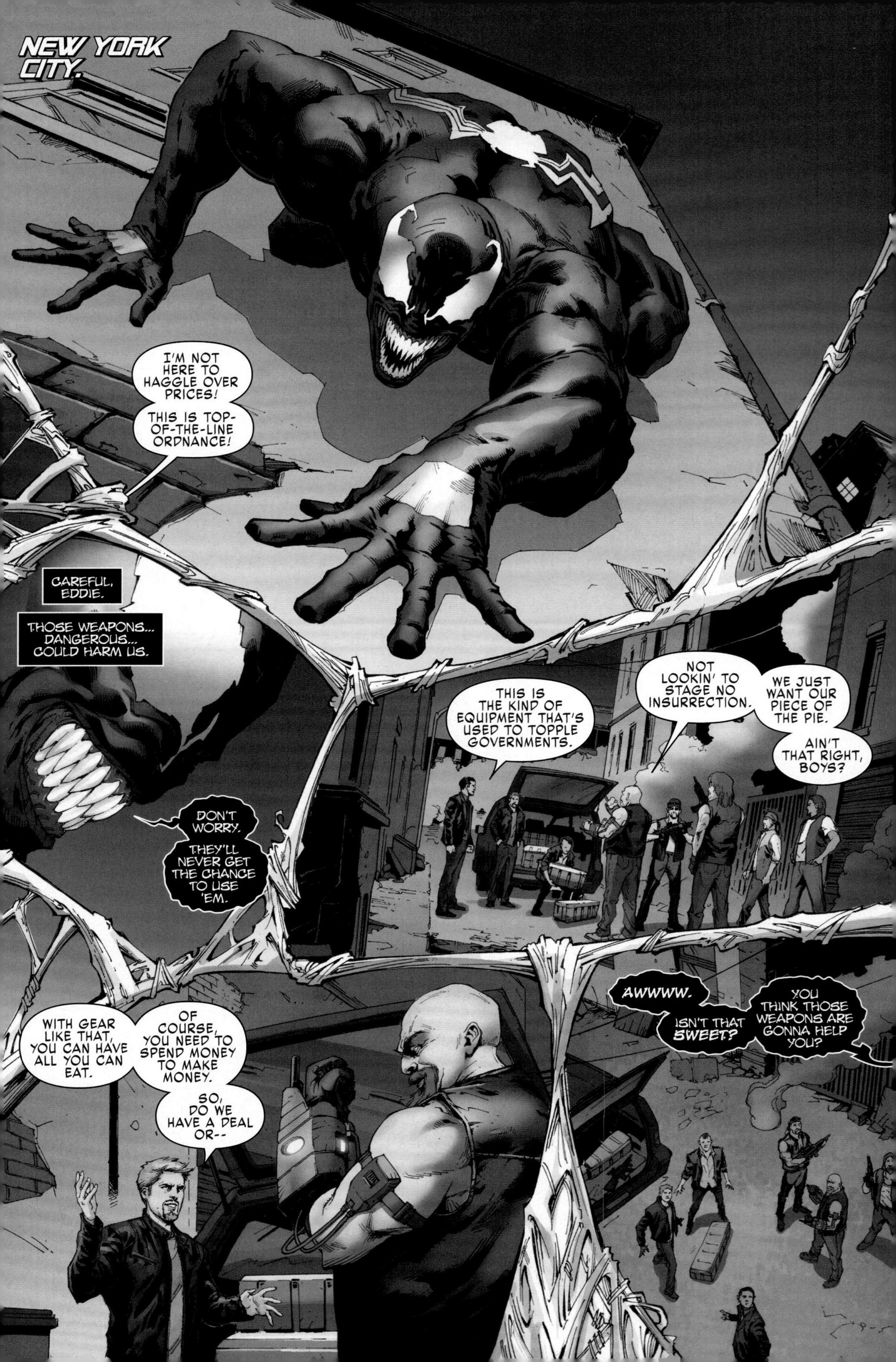
NEW YORK CITY.
I'M NOT HERE TO HAGGLE OVER PRICES!
THIS IS TOP-OF-THE-LINE ORDNANCE!
CAREFUL, EDDIE.
THOSE WEAPONS... DANGEROUS... COULD HARM US.
DON'T WORRY.
THEY'LL NEVER GET THE CHANCE TO USE 'EM.
THIS IS THE KIND OF EQUIPMENT THAT'S USED TO TOPPLE GOVERNMENTS.
NOT LOOKIN' TO STAGE NO INSURRECTION.
WE JUST WANT OUR PIECE OF THE PIE.
AIN'T THAT RIGHT, BOYS?
WITH GEAR LIKE THAT, YOU CAN HAVE ALL YOU CAN EAT.
OF COURSE, YOU NEED TO SPEND MONEY TO MAKE MONEY.
SO, DO WE HAVE A DEAL OR--
AWWWW.
ISN'T THAT SWEET?
YOU THINK THOSE WEAPONS ARE GONNA HELP YOU?

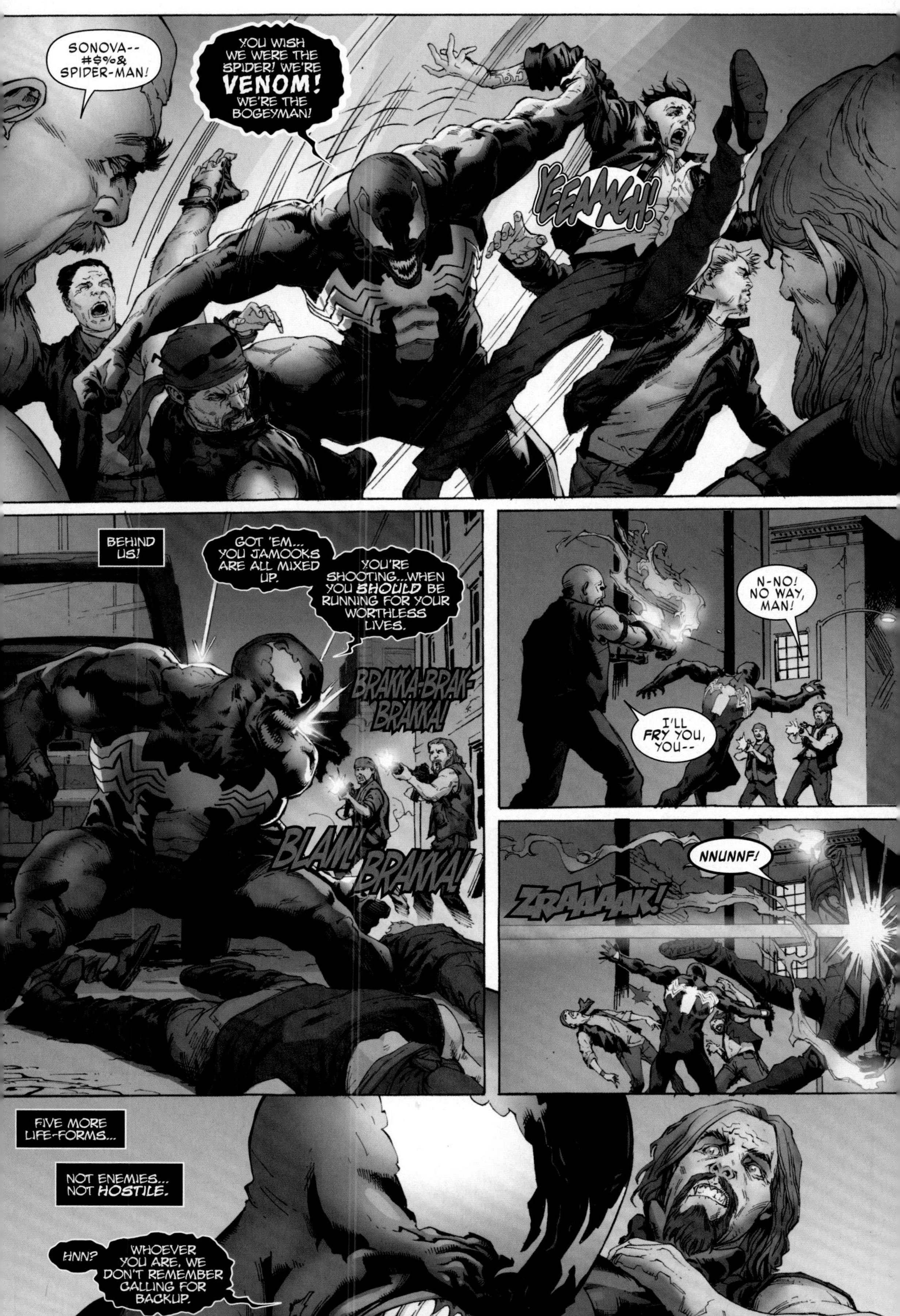
SONOVA-- #$%& SPIDER-MAN!
YOU WISH WE WERE THE SPIDER! WE'RE VENOM! WE'RE THE BOGEYMAN!
YEEAAAGH!
BEHIND US!
GOT 'EM... YOU JAMOOKS ARE ALL MIXED UP.
YOU'RE SHOOTING...WHEN YOU SHOULD BE RUNNING FOR YOUR WORTHLESS LIVES.
BRAKKA-BRAK-BRAKKA!
BLAM! BRAKKA!
N-NO! NO WAY, MAN!
I'LL FRY YOU, YOU--
NNUNNF!
ZRAAAAAK!
FIVE MORE LIFE-FORMS...
NOT ENEMIES... NOT HOSTILE.
HNN?
WHOEVER YOU ARE, WE DON'T REMEMBER CALLING FOR BACKUP.

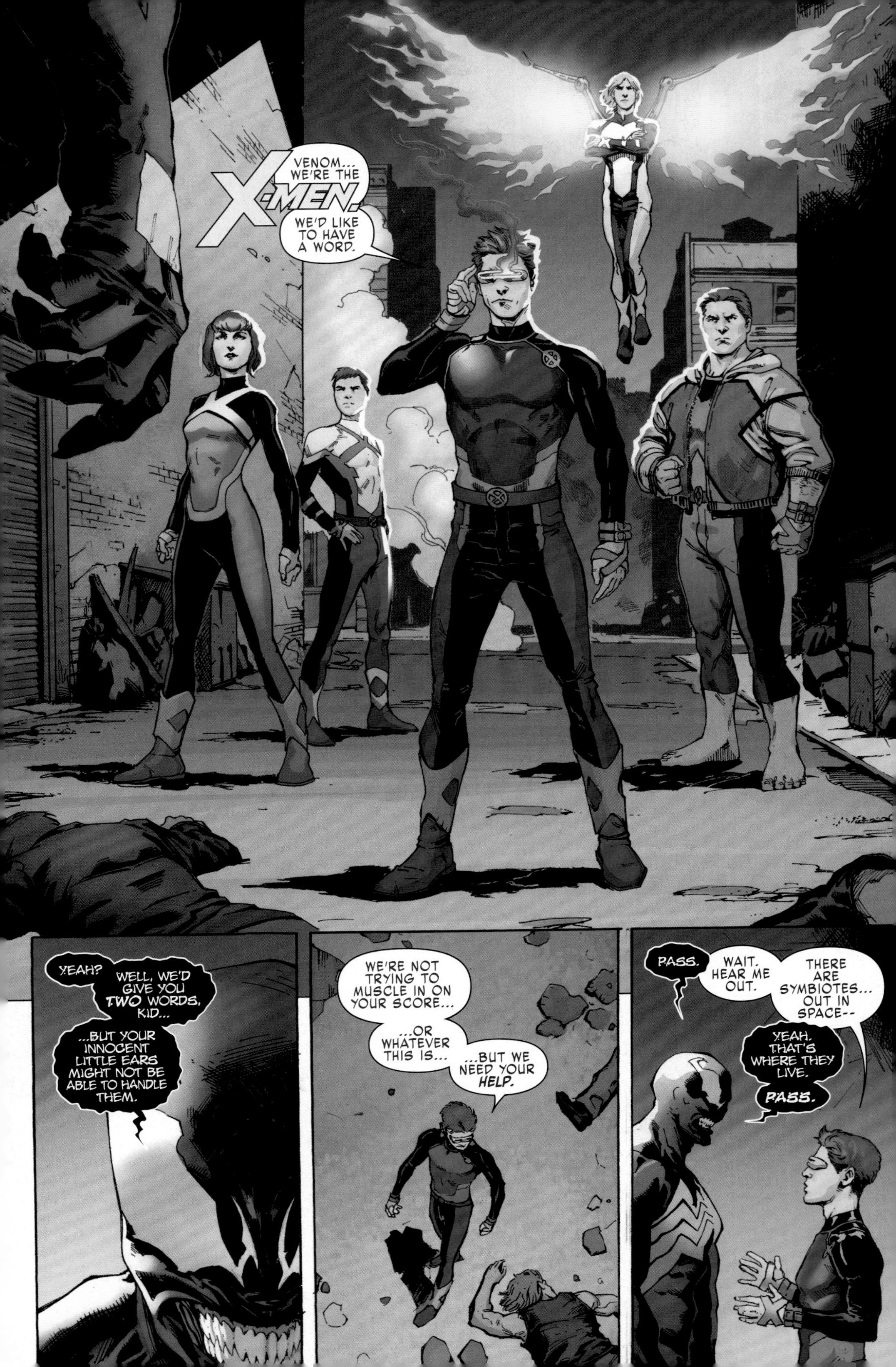
VENOM... WE'RE THE
X-MEN.
WE'D LIKE TO HAVE A WORD.
YEAH? WELL, WE'D GIVE YOU TWO WORDS, KID...
...BUT YOUR INNOCENT LITTLE EARS MIGHT NOT BE ABLE TO HANDLE THEM.
WE'RE NOT TRYING TO MUSCLE IN ON YOUR SCORE...
...OR WHATEVER THIS IS...
...BUT WE NEED YOUR HELP.
PASS.
WAIT. HEAR ME OUT.
THERE ARE SYMBIOTES... OUT IN SPACE--
YEAH. THAT'S WHERE THEY LIVE.
PASS.

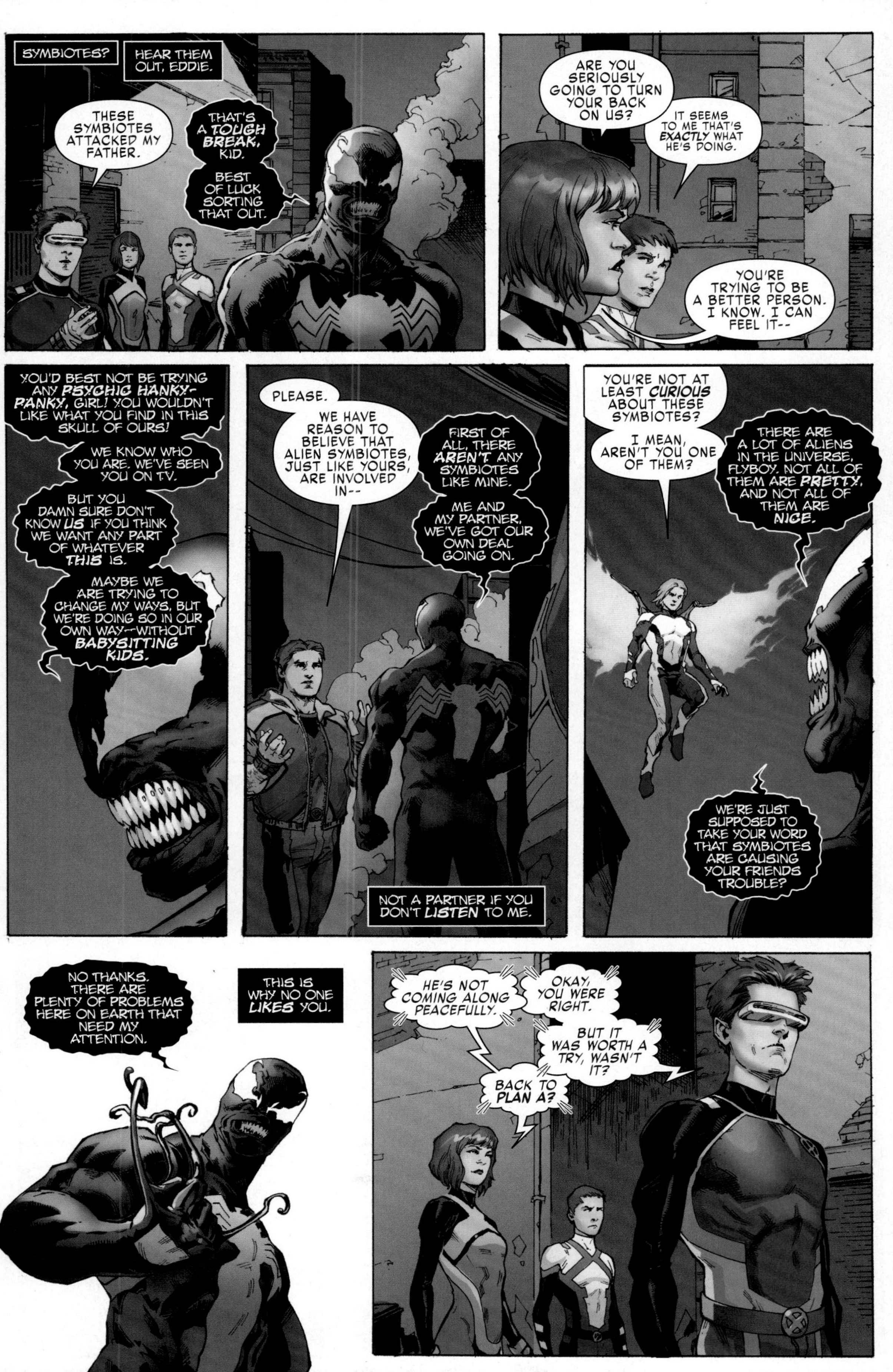
SYMBIOTES?
HEAR THEM OUT, EDDIE.
THESE SYMBIOTES ATTACKED MY FATHER.
THAT'S A TOUGH BREAK, KID.
BEST OF LUCK SORTING THAT OUT.
ARE YOU SERIOUSLY GOING TO TURN YOUR BACK ON US?
IT SEEMS TO ME THAT'S EXACTLY WHAT HE'S DOING.
YOU'RE TRYING TO BE A BETTER PERSON. I KNOW. I CAN FEEL IT--
YOU'D BEST NOT BE TRYING ANY PSYCHIC HANKY-PANKY, GIRL! YOU WOULDN'T LIKE WHAT YOU FIND IN THIS SKULL OF OURS!
WE KNOW WHO YOU ARE. WE'VE SEEN YOU ON T.V.
BUT YOU DAMN SURE DON'T KNOW US IF YOU THINK WE WANT ANY PART OF WHATEVER THIS IS.
MAYBE WE ARE TRYING TO CHANGE MY WAYS, BUT WE'RE DOING SO IN OUR OWN WAY--WITHOUT BABYSITTING KIDS.
PLEASE.
WE HAVE REASON TO BELIEVE THAT ALIEN SYMBIOTES, JUST LIKE YOURS, ARE INVOLVED IN--
FIRST OF ALL, THERE AREN'T ANY SYMBIOTES LIKE MINE.
ME AND MY PARTNER, WE'VE GOT OUR OWN DEAL GOING ON.
NOT A PARTNER IF YOU DON'T LISTEN TO ME.
YOU'RE NOT AT LEAST CURIOUS ABOUT THESE SYMBIOTES?
I MEAN, AREN'T YOU ONE OF THEM?
THERE ARE A LOT OF ALIENS IN THE UNIVERSE, FLYBOY. NOT ALL OF THEM ARE PRETTY, AND NOT ALL OF THEM ARE NICE.
WE'RE JUST SUPPOSED TO TAKE YOUR WORD THAT SYMBIOTES ARE CAUSING YOUR FRIENDS TROUBLE?
NO THANKS. THERE ARE PLENTY OF PROBLEMS HERE ON EARTH THAT NEED MY ATTENTION.
THIS IS WHY NO ONE LIKES YOU.
HE'S NOT COMING ALONG PEACEFULLY.
OKAY, YOU WERE RIGHT.
BUT IT WAS WORTH A TRY, WASN'T IT?
BACK TO PLAN A?

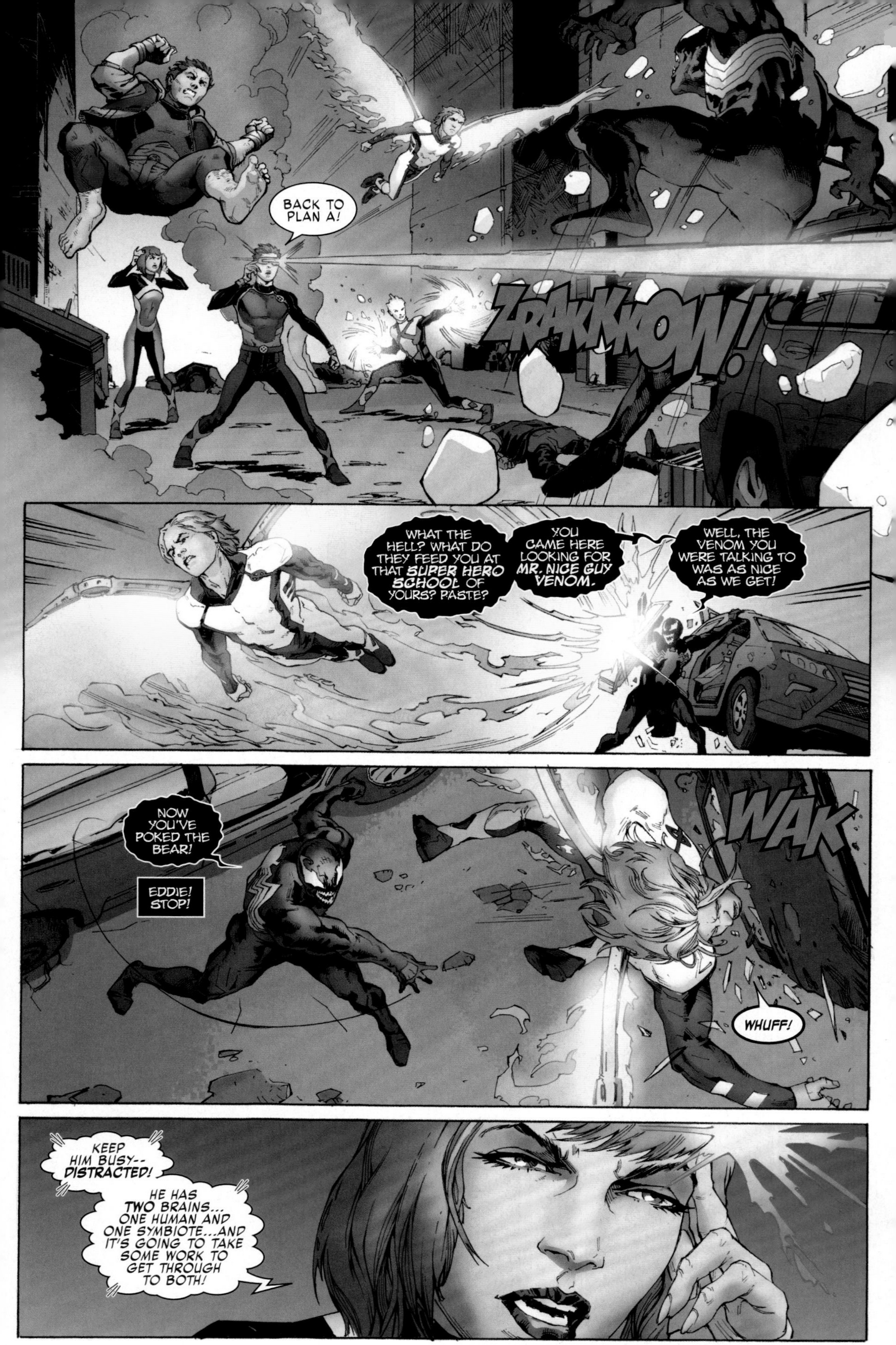
BACK TO PLAN A!
ZRAKKKOW!
WHAT THE HELL? WHAT DO THEY FEED YOU AT THAT SUPER HERO SCHOOL OF YOURS? PASTE?
YOU CAME HERE LOOKING FOR MR. NICE GUY VENOM.
WELL, THE VENOM YOU WERE TALKING TO WAS AS NICE AS WE GET!
NOW YOU'VE POKED THE BEAR!
EDDIE! STOP!
WAK
WHUFF!
KEEP HIM BUSY-- DISTRACTED!
HE HAS TWO BRAINS... ONE HUMAN AND ONE SYMBIOTE...AND IT'S GOING TO TAKE SOME WORK TO GET THROUGH TO BOTH!

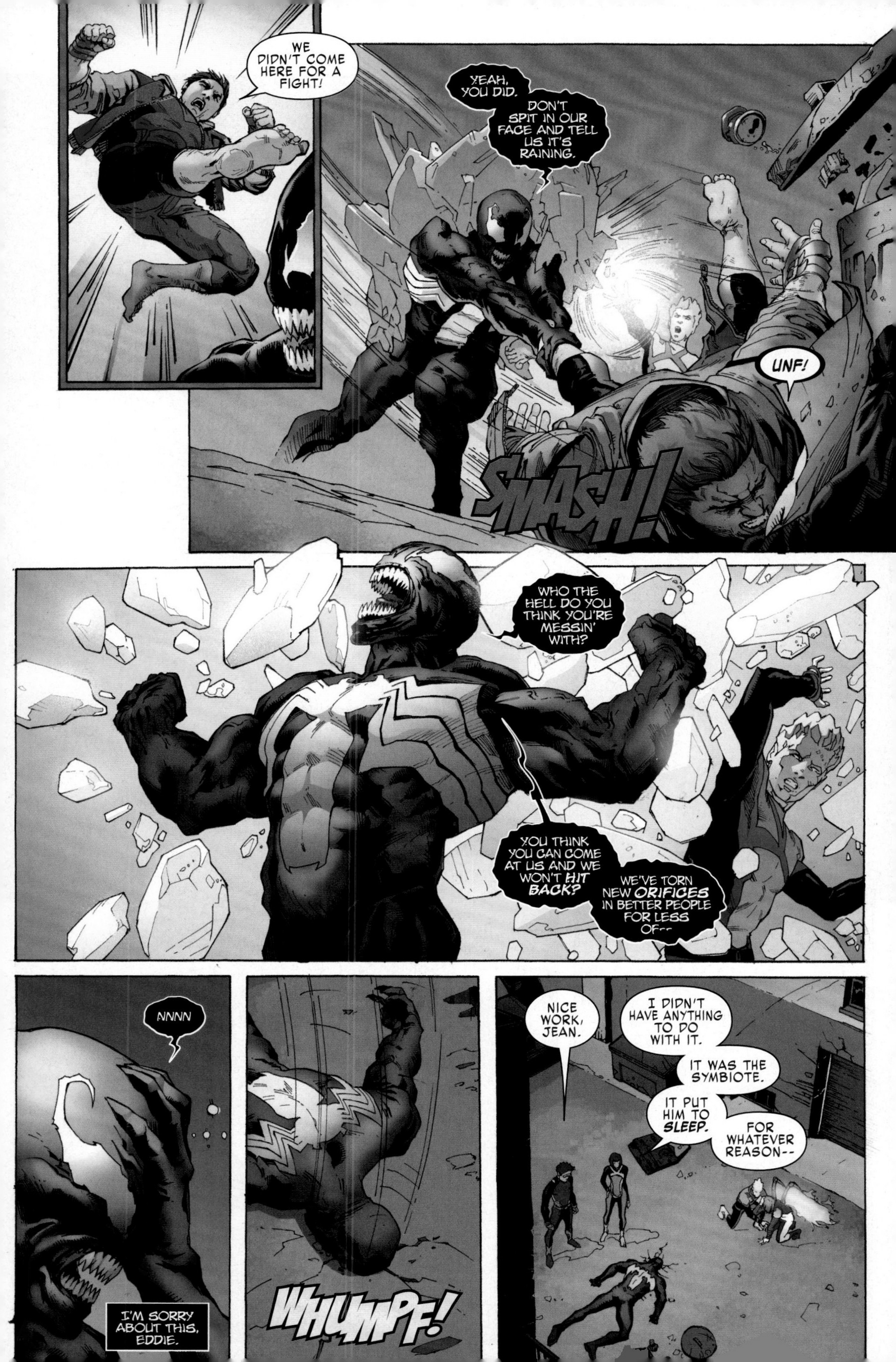
WE DIDN'T COME HERE FOR A FIGHT!
YEAH, YOU DID.
DON'T SPIT IN OUR FACE AND TELL US IT'S RAINING.
UNF!
SMASH!
WHO THE HELL DO YOU THINK YOU'RE MESSIN' WITH?
YOU THINK YOU CAN COME AT US AND WE WON'T HIT BACK?
WE'VE TORN NEW ORIFICES IN BETTER PEOPLE FOR LESS OF--
NNNN
I'M SORRY ABOUT THIS, EDDIE.
WHUMPF!
NICE WORK, JEAN.
I DIDN'T HAVE ANYTHING TO DO WITH IT.
IT WAS THE SYMBIOTE.
IT PUT HIM TO SLEEP.
FOR WHATEVER REASON--

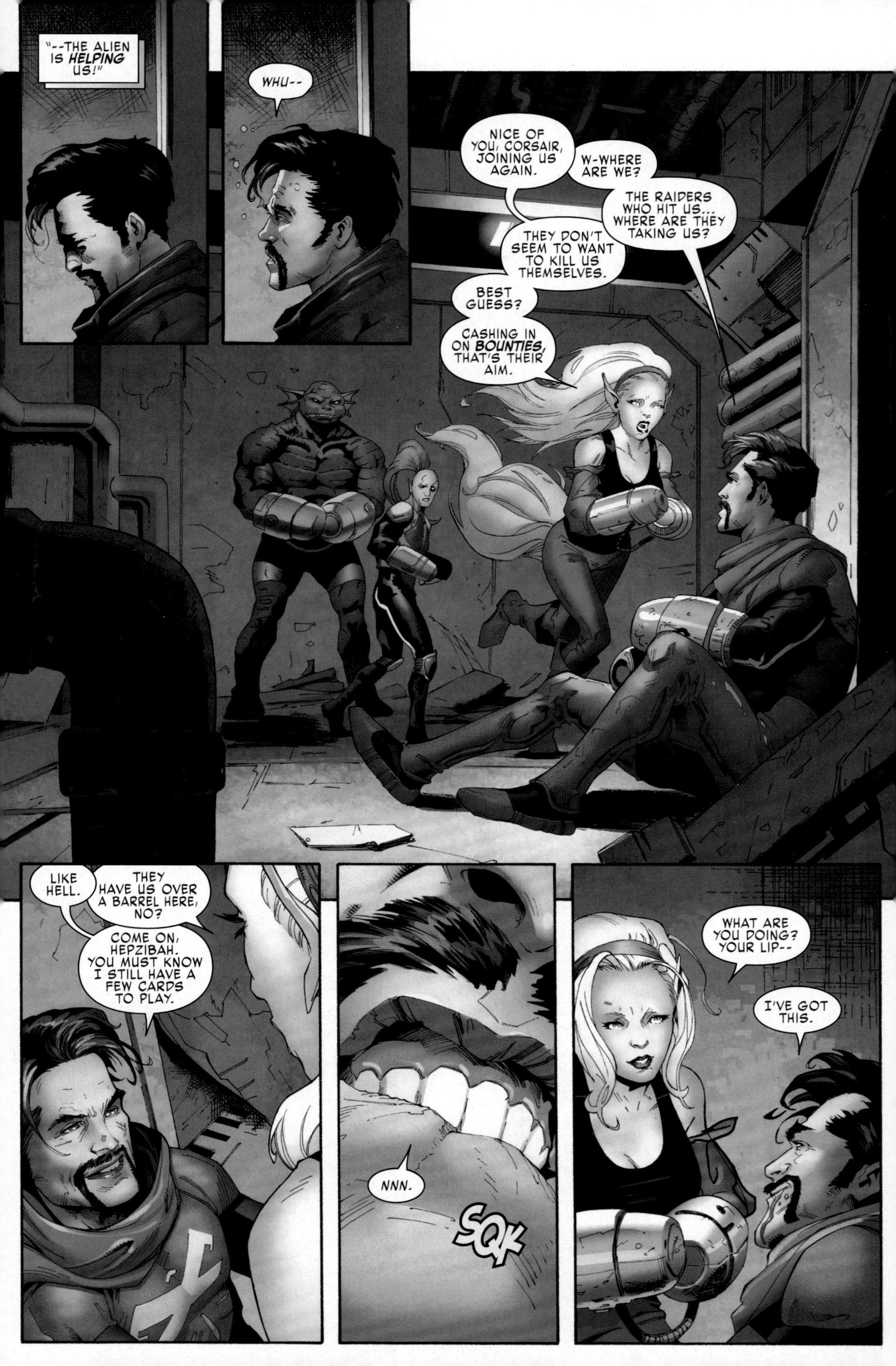
"--THE ALIEN IS HELPING US!"
WHU--
NICE OF YOU, CORSAIR, JOINING US AGAIN.
W-WHERE ARE WE?
THE RAIDERS WHO HIT US... WHERE ARE THEY TAKING US?
THEY DON'T SEEM TO WANT TO KILL US THEMSELVES.
BEST GUESS?
CASHING IN ON BOUNTIES, THAT'S THEIR AIM.
THEY HAVE US OVER A BARREL HERE, NO?
LIKE HELL.
COME ON, HEPZIBAH. YOU MUST KNOW I STILL HAVE A FEW CARDS TO PLAY.
NNN.
SQK
WHAT ARE YOU DOING? YOUR LIP--
I'VE GOT THIS.

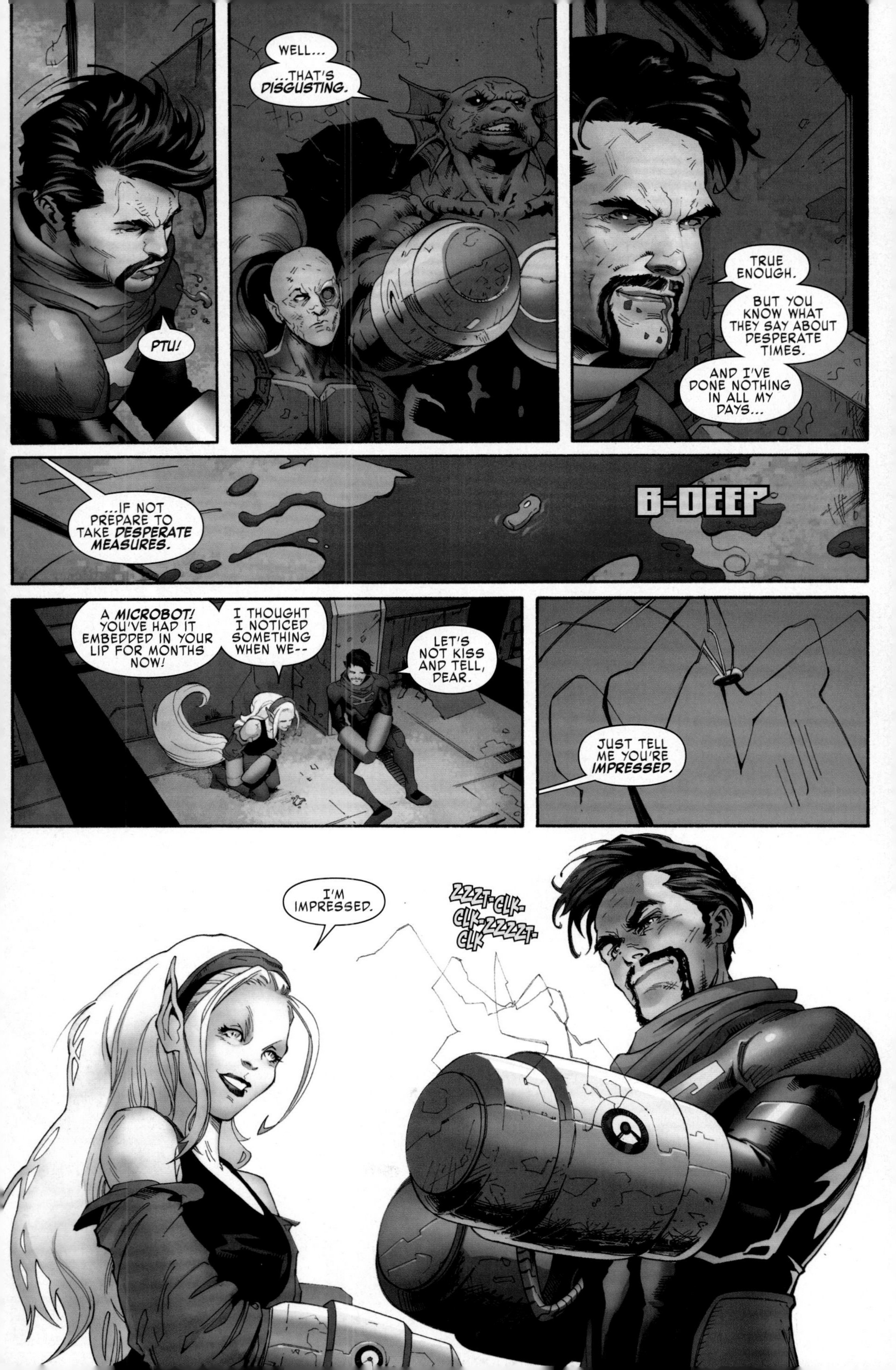
WELL...
...THAT'S DISGUSTING.
PTU!
TRUE ENOUGH.
BUT YOU KNOW WHAT THEY SAY ABOUT DESPERATE TIMES.
AND I'VE DONE NOTHING IN ALL MY DAYS...
...IF NOT PREPARE TO TAKE DESPERATE MEASURES.
B-DEEP
A MICROBOT! YOU'VE HAD IT EMBEDDED IN YOUR LIP FOR MONTHS NOW!
I THOUGHT I NOTICED SOMETHING WHEN WE--
LET'S NOT KISS AND TELL, DEAR.
JUST TELL ME YOU'RE IMPRESSED.
I'M IMPRESSED.
ZZZT-CLIK-CLIK-ZZZZT-CLIK

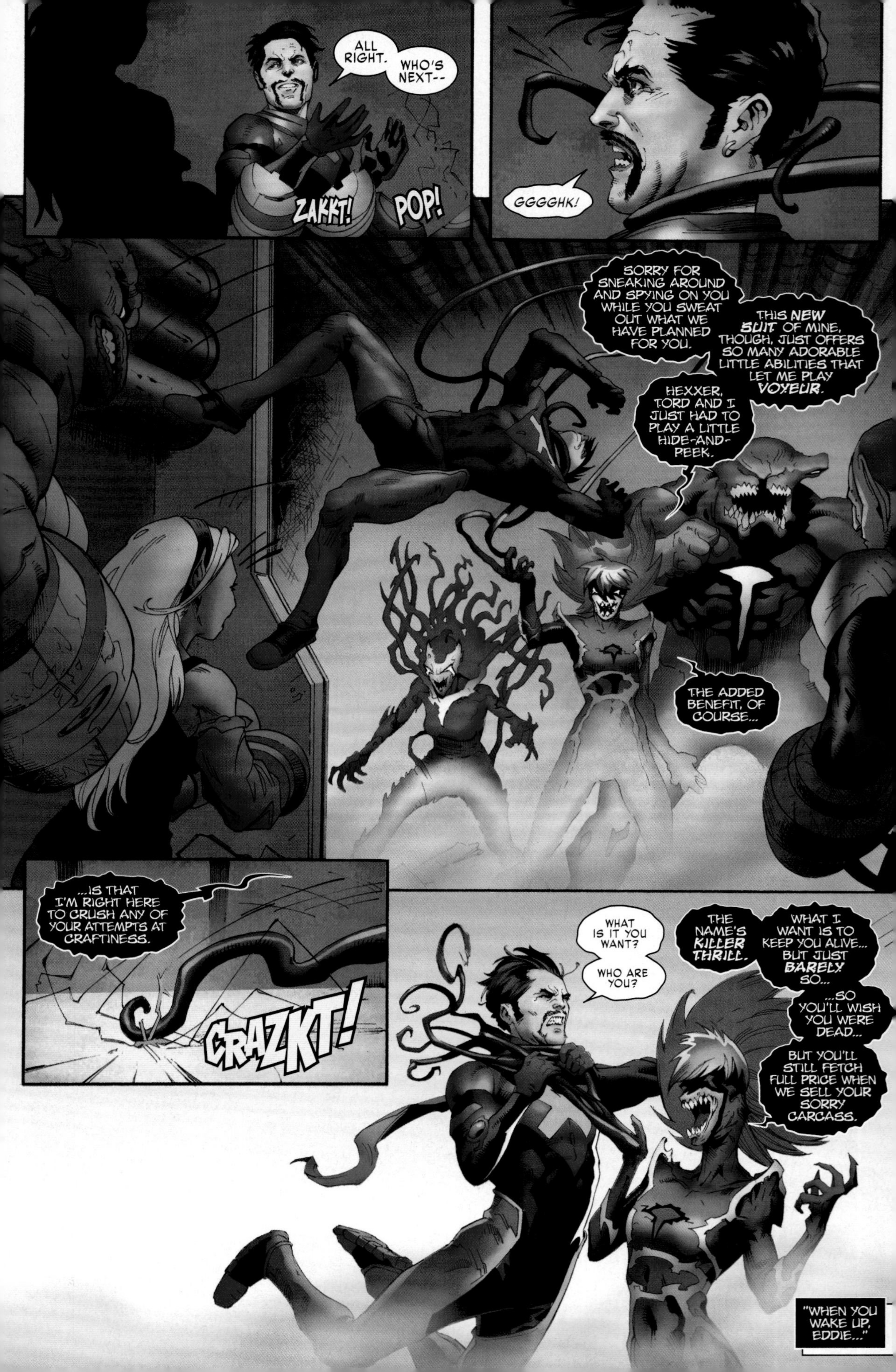
ALL RIGHT.
WHO'S NEXT--
ZAKKT!
POP!
GGGGHK!
SORRY FOR SNEAKING AROUND AND SPYING ON YOU WHILE YOU SWEAT OUT WHAT WE HAVE PLANNED FOR YOU.
THIS NEW SUIT OF MINE, THOUGH, JUST OFFERS SO MANY ADORABLE LITTLE ABILITIES THAT LET ME PLAY VOYEUR.
HEXXER, TORD AND I JUST HAD TO PLAY A LITTLE HIDE-AND-PEEK.
THE ADDED BENEFIT, OF COURSE...
...IS THAT I'M RIGHT HERE TO CRUSH ANY OF YOUR ATTEMPTS AT CRAFTINESS.
CRAZKT!
WHAT IS IT YOU WANT?
WHO ARE YOU?
THE NAME'S KILLER THRILL.
WHAT I WANT IS TO KEEP YOU ALIVE... BUT JUST BARELY SO...
...SO YOU'LL WISH YOU WERE DEAD...
BUT YOU'LL STILL FETCH FULL PRICE WHEN WE SELL YOUR SORRY CARCASS.
"WHEN YOU WAKE UP, EDDIE..."

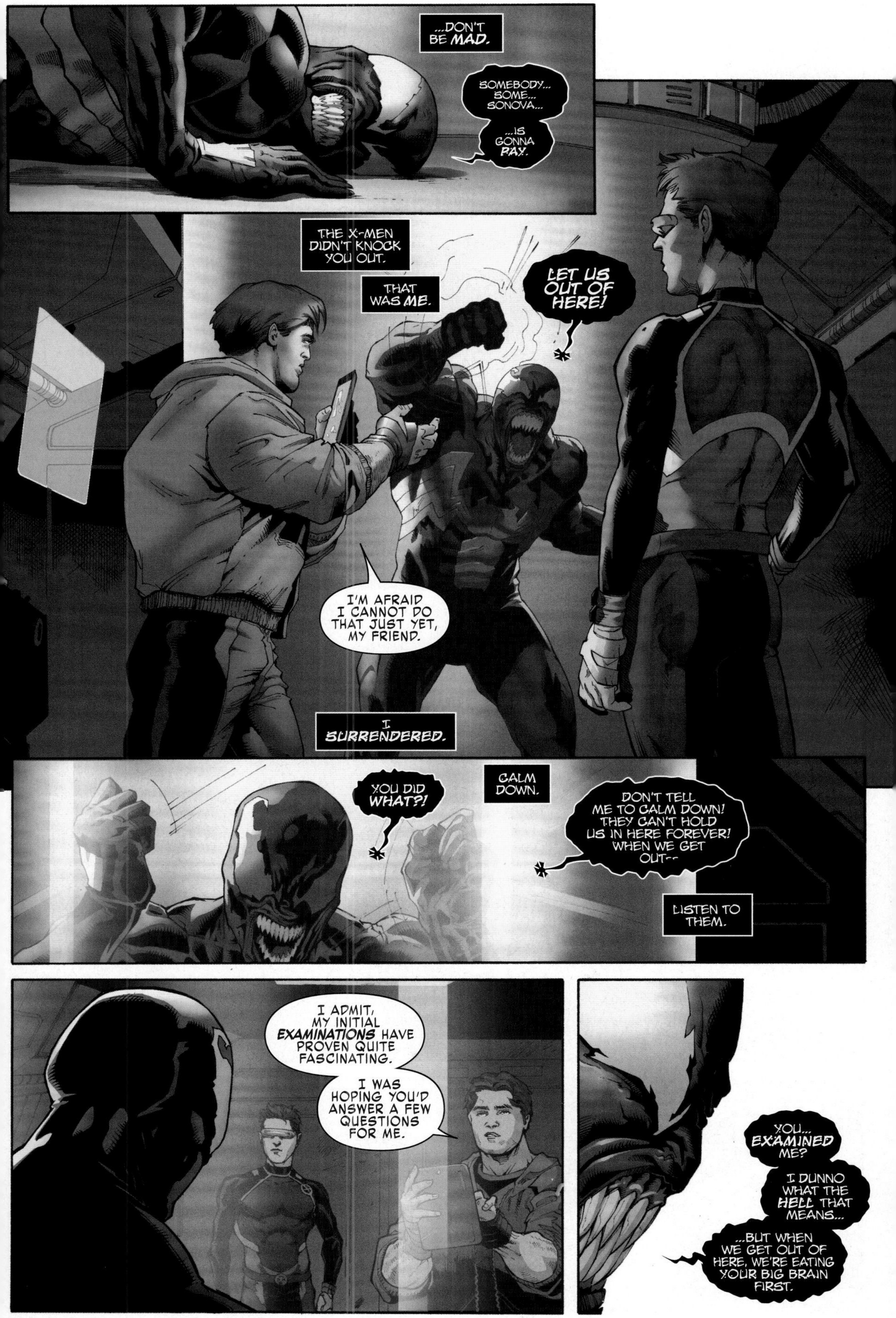
...DON'T BE MAD.
SOMEBODY... SOME... SONOVA...
...IS GONNA PAY.
THE X-MEN DIDN'T KNOCK YOU OUT.
THAT WAS ME.
LET US OUT OF HERE!
I'M AFRAID I CANNOT DO THAT JUST YET, MY FRIEND.
I SURRENDERED.
YOU DID WHAT?!
CALM DOWN.
DON'T TELL ME TO CALM DOWN! THEY CAN'T HOLD US IN HERE FOREVER! WHEN WE GET OUT--
LISTEN TO THEM.
I ADMIT, MY INITIAL EXAMINATIONS HAVE PROVEN QUITE FASCINATING.
I WAS HOPING YOU'D ANSWER A FEW QUESTIONS FOR ME.
YOU... EXAMINED ME?
I DUNNO WHAT THE HELL THAT MEANS...
...BUT WHEN WE GET OUT OF HERE, WE'RE EATING YOUR BIG BRAIN FIRST.

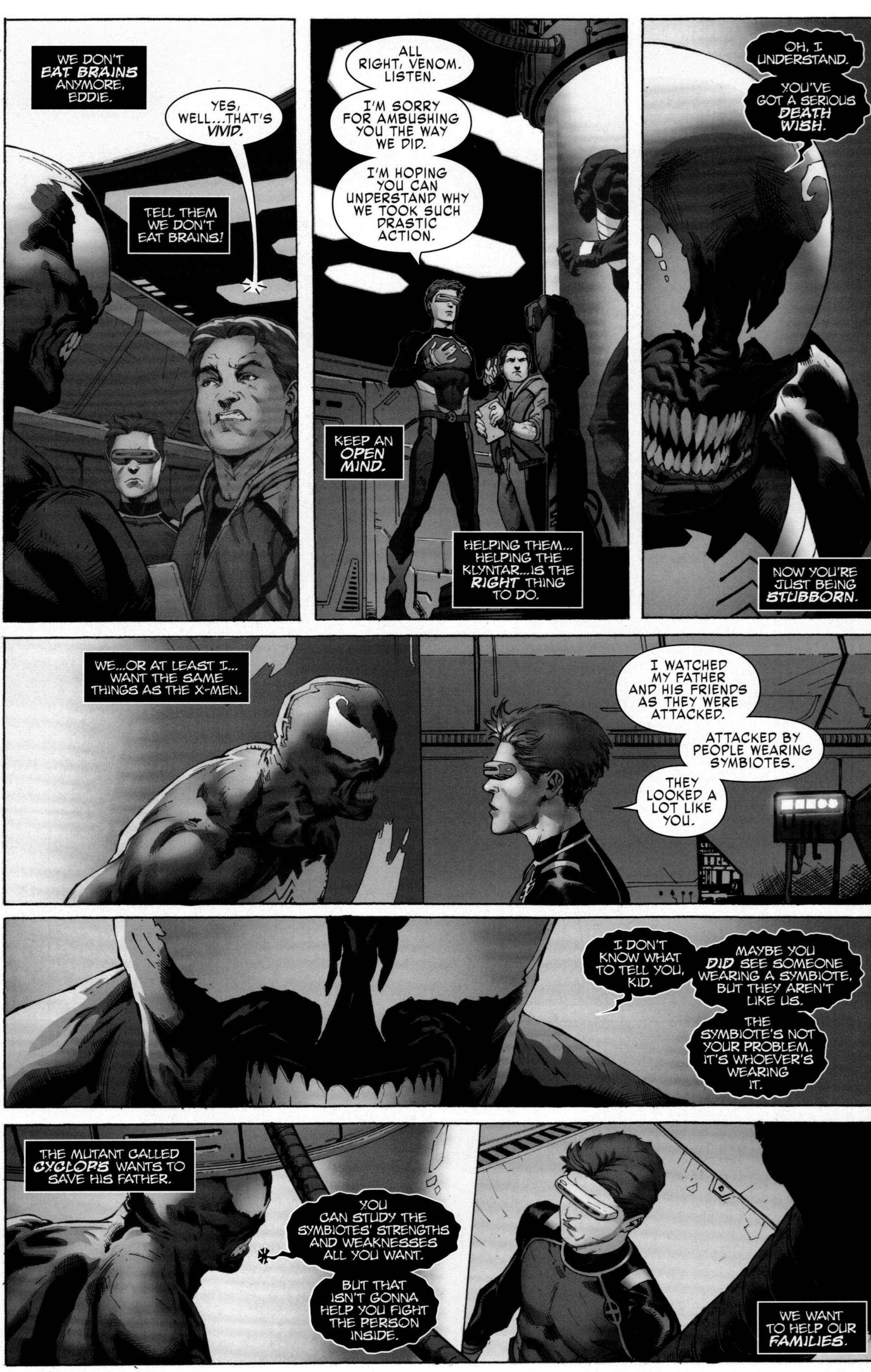
WE DON'T EAT BRAINS ANYMORE, EDDIE.
YES, WELL...THAT'S VIVID.
TELL THEM WE DON'T EAT BRAINS!
ALL RIGHT, VENOM. LISTEN.
I'M SORRY FOR AMBUSHING YOU THE WAY WE DID.
I'M HOPING YOU CAN UNDERSTAND WHY WE TOOK SUCH DRASTIC ACTION.
KEEP AN OPEN MIND.
HELPING THEM... HELPING THE KLYNTAR...IS THE RIGHT THING TO DO.
OH, I UNDERSTAND.
YOU'VE GOT A SERIOUS DEATH WISH.
NOW YOU'RE JUST BEING STUBBORN.
WE...OR AT LEAST I... WANT THE SAME THINGS AS THE X-MEN.
I WATCHED MY FATHER AND HIS FRIENDS AS THEY WERE ATTACKED.
ATTACKED BY PEOPLE WEARING SYMBIOTES.
THEY LOOKED A LOT LIKE YOU.
I DON'T KNOW WHAT TO TELL YOU, KID.
MAYBE YOU DID SEE SOMEONE WEARING A SYMBIOTE, BUT THEY AREN'T LIKE US.
THE SYMBIOTE'S NOT YOUR PROBLEM. IT'S WHOEVER'S WEARING IT.
THE MUTANT CALLED CYCLOPS WANTS TO SAVE HIS FATHER.
YOU CAN STUDY THE SYMBIOTES' STRENGTHS AND WEAKNESSES ALL YOU WANT.
BUT THAT ISN'T GONNA HELP YOU FIGHT THE PERSON INSIDE.
WE WANT TO HELP OUR FAMILIES.

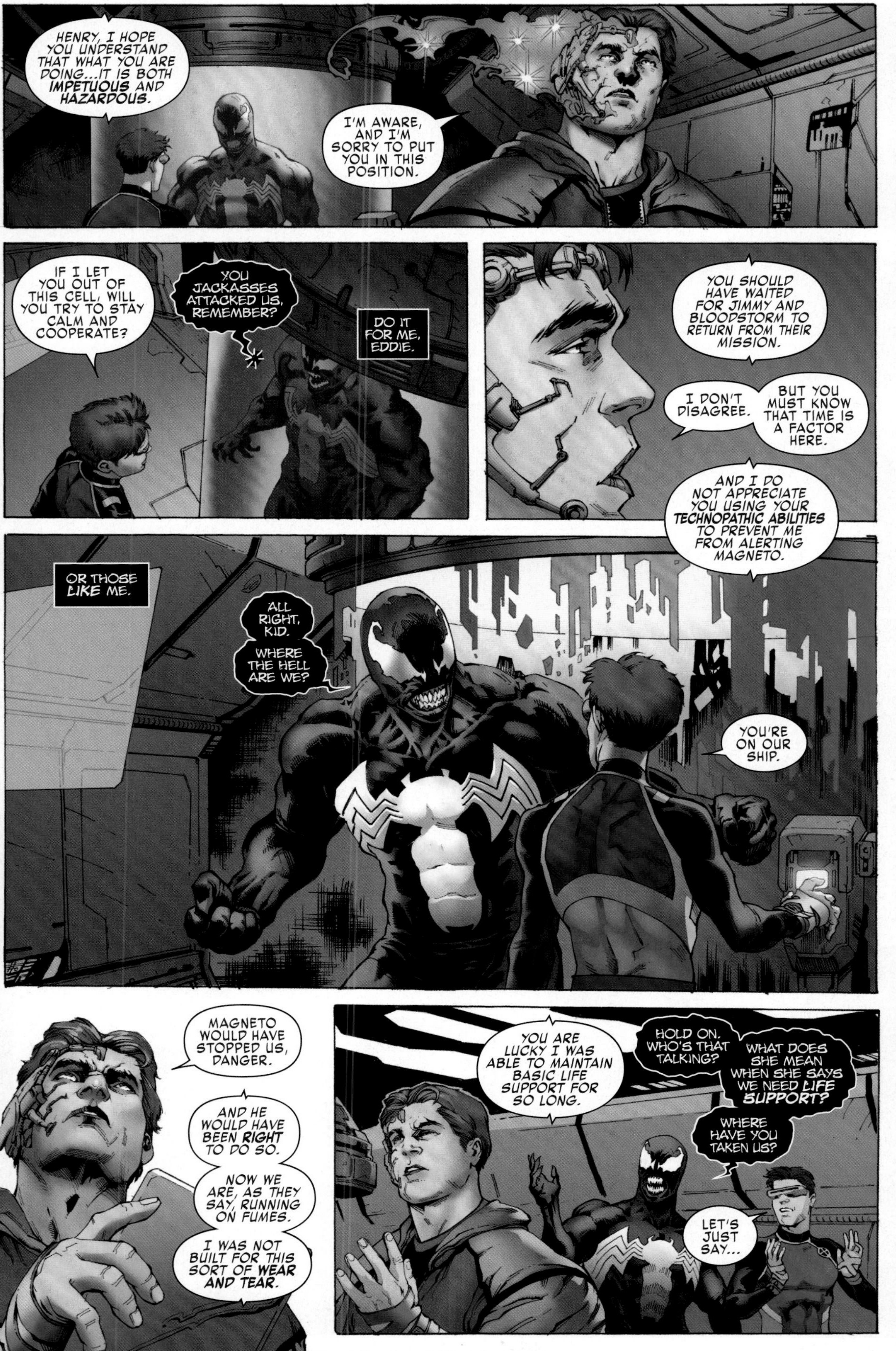
HENRY, I HOPE YOU UNDERSTAND THAT WHAT YOU ARE DOING...IT IS BOTH IMPETUOUS AND HAZARDOUS.
I'M AWARE, AND I'M SORRY TO PUT YOU IN THIS POSITION.
IF I LET YOU OUT OF THIS CELL, WILL YOU TRY TO STAY CALM AND COOPERATE?
YOU JACKASSES ATTACKED US, REMEMBER?
DO IT FOR ME, EDDIE.
YOU SHOULD HAVE WAITED FOR JIMMY AND BLOODSTORM TO RETURN FROM THEIR MISSION.
I DON'T DISAGREE.
BUT YOU MUST KNOW THAT TIME IS A FACTOR HERE.
AND I DO NOT APPRECIATE YOU USING YOUR TECHNOPATHIC ABILITIES TO PREVENT ME FROM ALERTING MAGNETO.
OR THOSE LIKE ME.
ALL RIGHT, KID.
WHERE THE HELL ARE WE?
YOU'RE ON OUR SHIP.
MAGNETO WOULD HAVE STOPPED US, DANGER.
AND HE WOULD HAVE BEEN RIGHT TO DO SO.
NOW WE ARE, AS THEY SAY, RUNNING ON FUMES.
I WAS NOT BUILT FOR THIS SORT OF WEAR AND TEAR.
YOU ARE LUCKY I WAS ABLE TO MAINTAIN BASIC LIFE SUPPORT FOR SO LONG.
HOLD ON. WHO'S THAT TALKING?
WHAT DOES SHE MEAN WHEN SHE SAYS WE NEED LIFE SUPPORT?
WHERE HAVE YOU TAKEN US?
LET'S JUST SAY...

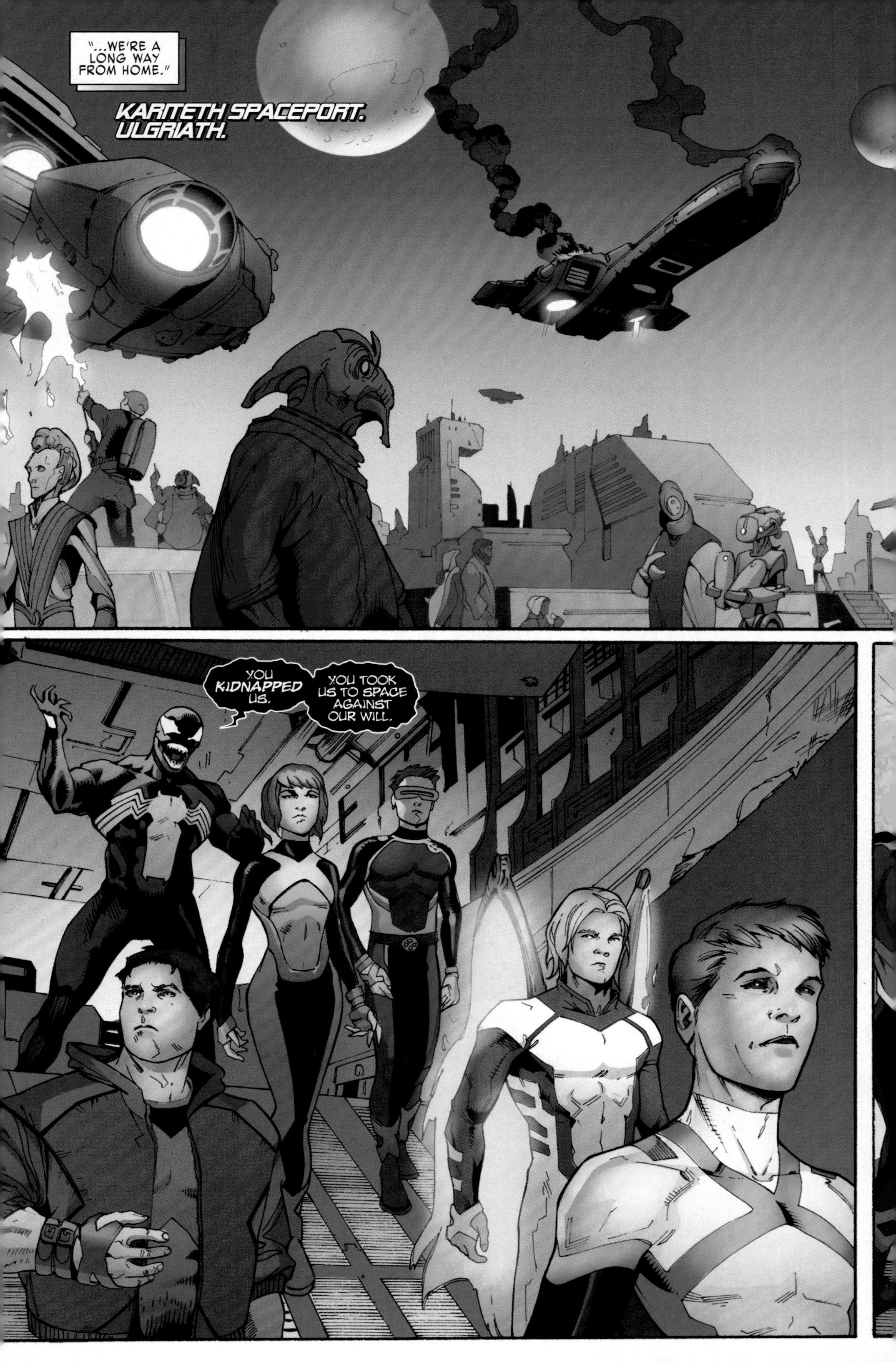
"...WE'RE A LONG WAY FROM HOME."
KARITETH SPACEPORT. ULGRIATH.
YOU KIDNAPPED US.
YOU TOOK US TO SPACE AGAINST OUR WILL.

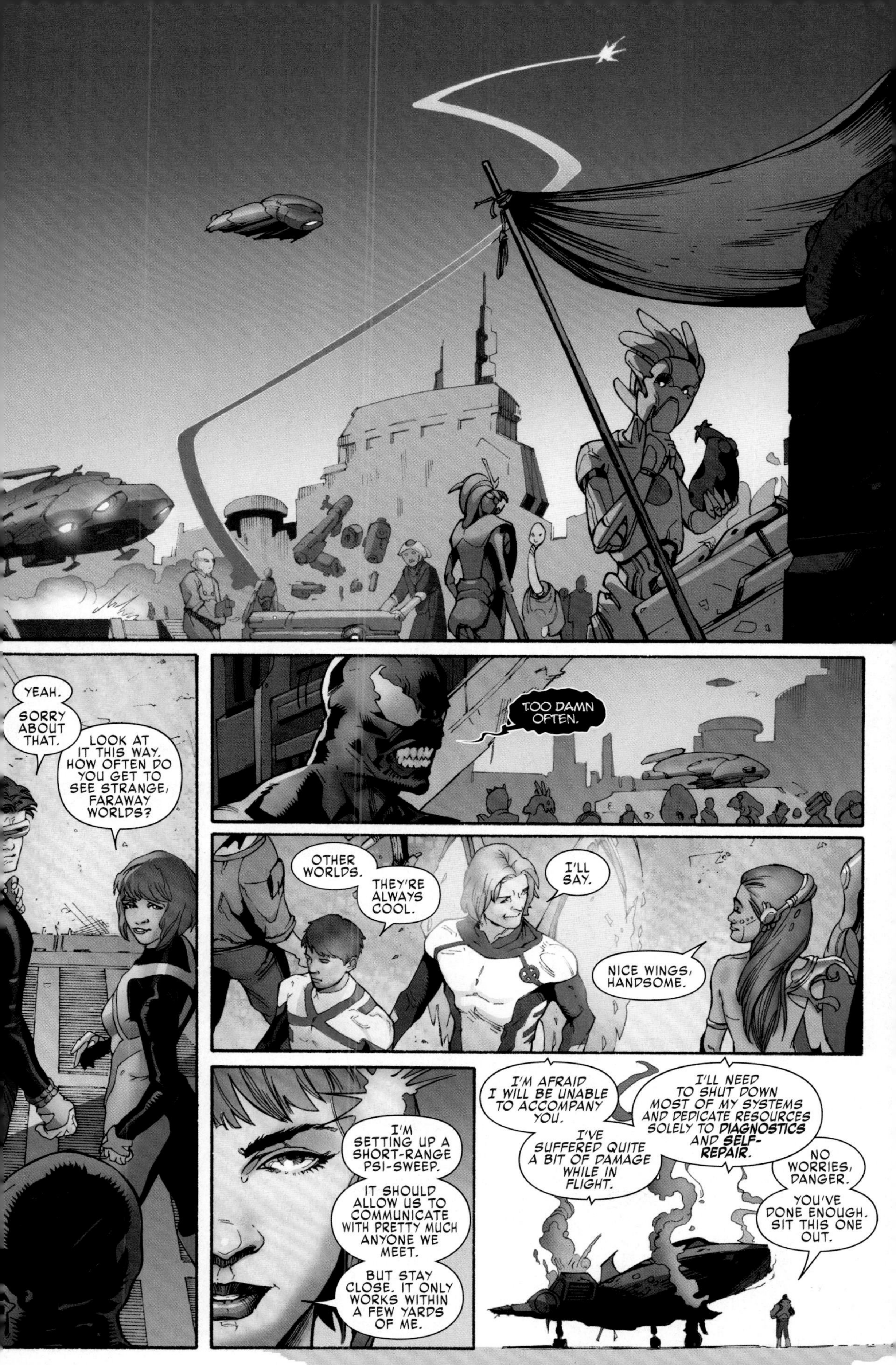
YEAH.
SORRY ABOUT THAT.
LOOK AT IT THIS WAY. HOW OFTEN DO YOU GET TO SEE STRANGE, FARAWAY WORLDS?
TOO DAMN OFTEN.
OTHER WORLDS.
THEY'RE ALWAYS COOL.
I'LL SAY.
NICE WINGS, HANDSOME.
I'M SETTING UP A SHORT-RANGE PSI-SWEEP.
IT SHOULD ALLOW US TO COMMUNICATE WITH PRETTY MUCH ANYONE WE MEET.
BUT STAY CLOSE. IT ONLY WORKS WITHIN A FEW YARDS OF ME.
I'M AFRAID I WILL BE UNABLE TO ACCOMPANY YOU.
I'VE SUFFERED QUITE A BIT OF DAMAGE WHILE IN FLIGHT.
I'LL NEED TO SHUT DOWN MOST OF MY SYSTEMS AND DEDICATE RESOURCES SOLELY TO DIAGNOSTICS AND SELF-REPAIR.
NO WORRIES, DANGER.
YOU'VE DONE ENOUGH. SIT THIS ONE OUT.

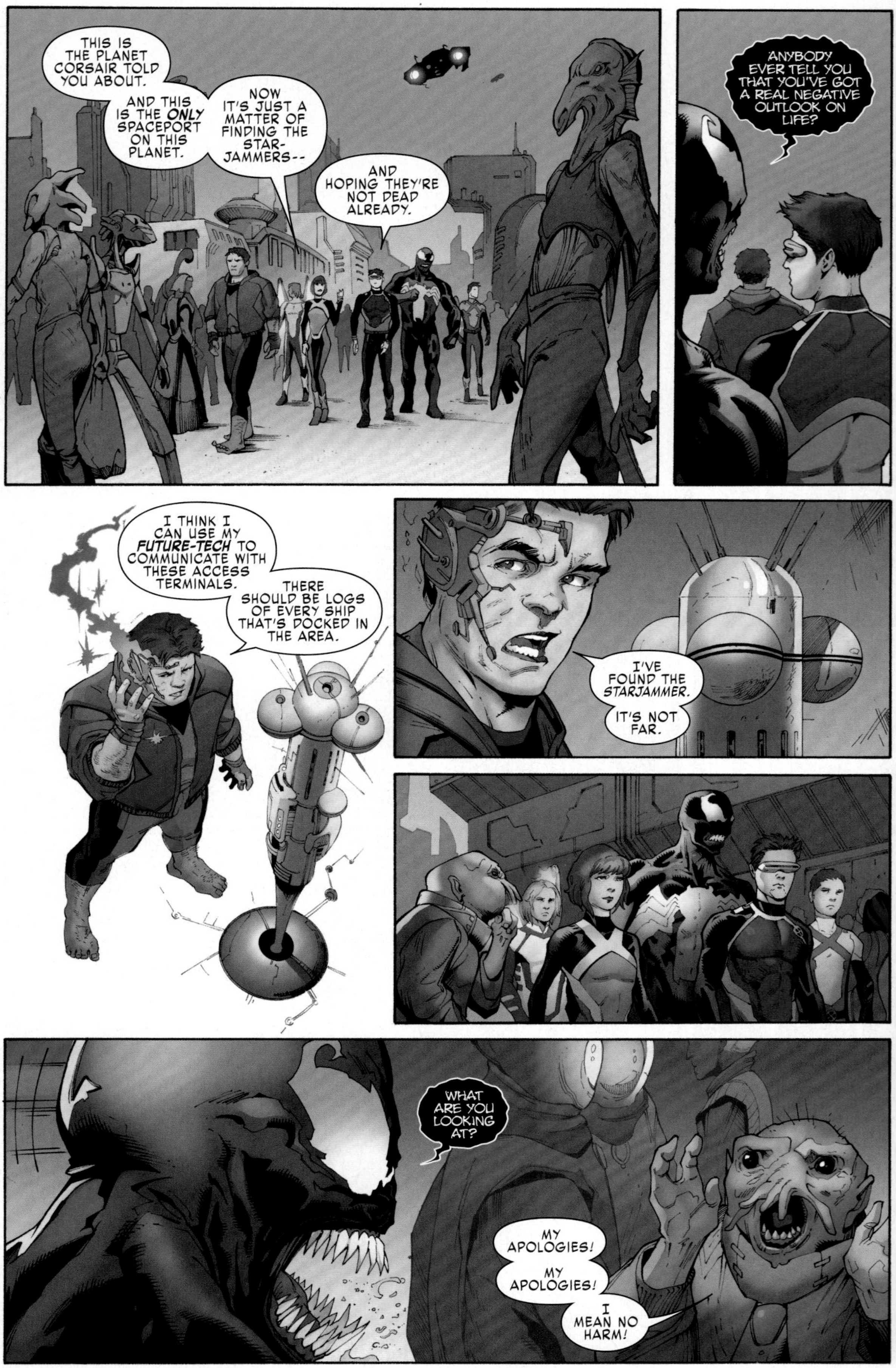
THIS IS THE PLANET CORSAIR TOLD YOU ABOUT.
AND THIS IS THE ONLY SPACEPORT ON THIS PLANET.
NOW IT'S JUST A MATTER OF FINDING THE STAR-JAMMERS--
AND HOPING THEY'RE NOT DEAD ALREADY.
ANYBODY EVER TELL YOU THAT YOU'VE GOT A REAL NEGATIVE OUTLOOK ON LIFE?
I THINK I CAN USE MY FUTURE-TECH TO COMMUNICATE WITH THESE ACCESS TERMINALS.
THERE SHOULD BE LOGS OF EVERY SHIP THAT'S DOCKED IN THE AREA.
I'VE FOUND THE STARJAMMER.
IT'S NOT FAR.
WHAT ARE YOU LOOKING AT?
MY APOLOGIES!
MY APOLOGIES!
I MEAN NO HARM!

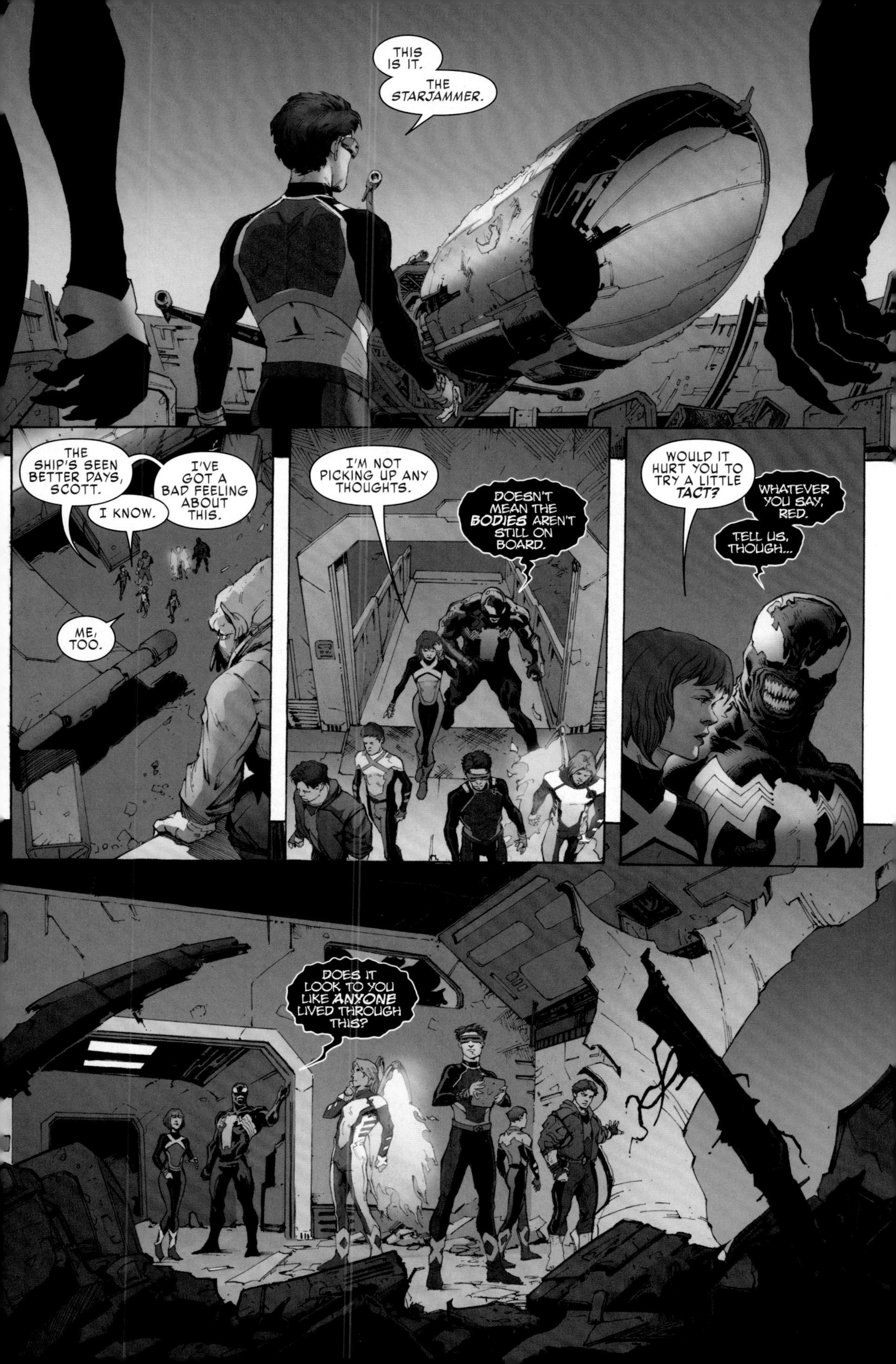
THIS IS IT. THE STARJAMMER.
THE SHIP'S SEEN BETTER DAYS, SCOTT.
I KNOW.
I'VE GOT A BAD FEELING ABOUT THIS.
ME, TOO.
I'M NOT PICKING UP ANY THOUGHTS.
DOESN'T MEAN THE BODIES AREN'T STILL ON BOARD.
WOULD IT HURT YOU TO TRY A LITTLE TACT?
WHATEVER YOU SAY, RED.
TELL US, THOUGH...
DOES IT LOOK TO YOU LIKE ANYONE LIVED THROUGH THIS?

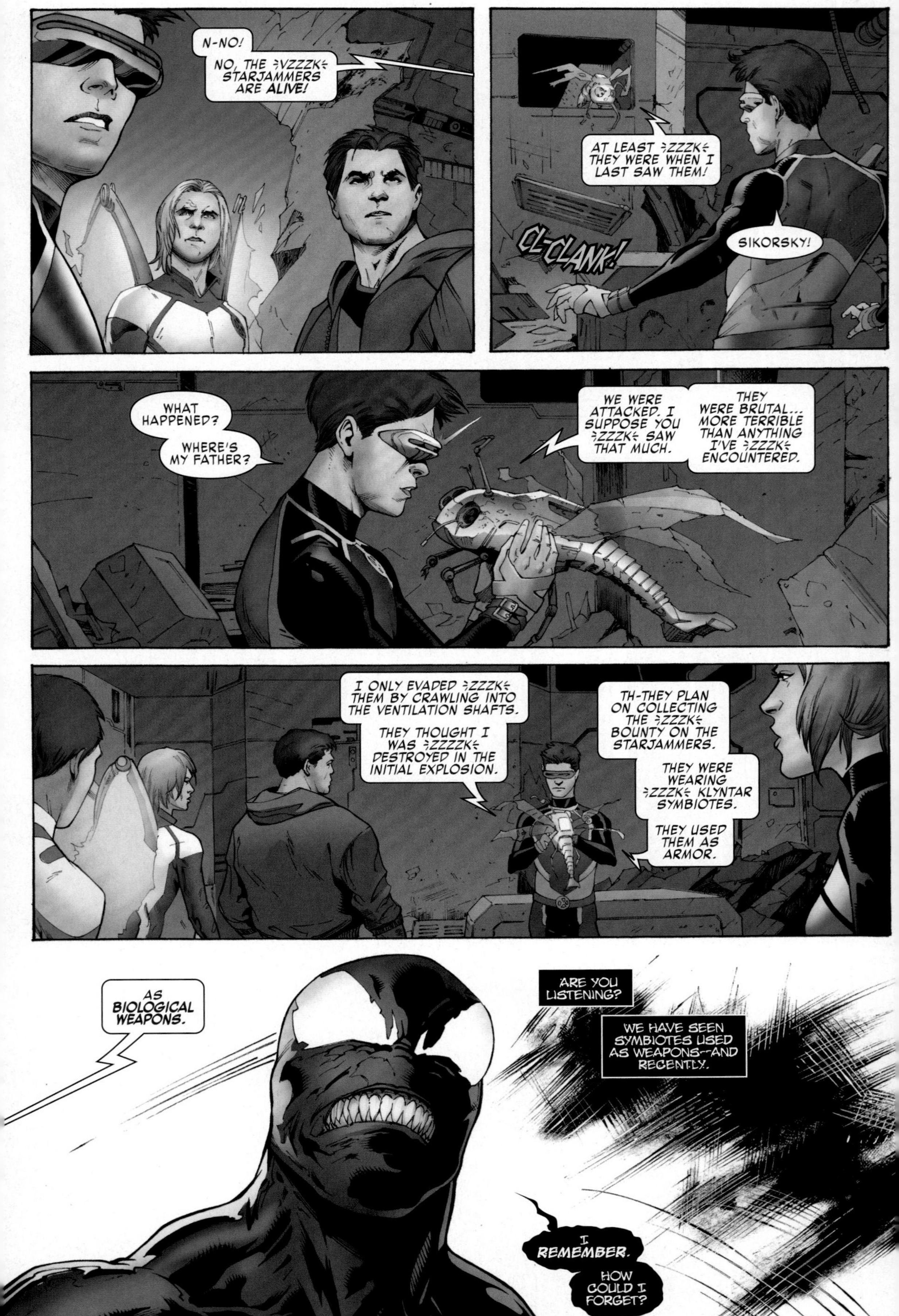

N-NO!
NO, THE ⋟VZZZK⋞ STARJAMMERS ARE ALIVE!
AT LEAST ⋟ZZZK⋞ THEY WERE WHEN I LAST SAW THEM!
CL-CLANK!
SIKORSKY!
WHAT HAPPENED?
WHERE'S MY FATHER?
WE WERE ATTACKED. I SUPPOSE YOU ⋟ZZZK⋞ SAW THAT MUCH.
THEY WERE BRUTAL... MORE TERRIBLE THAN ANYTHING I'VE ⋟ZZZK⋞ ENCOUNTERED.
I ONLY EVADED ⋟ZZZK⋞ THEM BY CRAWLING INTO THE VENTILATION SHAFTS.
THEY THOUGHT I WAS ⋟ZZZK⋞ DESTROYED IN THE INITIAL EXPLOSION.
TH-THEY PLAN ON COLLECTING THE ⋟ZZZK⋞ BOUNTY ON THE STARJAMMERS.
THEY WERE WEARING ⋟ZZZK⋞ KLYNTAR SYMBIOTES.
THEY USED THEM AS ARMOR.
AS BIOLOGICAL WEAPONS.
ARE YOU LISTENING?
WE HAVE SEEN SYMBIOTES USED AS WEAPONS--AND RECENTLY.
I REMEMBER.
HOW COULD I FORGET?

THIS IS WHY WE MUST HELP THE X-MEN.

LISTEN-- THESE SYMBIOTES... THEY'RE BAD NEWS.

AT LEAST, THE PEOPLE INSIDE THEM ARE.

IN ANOTHER UNIVERSE... KLYNTAR... VENOM SYMBIOTES...

...THEY WERE USED TO DESTROY...

AND YOU GUYS ARE JUST KIDS.

MAYBE YOU SHOULD CALL ON--I DUNNO--THE *GROWN-UP* X-MEN TO HANDLE THIS ONE.

...ALMOST WIPED OUT.

NO FREE WILL...

WE DON'T HAVE TIME TO CALL FOR BACKUP.

THE PEOPLE WHO HAVE MY FATHER...WE HAVE TO FIND THEM AND STOP THEM.

IF WE DON'T, THEY'LL TURN THEM OVER TO GOD-KNOWS- WHO.

I'LL NEVER SEE HIM AGAIN.

...WASTED AND USED UP...

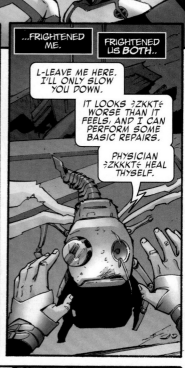

...FRIGHTENED ME.

FRIGHTENED US *BOTH*..

L-LEAVE ME HERE. I'LL ONLY SLOW YOU DOWN.

IT LOOKS ⁑ZKKT⁑ WORSE THAN IT FEELS, AND I CAN PERFORM SOME BASIC REPAIRS.

PHYSICIAN ⁑ZKKKT⁑ HEAL THYSELF.

I KNOW YOU DON'T WANT TO BE DRAWN INTO ANOTHER FIGHT TO SAVE MY SPECIES.

WE'RE GOING TO GET OURSELVES KILLED!

WE HAVE NO CHOICE.

AW, CRAP.

I'M GONNA HAVE TO WATCH OVER THESE DAMN KIDS, AIN'T I?

WHATEVER MAKES THIS WORK FOR YOU, EDDIE.

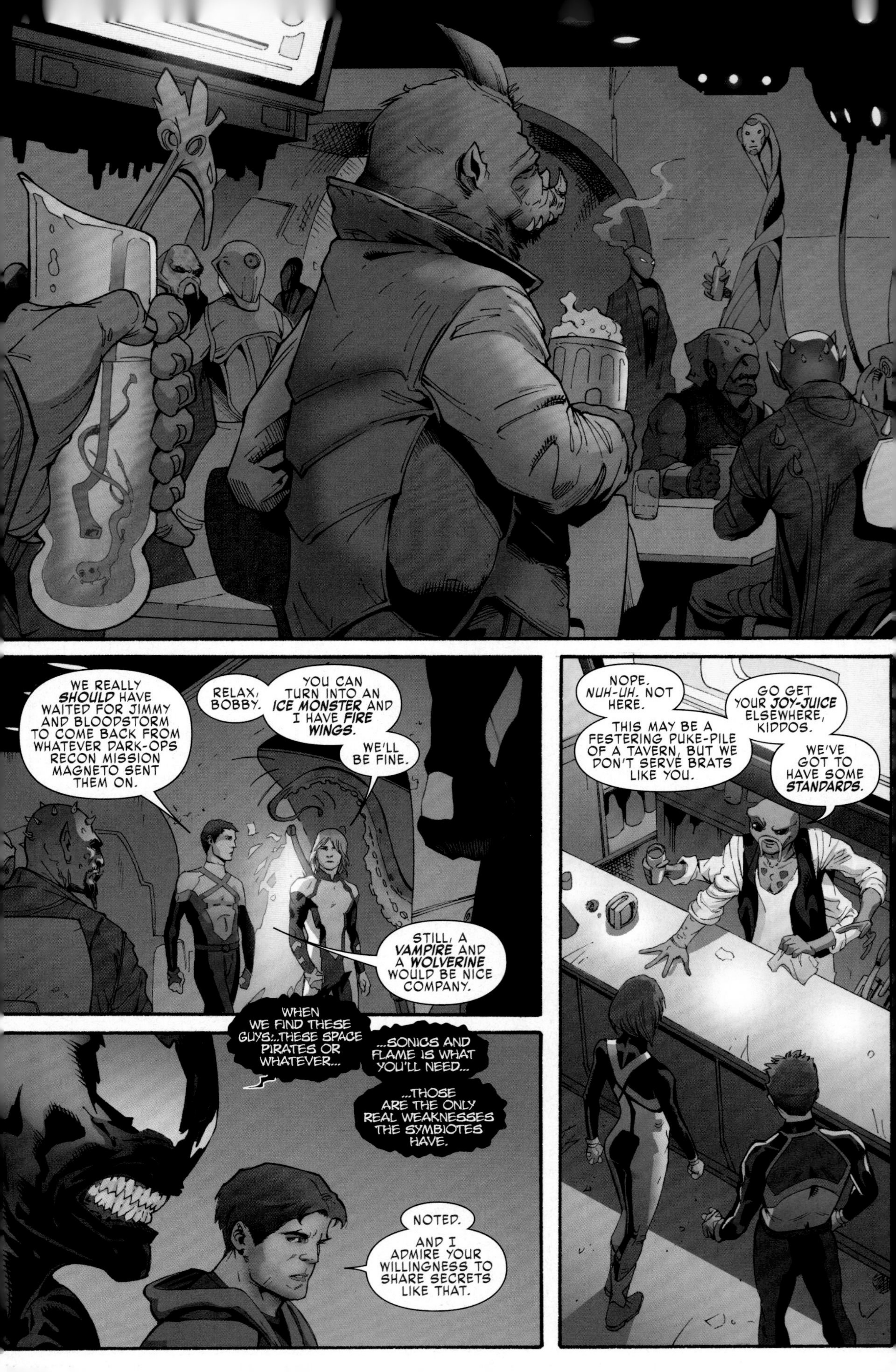

WE REALLY SHOULD HAVE WAITED FOR JIMMY AND BLOODSTORM TO COME BACK FROM WHATEVER DARK-OPS RECON MISSION MAGNETO SENT THEM ON.
RELAX, BOBBY.
YOU CAN TURN INTO AN ICE MONSTER AND I HAVE FIRE WINGS.
WE'LL BE FINE.
STILL, A VAMPIRE AND A WOLVERINE WOULD BE NICE COMPANY.
NOPE. NUH-UH. NOT HERE.
THIS MAY BE A FESTERING PUKE-PILE OF A TAVERN, BUT WE DON'T SERVE BRATS LIKE YOU.
GO GET YOUR JOY-JUICE ELSEWHERE, KIDDOS.
WE'VE GOT TO HAVE SOME STANDARDS.
WHEN WE FIND THESE GUYS...THESE SPACE PIRATES OR WHATEVER...
...SONICS AND FLAME IS WHAT YOU'LL NEED...
...THOSE ARE THE ONLY REAL WEAKNESSES THE SYMBIOTES HAVE.
NOTED.
AND I ADMIRE YOUR WILLINGNESS TO SHARE SECRETS LIKE THAT.

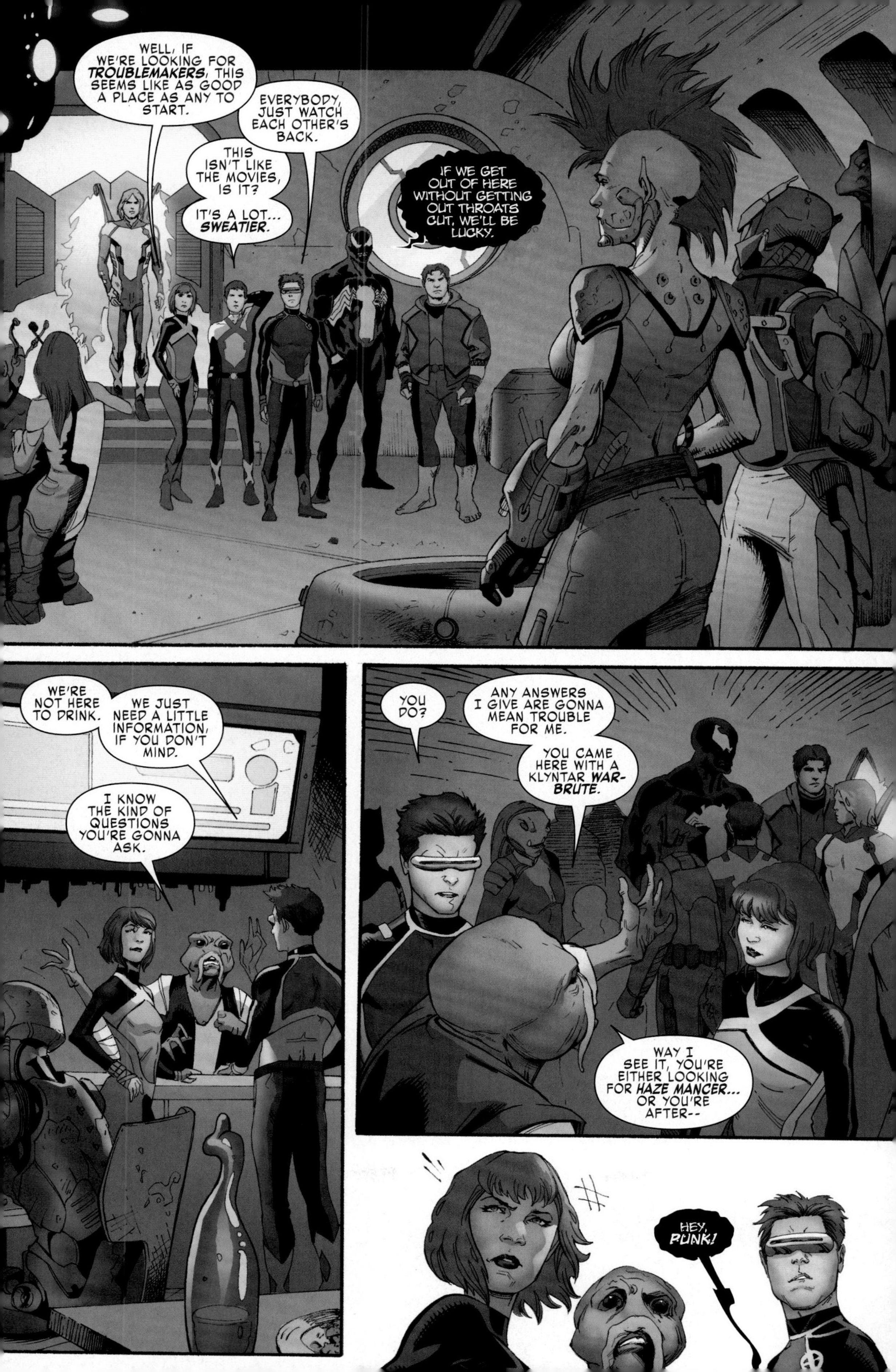
WELL, IF WE'RE LOOKING FOR TROUBLEMAKERS, THIS SEEMS LIKE AS GOOD A PLACE AS ANY TO START.
EVERYBODY, JUST WATCH EACH OTHER'S BACK.
THIS ISN'T LIKE THE MOVIES, IS IT?
IT'S A LOT... SWEATIER.
IF WE GET OUT OF HERE WITHOUT GETTING OUT THROATS CUT, WE'LL BE LUCKY.
WE'RE NOT HERE TO DRINK.
WE JUST NEED A LITTLE INFORMATION, IF YOU DON'T MIND.
I KNOW THE KIND OF QUESTIONS YOU'RE GONNA ASK.
YOU DO?
ANY ANSWERS I GIVE ARE GONNA MEAN TROUBLE FOR ME.
YOU CAME HERE WITH A KLYNTAR WAR-BRUTE.
WAY I SEE IT, YOU'RE EITHER LOOKING FOR HAZE MANCER... OR YOU'RE AFTER--
HEY, PUNK!

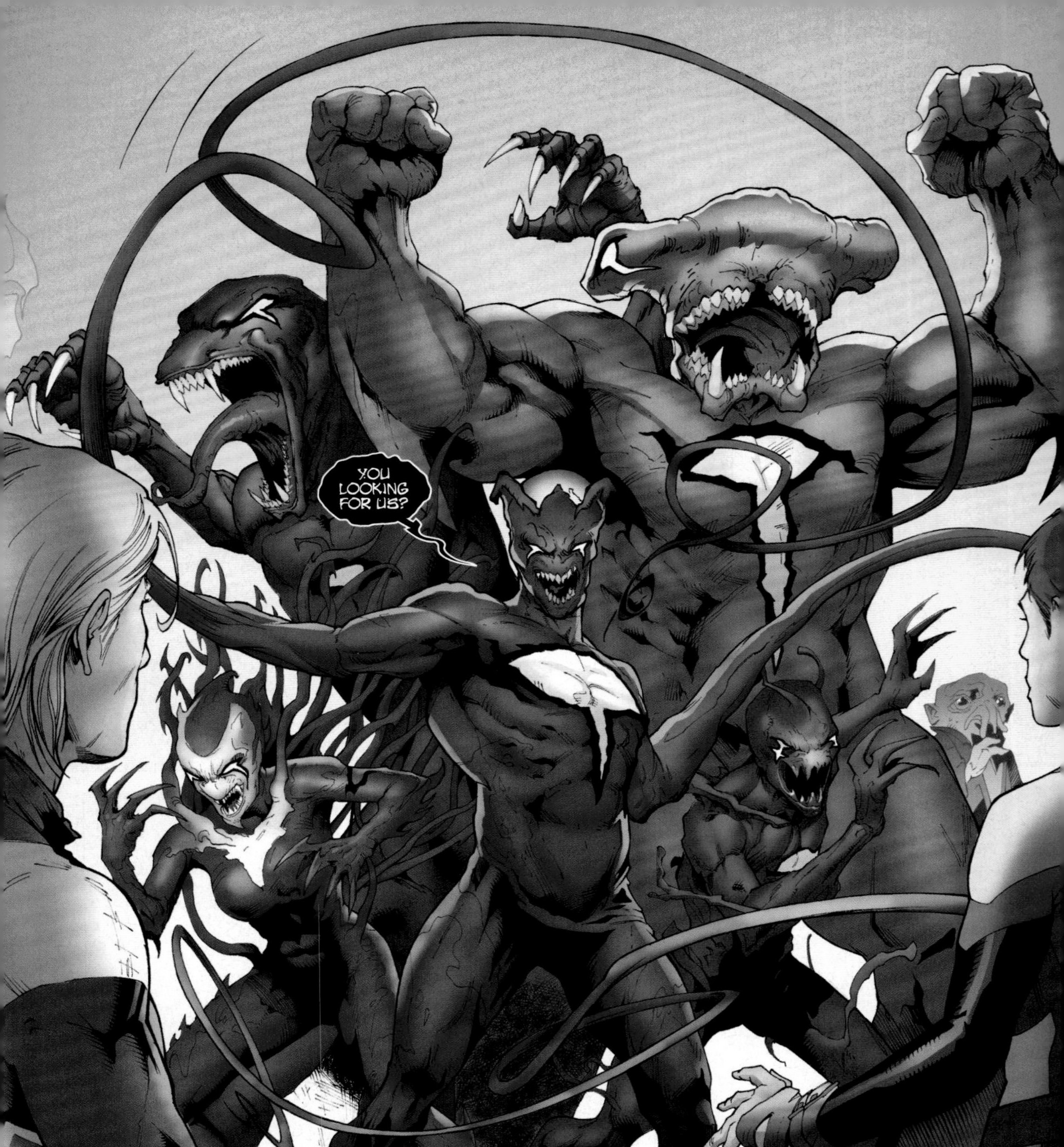
YOU LOOKING FOR US?

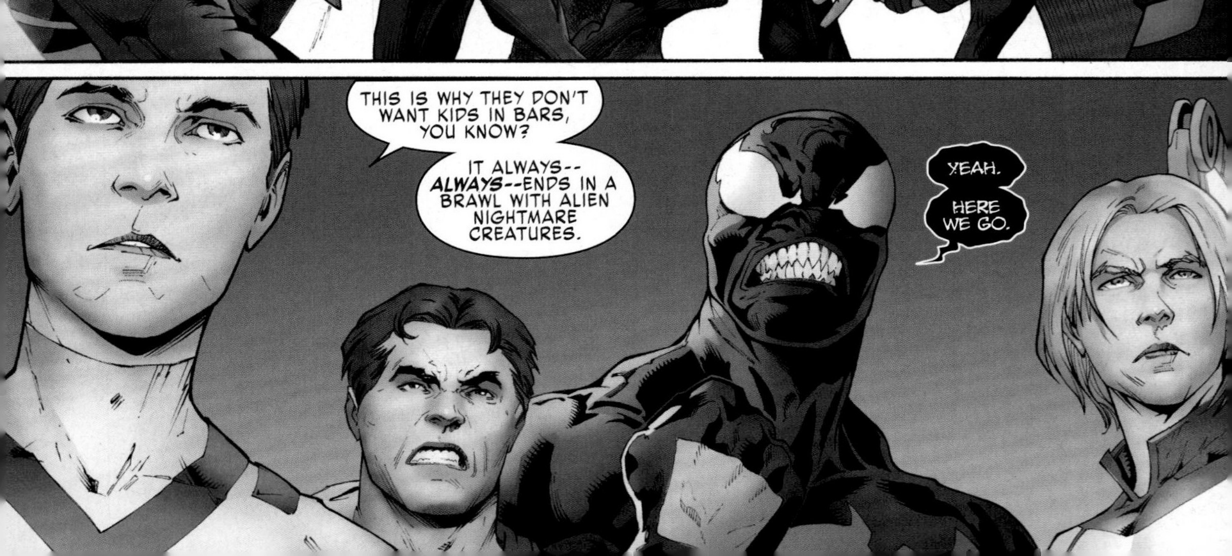
THIS IS WHY THEY DON'T WANT KIDS IN BARS, YOU KNOW?
IT ALWAYS-- ALWAYS--ENDS IN A BRAWL WITH ALIEN NIGHTMARE CREATURES.
YEAH.
HERE WE GO.

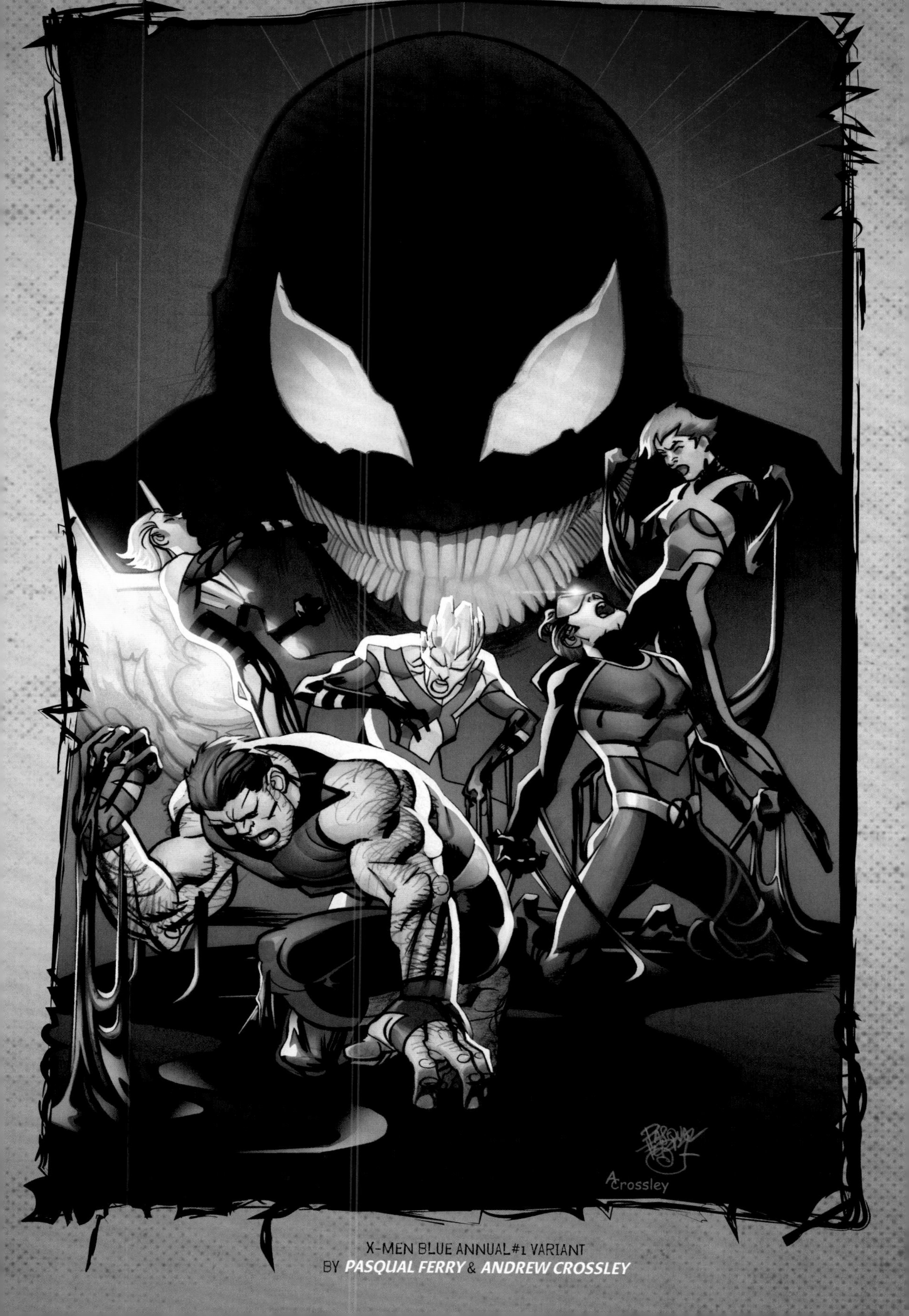
A Crossley

X-MEN BLUE ANNUAL #1 VARIANT
BY **PASQUAL FERRY** & **ANDREW CROSSLEY**

X-MEN BLUE 21

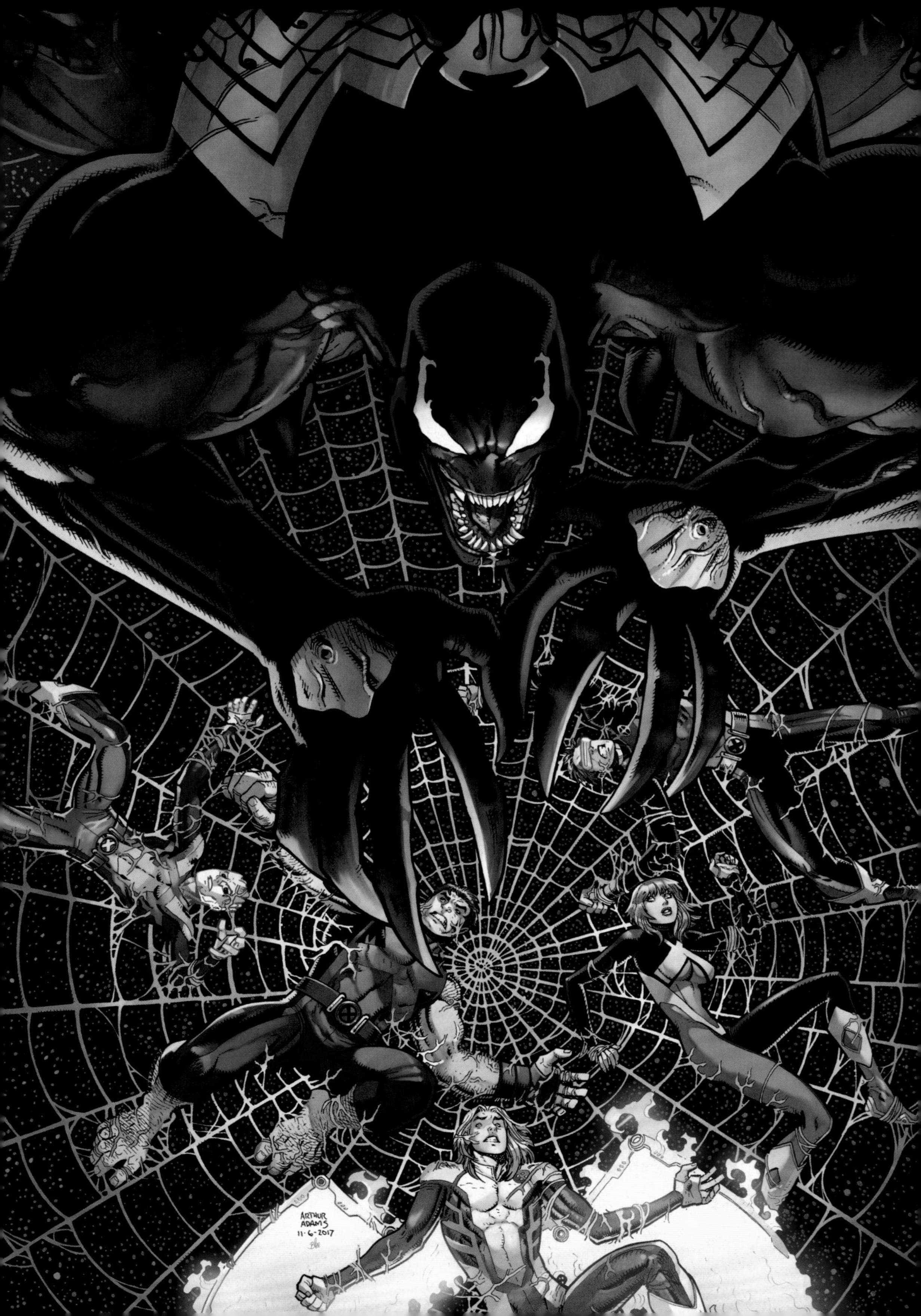
ARTHUR ADAMS
11-6-2017

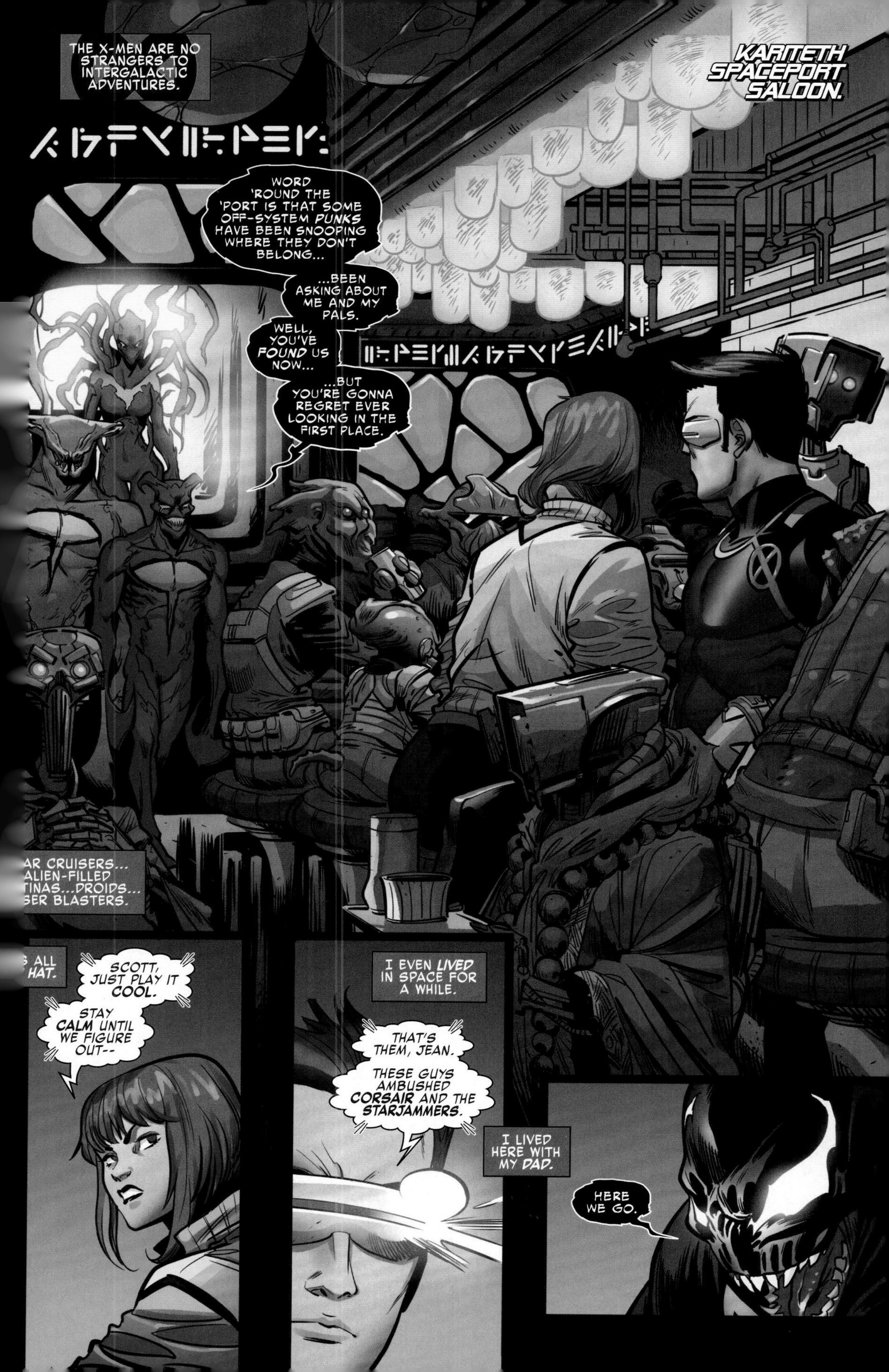

THE X-MEN ARE NO STRANGERS TO INTERGALACTIC ADVENTURES.
KARITETH SPACEPORT SALOON.
WORD 'ROUND THE 'PORT IS THAT SOME OFF-SYSTEM PUNKS HAVE BEEN SNOOPING WHERE THEY DON'T BELONG...
...BEEN ASKING ABOUT ME AND MY PALS.
WELL, YOU'VE FOUND US NOW...
...BUT YOU'RE GONNA REGRET EVER LOOKING IN THE FIRST PLACE.
AR CRUISERS... ALIEN-FILLED TINAS...DROIDS... SER BLASTERS.
S ALL HAT.
SCOTT, JUST PLAY IT COOL.
STAY CALM UNTIL WE FIGURE OUT--
I EVEN LIVED IN SPACE FOR A WHILE.
THAT'S THEM, JEAN.
THESE GUYS AMBUSHED CORSAIR AND THE STARJAMMERS.
I LIVED HERE WITH MY DAD.
HERE WE GO.

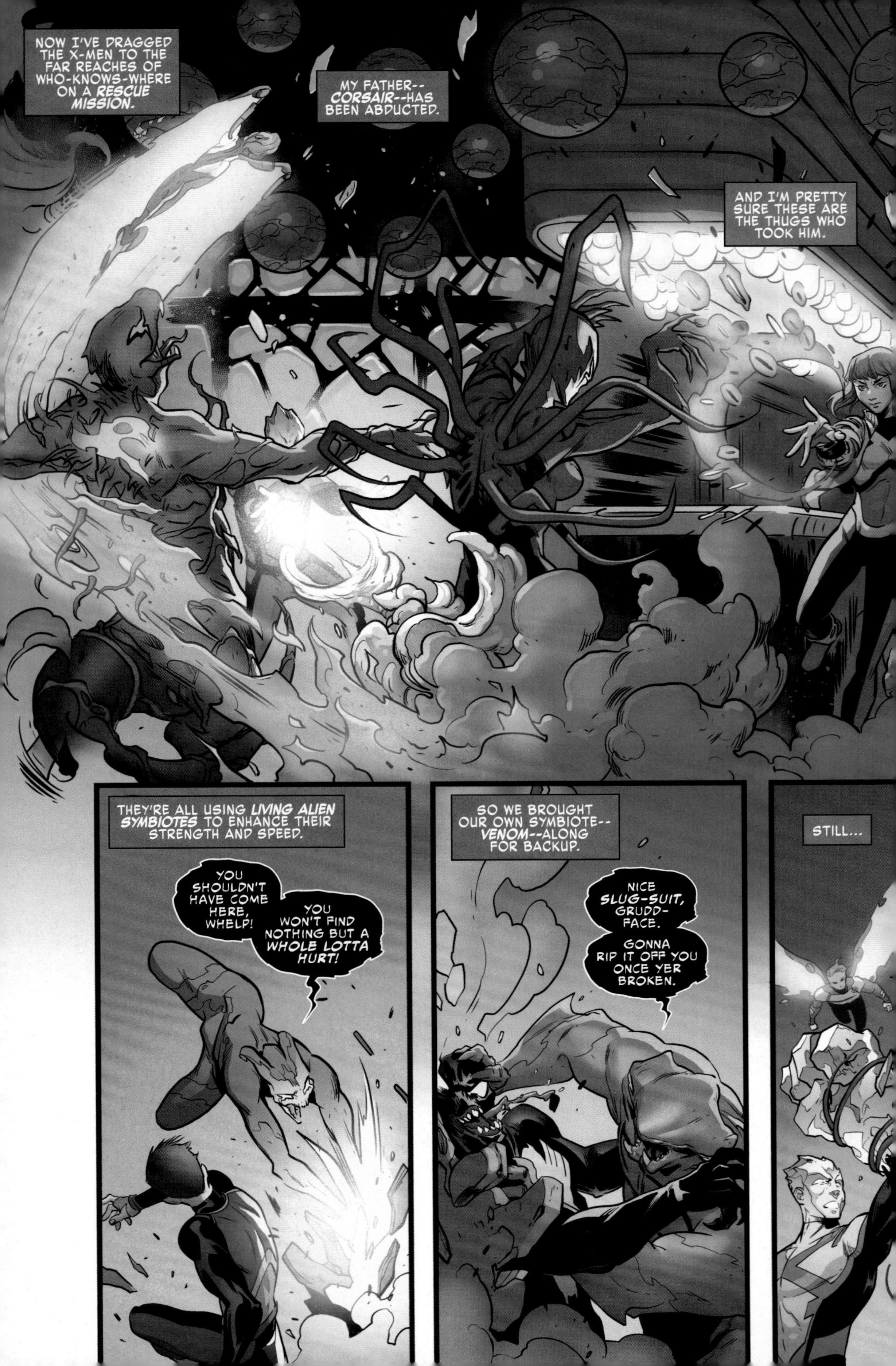
NOW I'VE DRAGGED THE X-MEN TO THE FAR REACHES OF WHO-KNOWS-WHERE ON A RESCUE MISSION.
MY FATHER--CORSAIR--HAS BEEN ABDUCTED.
AND I'M PRETTY SURE THESE ARE THE THUGS WHO TOOK HIM.
THEY'RE ALL USING LIVING ALIEN SYMBIOTES TO ENHANCE THEIR STRENGTH AND SPEED.
YOU SHOULDN'T HAVE COME HERE, WHELP!
YOU WON'T FIND NOTHING BUT A WHOLE LOTTA HURT!
SO WE BROUGHT OUR OWN SYMBIOTE--VENOM--ALONG FOR BACKUP.
NICE SLUG-SUIT, GRUDD-FACE.
GONNA RIP IT OFF YOU ONCE YER BROKEN.
STILL...

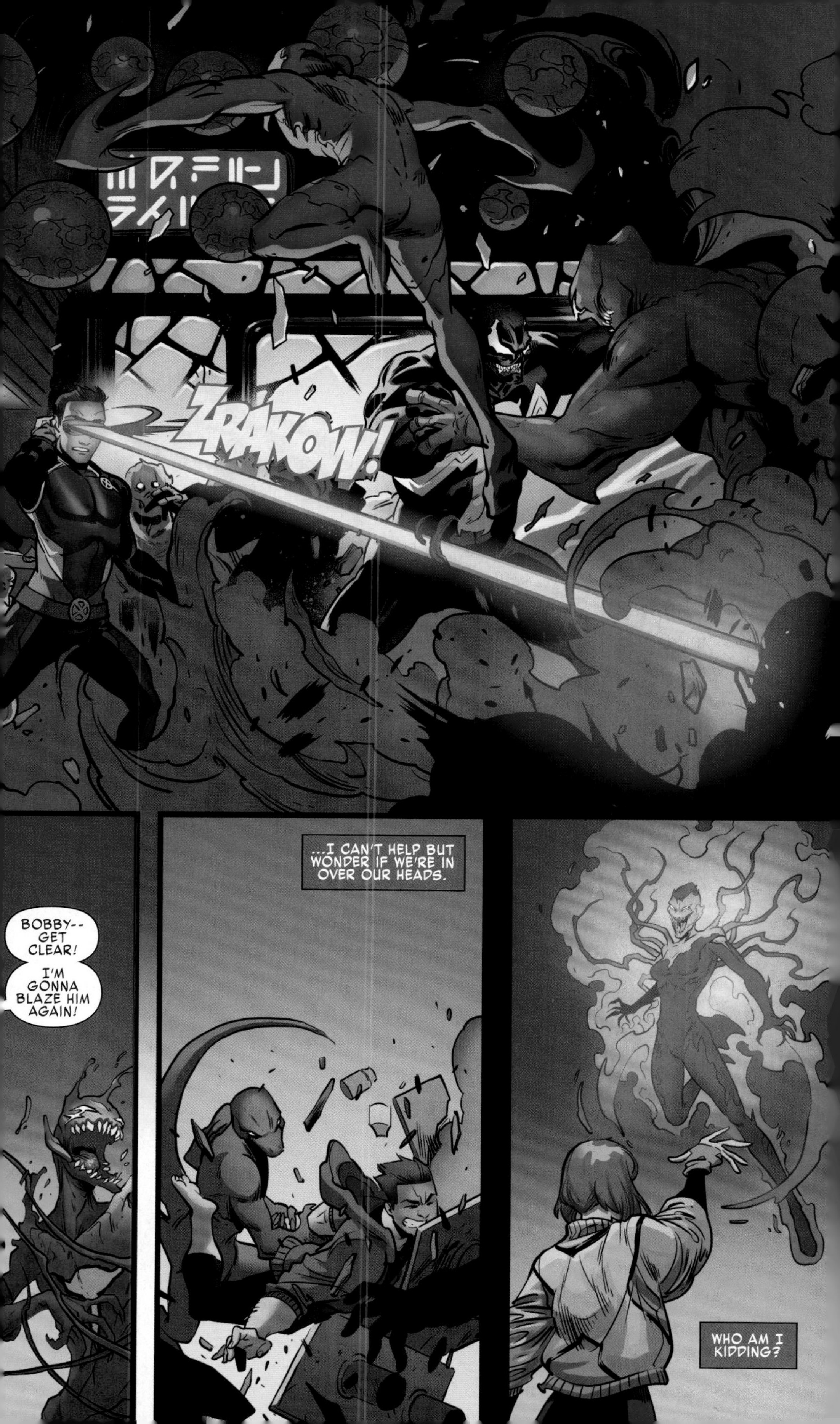
ZRAKOW!
BOBBY-- GET CLEAR!
I'M GONNA BLAZE HIM AGAIN!
...I CAN'T HELP BUT WONDER IF WE'RE IN OVER OUR HEADS.
WHO AM I KIDDING?

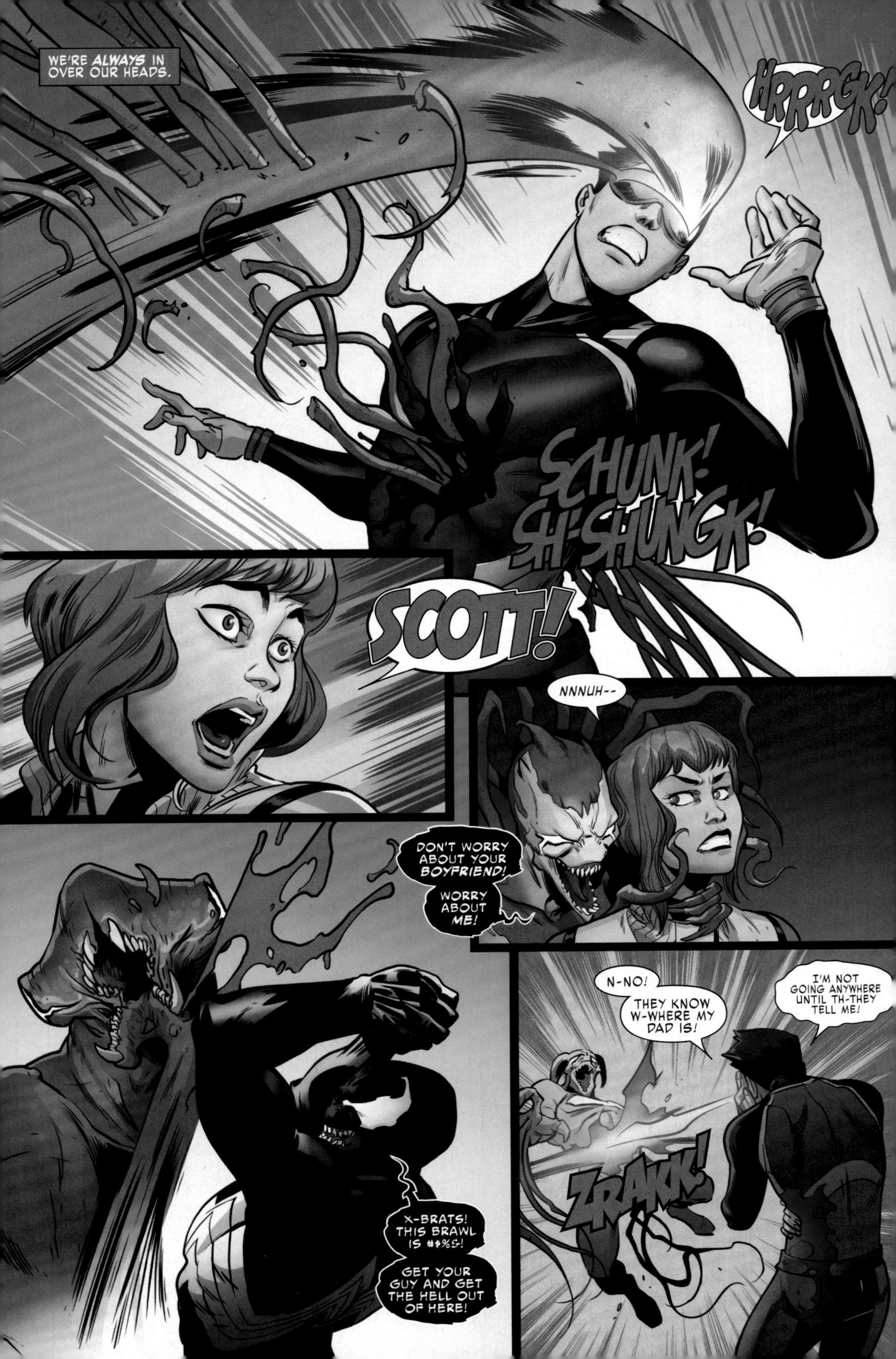
WE'RE ALWAYS IN OVER OUR HEADS.
HRRRGK!
SCHUNK! SH-SHUNGK!
SCOTT!
NNNUH--
DON'T WORRY ABOUT YOUR BOYFRIEND!
WORRY ABOUT ME!
X-BRATS! THIS BRAWL IS #$%&!
GET YOUR GUY AND GET THE HELL OUT OF HERE!
N-NO!
THEY KNOW W-WHERE MY DAD IS!
I'M NOT GOING ANYWHERE UNTIL TH-THEY TELL ME!
ZRAKK!

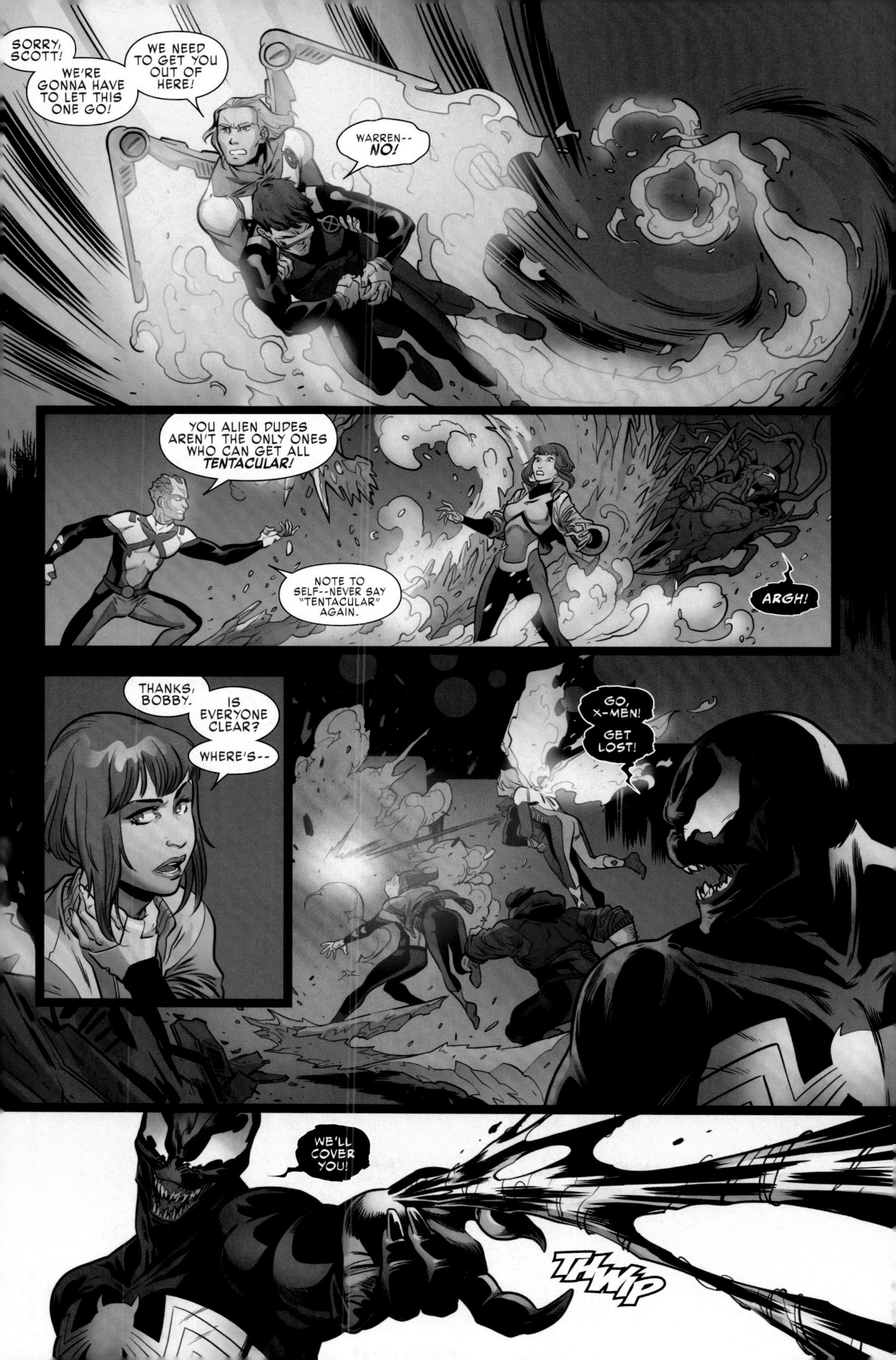
SORRY, SCOTT!
WE'RE GONNA HAVE TO LET THIS ONE GO!
WE NEED TO GET YOU OUT OF HERE!
WARREN-- NO!
YOU ALIEN DUDES AREN'T THE ONLY ONES WHO CAN GET ALL TENTACULAR!
NOTE TO SELF--NEVER SAY "TENTACULAR" AGAIN.
ARGH!
THANKS, BOBBY.
IS EVERYONE CLEAR?
WHERE'S--
GO, X-MEN!
GET LOST!
WE'LL COVER YOU!
THWIP

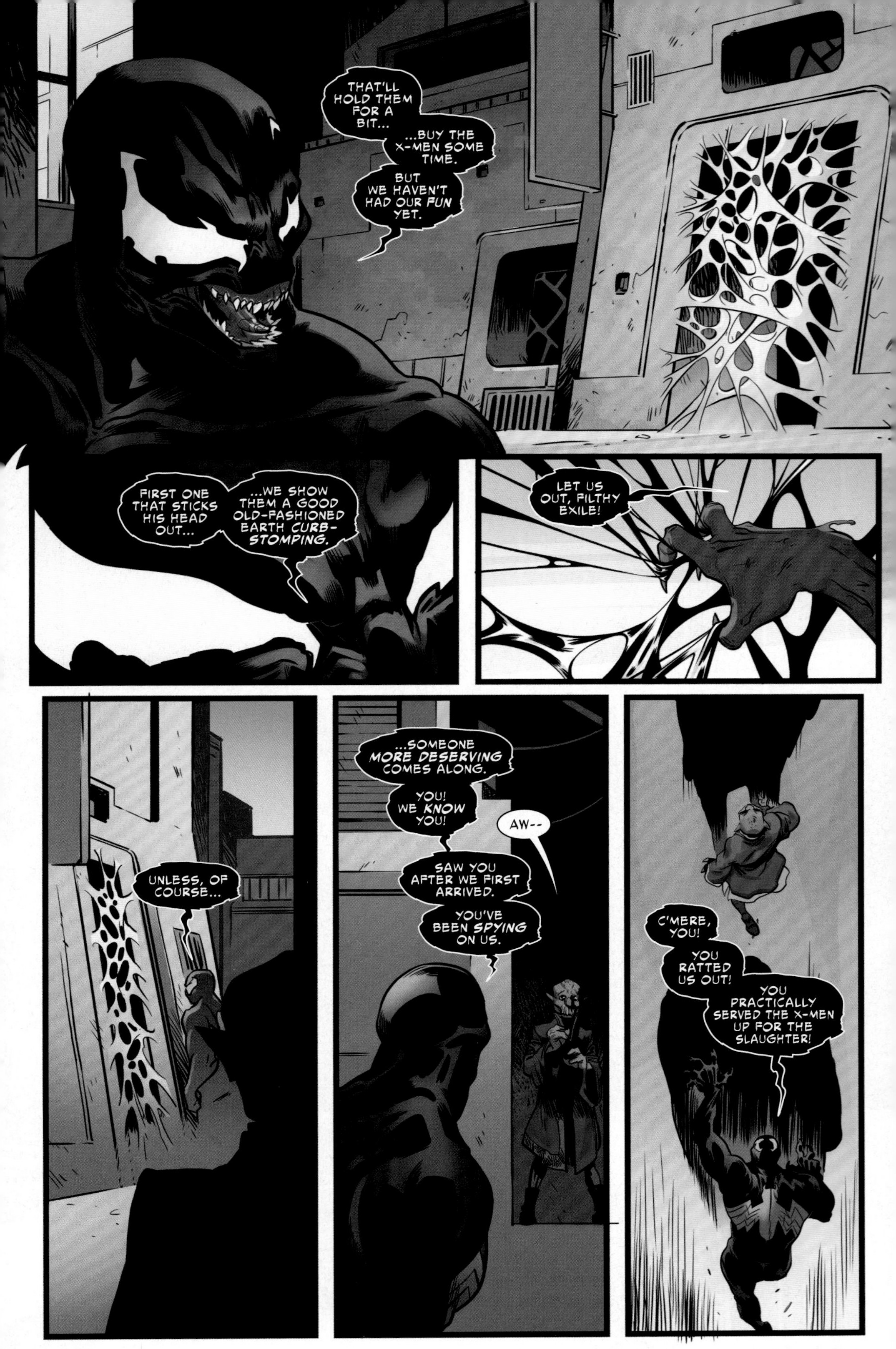
THAT'LL HOLD THEM FOR A BIT...
...BUY THE X-MEN SOME TIME.
BUT WE HAVEN'T HAD OUR FUN YET.
FIRST ONE THAT STICKS HIS HEAD OUT...
...WE SHOW THEM A GOOD OLD-FASHIONED EARTH CURB-STOMPING.
LET US OUT, FILTHY EXILE!
UNLESS, OF COURSE...
...SOMEONE MORE DESERVING COMES ALONG.
YOU! WE KNOW YOU!
AW--
SAW YOU AFTER WE FIRST ARRIVED.
YOU'VE BEEN SPYING ON US.
C'MERE, YOU!
YOU RATTED US OUT!
YOU PRACTICALLY SERVED THE X-MEN UP FOR THE SLAUGHTER!

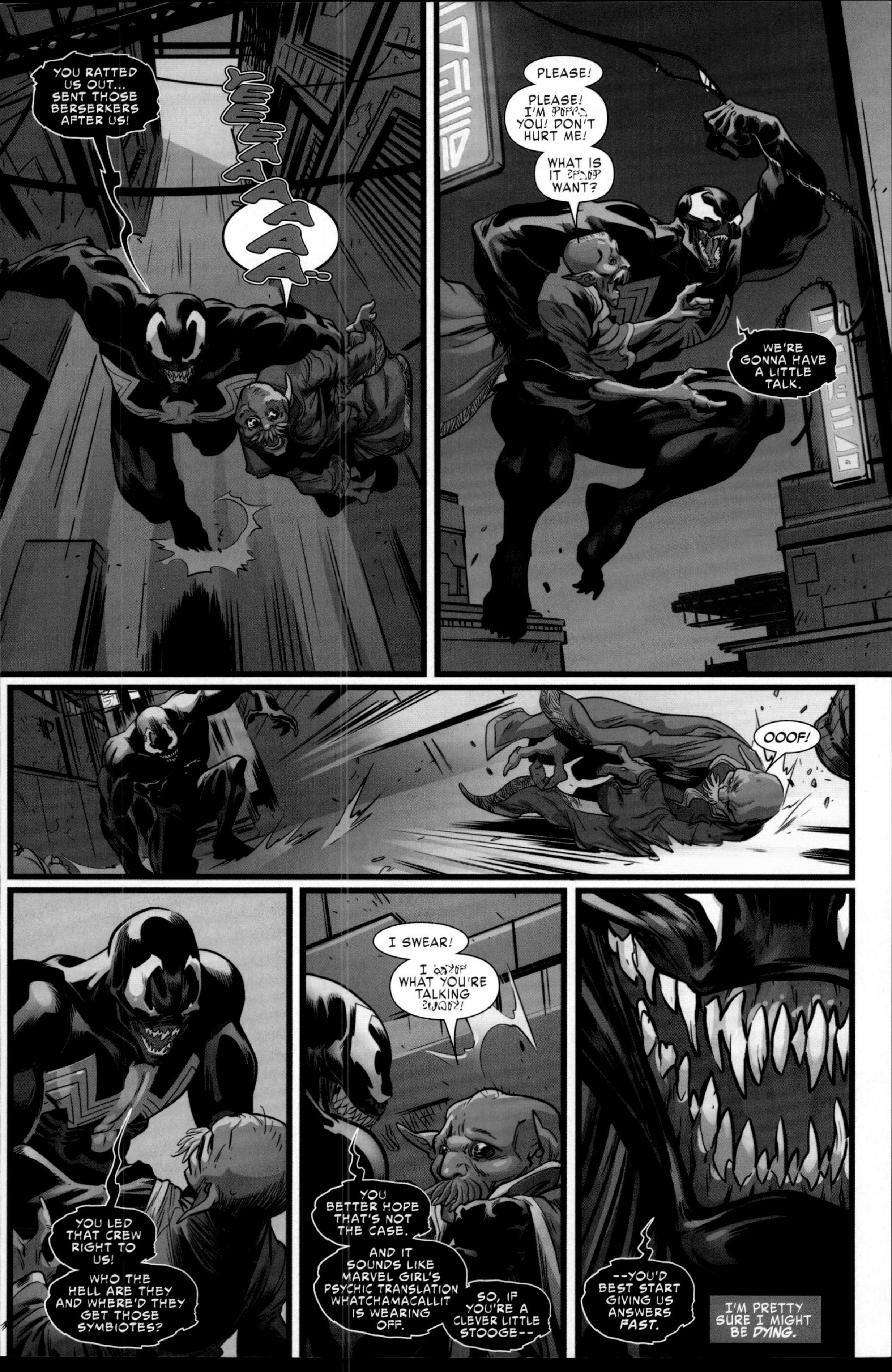
YOU RATTED US OUT... SENT THOSE BERSERKERS AFTER US!
YEEAAAAAAA...
PLEASE!
PLEASE! I'M YOU! DON'T HURT ME!
WHAT IS IT WANT?
WE'RE GONNA HAVE A LITTLE TALK.
OOOF!
YOU LED THAT CREW RIGHT TO US!
WHO THE HELL ARE THEY AND WHERE'D THEY GET THOSE SYMBIOTES?
I SWEAR!
I WHAT YOU'RE TALKING !
YOU BETTER HOPE THAT'S NOT THE CASE.
AND IT SOUNDS LIKE MARVEL GIRL'S PSYCHIC TRANSLATION WHATCHAMACALLIT IS WEARING OFF.
SO, IF YOU'RE A CLEVER LITTLE STOOGE--
--YOU'D BEST START GIVING US ANSWERS *FAST*.
I'M PRETTY SURE I MIGHT BE *DYING*.

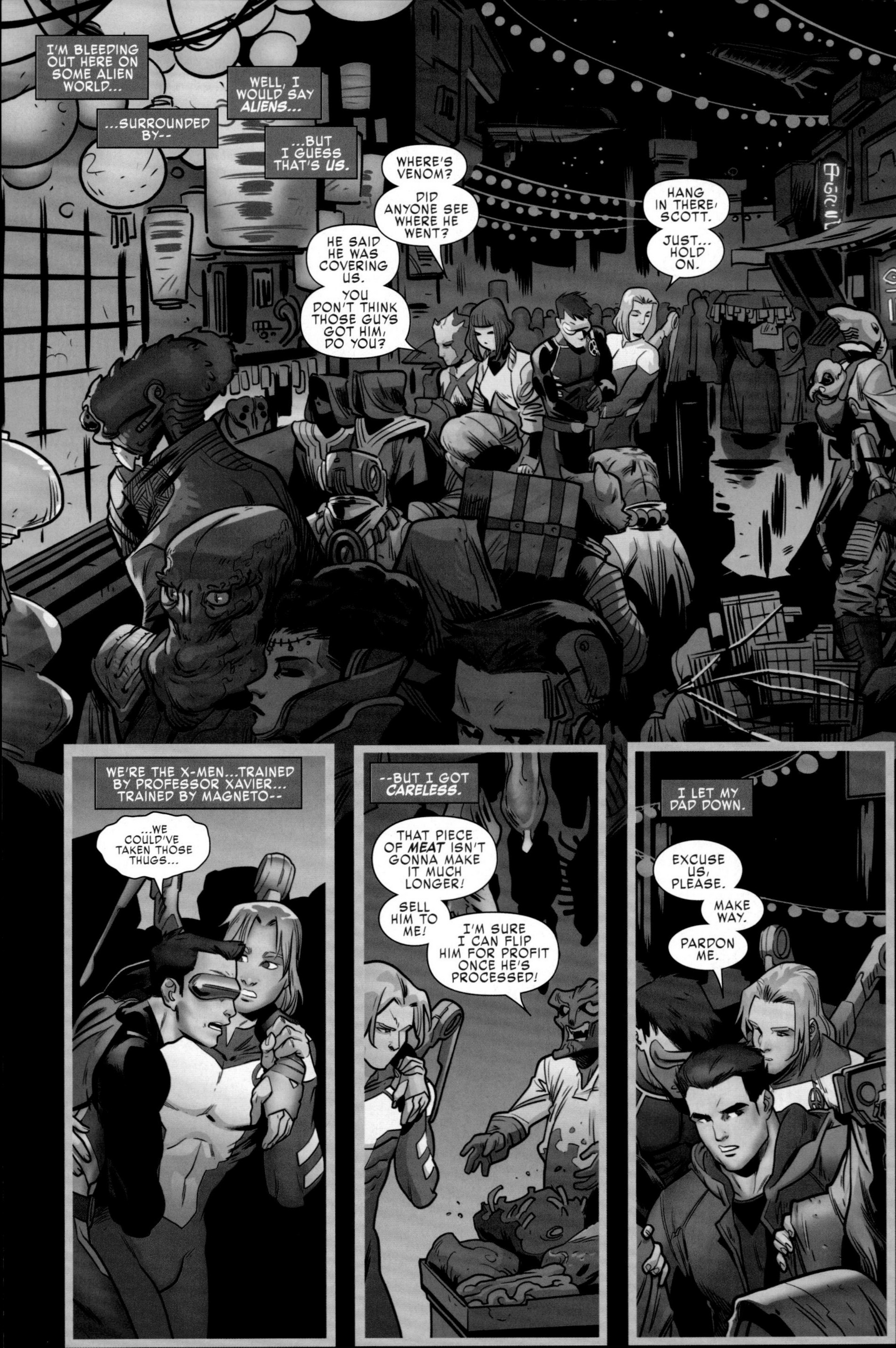
I'M BLEEDING OUT HERE ON SOME ALIEN WORLD...
...SURROUNDED BY--
WELL, I WOULD SAY ALIENS...
...BUT I GUESS THAT'S US.
WHERE'S VENOM?
DID ANYONE SEE WHERE HE WENT?
HE SAID HE WAS COVERING US.
YOU DON'T THINK THOSE GUYS GOT HIM, DO YOU?
HANG IN THERE, SCOTT.
JUST... HOLD ON.
WE'RE THE X-MEN...TRAINED BY PROFESSOR XAVIER... TRAINED BY MAGNETO--
...WE COULD'VE TAKEN THOSE THUGS...
--BUT I GOT CARELESS.
THAT PIECE OF MEAT ISN'T GONNA MAKE IT MUCH LONGER!
SELL HIM TO ME!
I'M SURE I CAN FLIP HIM FOR PROFIT ONCE HE'S PROCESSED!
I LET MY DAD DOWN.
EXCUSE US, PLEASE.
MAKE WAY.
PARDON ME.

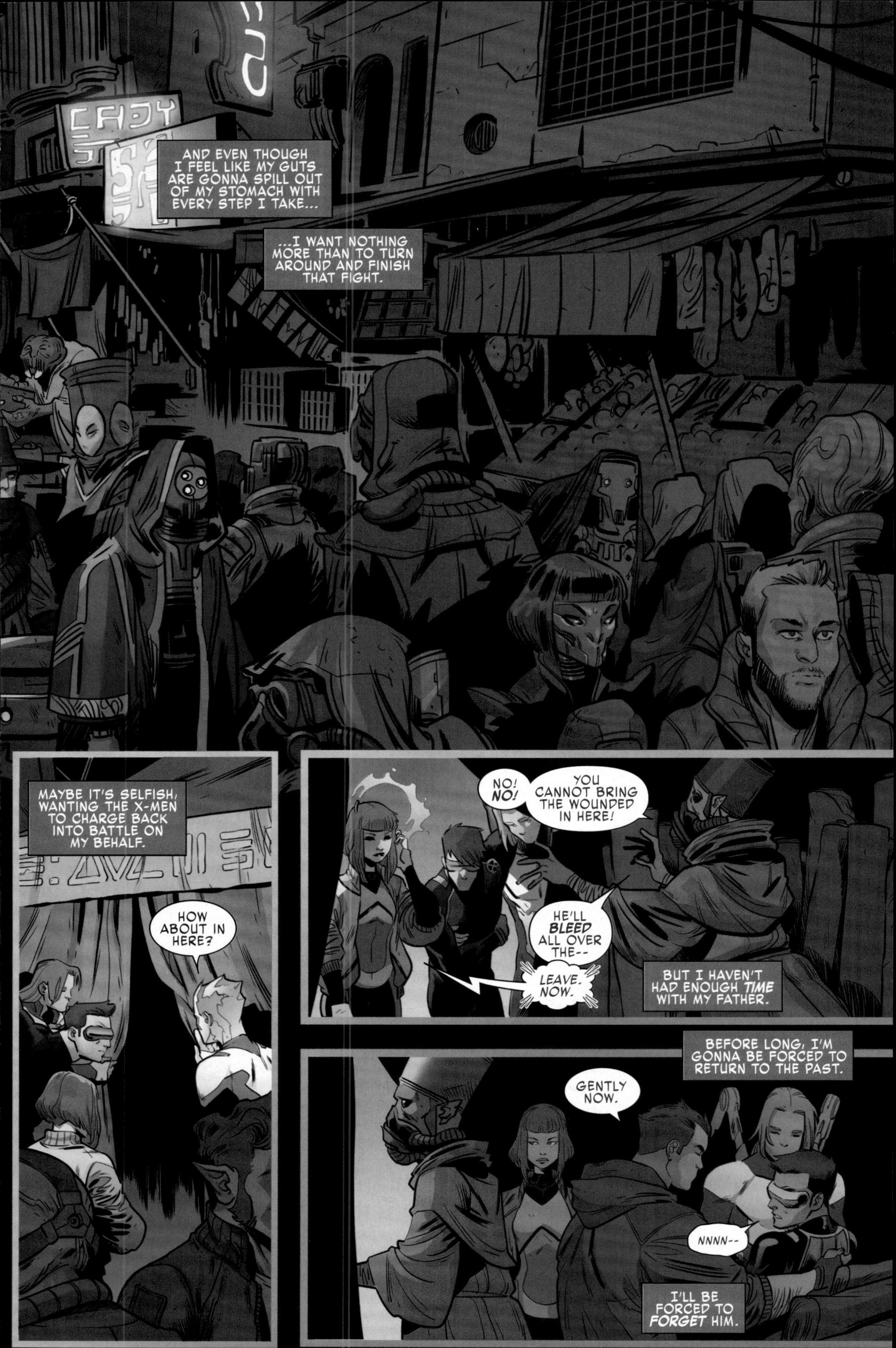
AND EVEN THOUGH I FEEL LIKE MY GUTS ARE GONNA SPILL OUT OF MY STOMACH WITH EVERY STEP I TAKE...
...I WANT NOTHING MORE THAN TO TURN AROUND AND FINISH THAT FIGHT.
MAYBE IT'S SELFISH, WANTING THE X-MEN TO CHARGE BACK INTO BATTLE ON MY BEHALF.
HOW ABOUT IN HERE?
NO! NO!
YOU CANNOT BRING THE WOUNDED IN HERE!
HE'LL BLEED ALL OVER THE--
LEAVE. NOW.
BUT I HAVEN'T HAD ENOUGH TIME WITH MY FATHER.
BEFORE LONG, I'M GONNA BE FORCED TO RETURN TO THE PAST.
GENTLY NOW.
NNNN--
I'LL BE FORCED TO FORGET HIM.

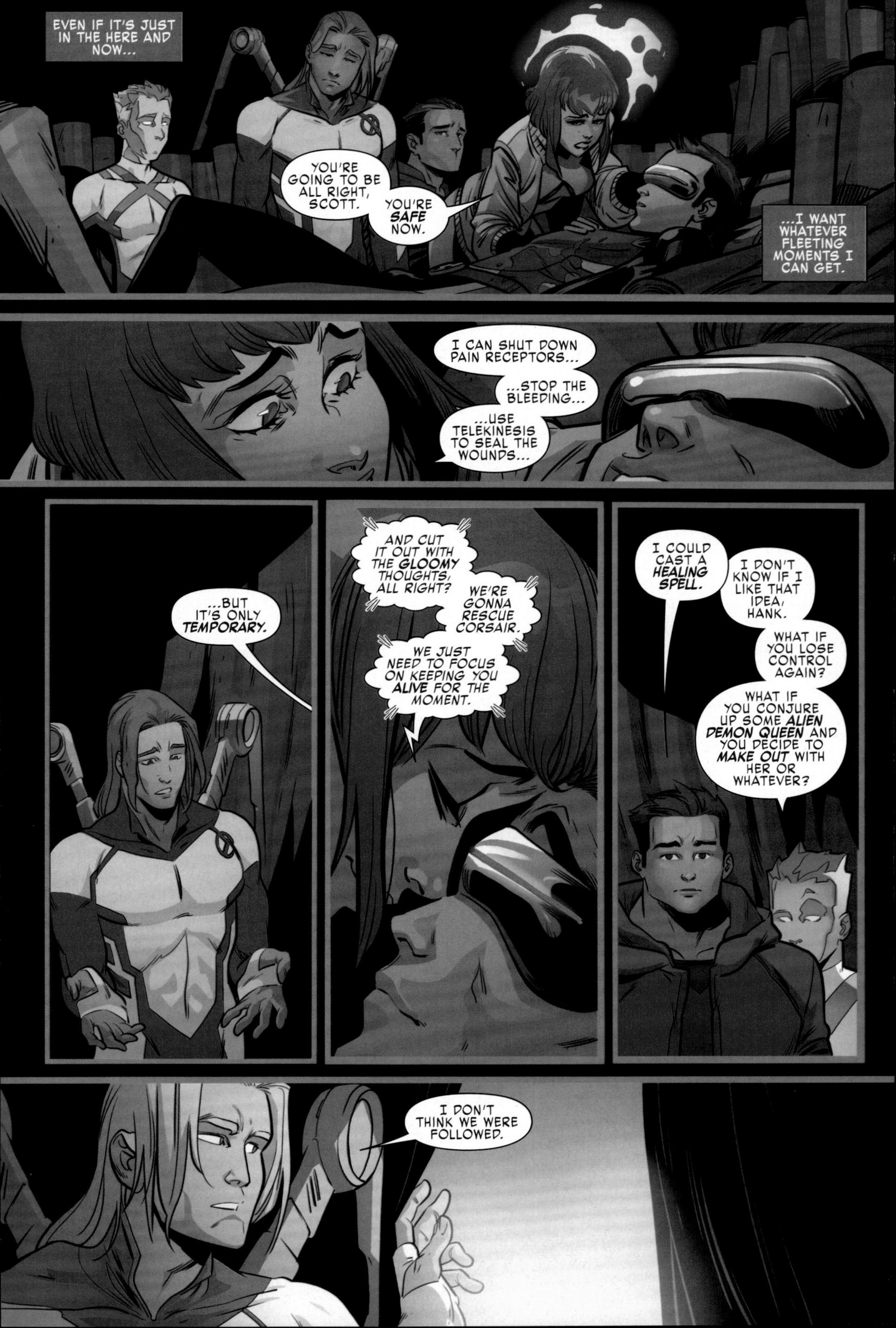
EVEN IF IT'S JUST IN THE HERE AND NOW...
YOU'RE GOING TO BE ALL RIGHT, SCOTT.
YOU'RE SAFE NOW.
...I WANT WHATEVER FLEETING MOMENTS I CAN GET.
I CAN SHUT DOWN PAIN RECEPTORS...
...STOP THE BLEEDING...
...USE TELEKINESIS TO SEAL THE WOUNDS...
...BUT IT'S ONLY TEMPORARY.
AND CUT IT OUT WITH THE GLOOMY THOUGHTS, ALL RIGHT?
WE'RE GONNA RESCUE CORSAIR.
WE JUST NEED TO FOCUS ON KEEPING YOU ALIVE FOR THE MOMENT.
I COULD CAST A HEALING SPELL.
I DON'T KNOW IF I LIKE THAT IDEA, HANK.
WHAT IF YOU LOSE CONTROL AGAIN?
WHAT IF YOU CONJURE UP SOME ALIEN DEMON QUEEN AND YOU DECIDE TO MAKE OUT WITH HER OR WHATEVER?
I DON'T THINK WE WERE FOLLOWED.

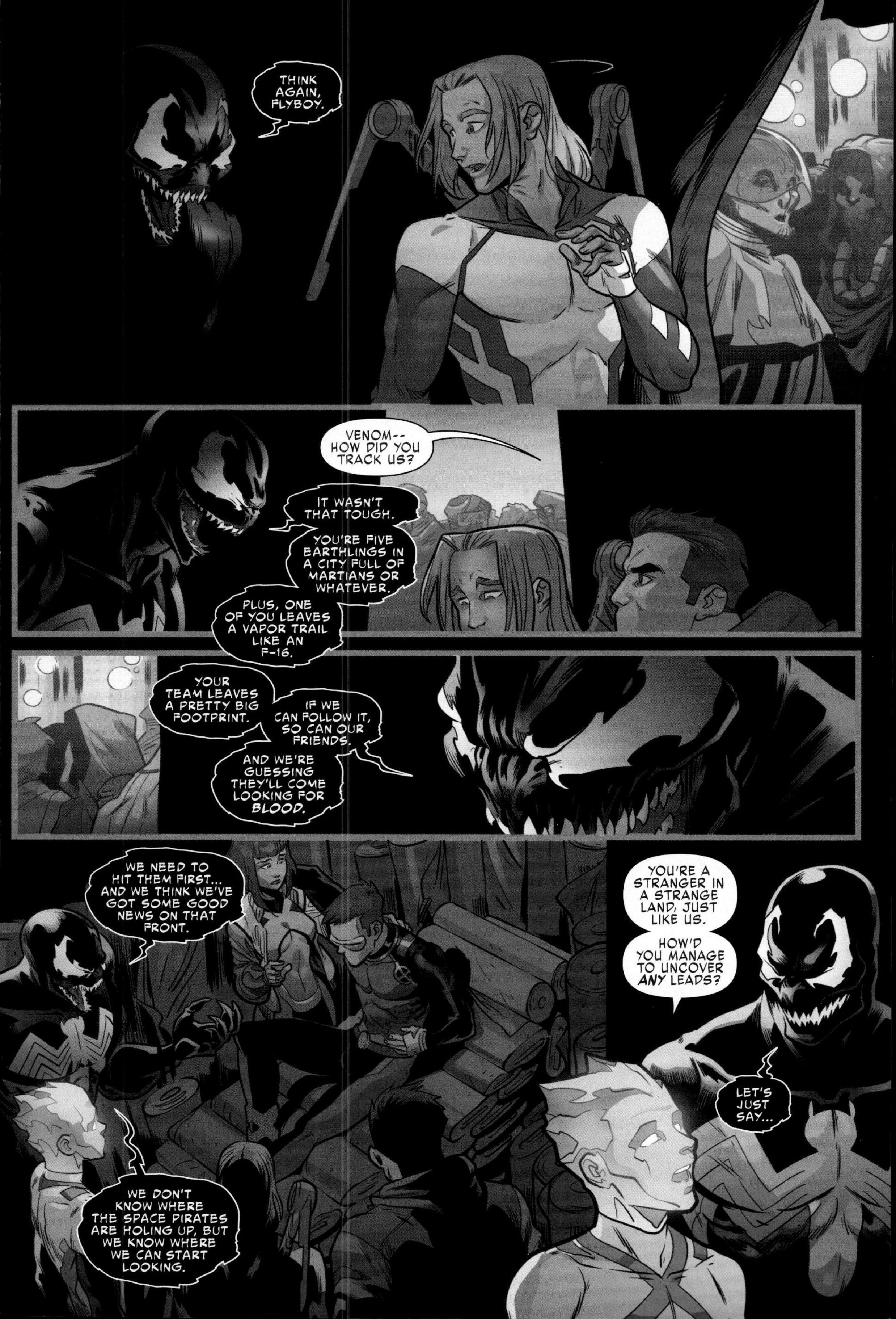
THINK AGAIN, FLYBOY.
VENOM-- HOW DID YOU TRACK US?
IT WASN'T THAT TOUGH.
YOU'RE FIVE EARTHLINGS IN A CITY FULL OF MARTIANS OR WHATEVER.
PLUS, ONE OF YOU LEAVES A VAPOR TRAIL LIKE AN F-16.
YOUR TEAM LEAVES A PRETTY BIG FOOTPRINT.
IF WE CAN FOLLOW IT, SO CAN OUR FRIENDS.
AND WE'RE GUESSING THEY'LL COME LOOKING FOR *BLOOD.*
WE NEED TO HIT THEM FIRST... AND WE THINK WE'VE GOT SOME GOOD NEWS ON THAT FRONT.
WE DON'T KNOW WHERE THE SPACE PIRATES ARE HOLING UP, BUT WE KNOW WHERE WE CAN START LOOKING.
YOU'RE A STRANGER IN A STRANGE LAND, JUST LIKE US.
HOW'D YOU MANAGE TO UNCOVER *ANY* LEADS?
LET'S JUST SAY...

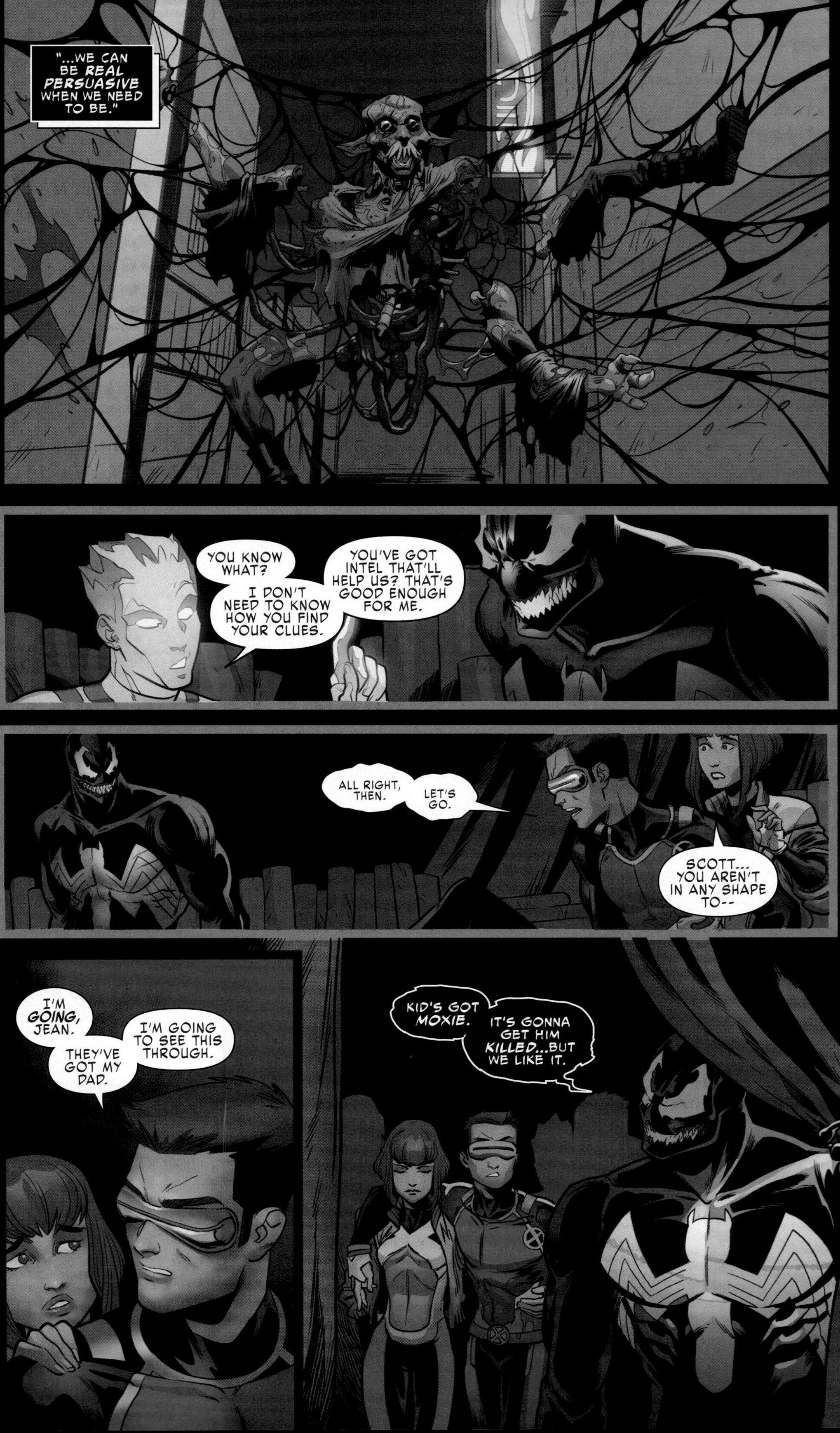
"...WE CAN BE *REAL PERSUASIVE* WHEN WE NEED TO BE."
YOU KNOW WHAT?
I DON'T NEED TO KNOW HOW YOU FIND YOUR CLUES.
YOU'VE GOT INTEL THAT'LL HELP US? THAT'S GOOD ENOUGH FOR ME.
ALL RIGHT, THEN.
LET'S GO.
SCOTT... YOU AREN'T IN ANY SHAPE TO--
I'M *GOING*, JEAN.
THEY'VE GOT MY DAD.
I'M GOING TO SEE THIS THROUGH.
KID'S GOT *MOXIE*.
IT'S GONNA GET HIM *KILLED*...BUT WE LIKE IT.

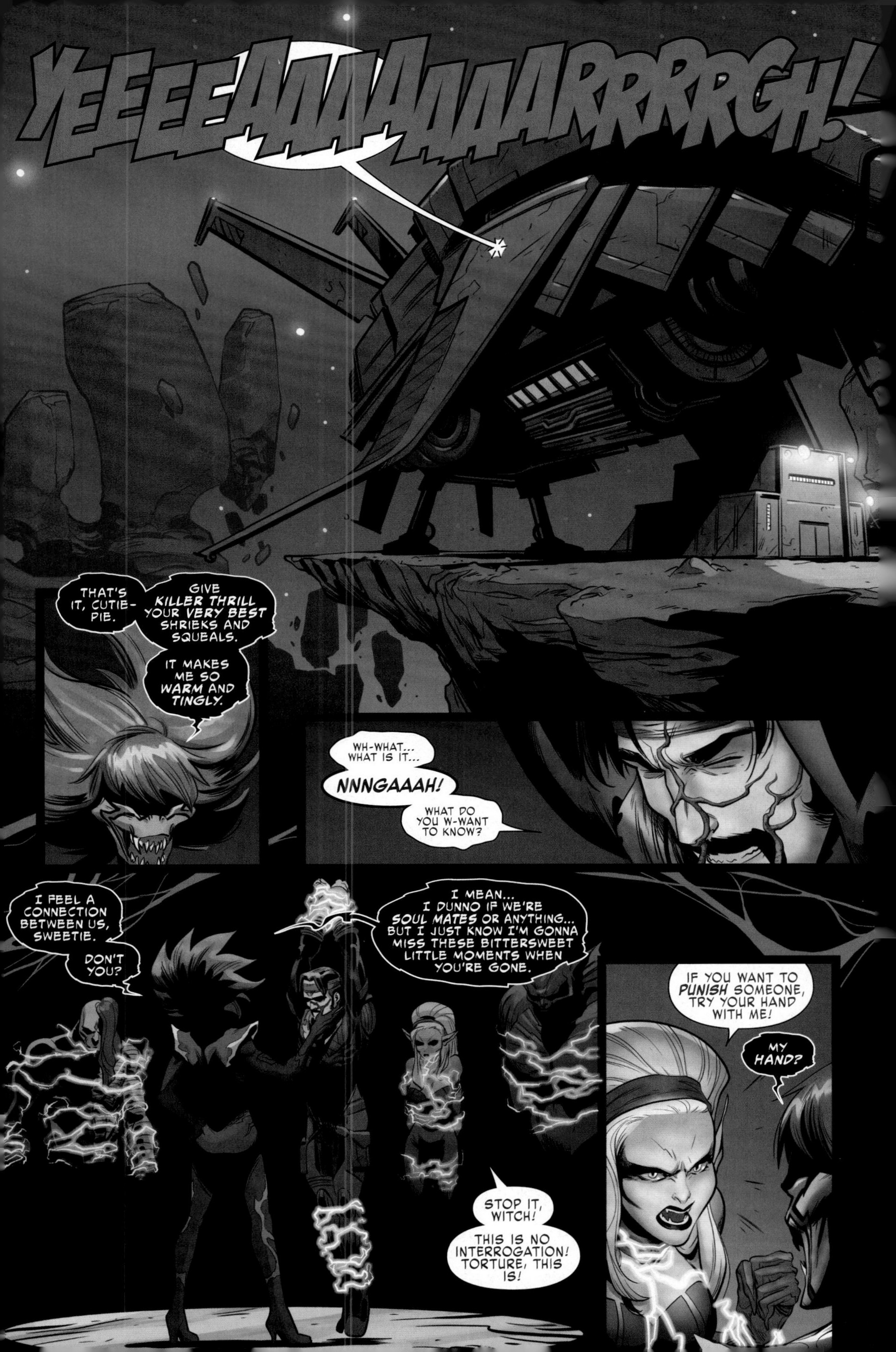
YEEEEAAAAAAAARRRRRGH!
THAT'S IT, CUTIE-PIE.
GIVE KILLER THRILL YOUR VERY BEST SHRIEKS AND SQUEALS.
IT MAKES ME SO WARM AND TINGLY.
WH-WHAT... WHAT IS IT...
NNNGAAAH!
WHAT DO YOU W-WANT TO KNOW?
I FEEL A CONNECTION BETWEEN US, SWEETIE.
DON'T YOU?
I MEAN... I DUNNO IF WE'RE SOUL MATES OR ANYTHING... BUT I JUST KNOW I'M GONNA MISS THESE BITTERSWEET LITTLE MOMENTS WHEN YOU'RE GONE.
STOP IT, WITCH!
THIS IS NO INTERROGATION! TORTURE, THIS IS!
IF YOU WANT TO PUNISH SOMEONE, TRY YOUR HAND WITH ME!
MY HAND?

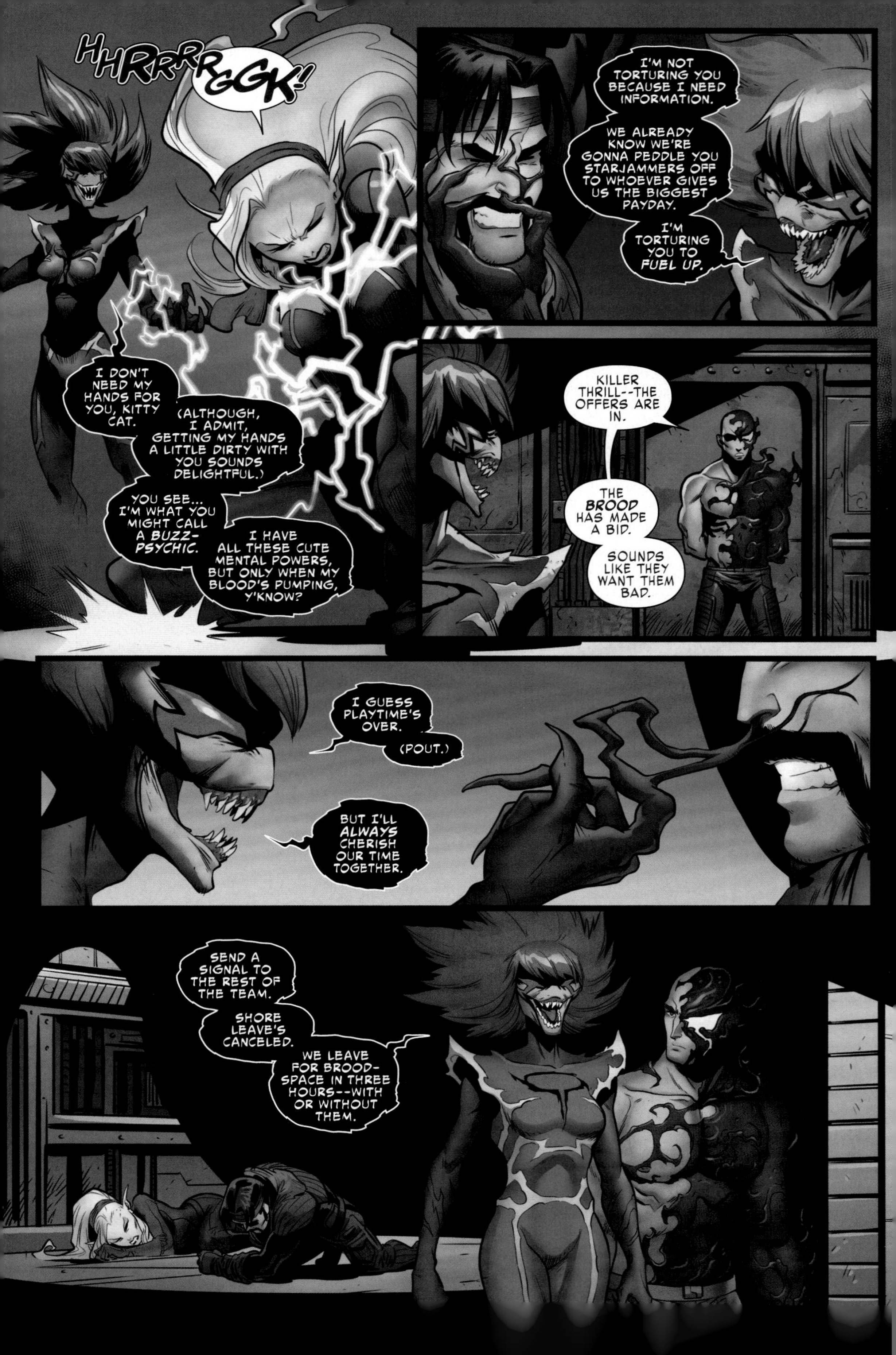
HHRRRRGGK!
I DON'T NEED MY HANDS FOR YOU, KITTY CAT.
(ALTHOUGH, I ADMIT, GETTING MY HANDS A LITTLE DIRTY WITH YOU SOUNDS DELIGHTFUL.)
YOU SEE... I'M WHAT YOU MIGHT CALL A BUZZ-PSYCHIC.
I HAVE ALL THESE CUTE MENTAL POWERS, BUT ONLY WHEN MY BLOOD'S PUMPING, Y'KNOW?
I'M NOT TORTURING YOU BECAUSE I NEED INFORMATION.
WE ALREADY KNOW WE'RE GONNA PEDDLE YOU STARJAMMERS OFF TO WHOEVER GIVES US THE BIGGEST PAYDAY.
I'M TORTURING YOU TO FUEL UP.
KILLER THRILL--THE OFFERS ARE IN.
THE BROOD HAS MADE A BID.
SOUNDS LIKE THEY WANT THEM BAD.
I GUESS PLAYTIME'S OVER.
(POUT.)
BUT I'LL ALWAYS CHERISH OUR TIME TOGETHER.
SEND A SIGNAL TO THE REST OF THE TEAM.
SHORE LEAVE'S CANCELED.
WE LEAVE FOR BROOD-SPACE IN THREE HOURS--WITH OR WITHOUT THEM.

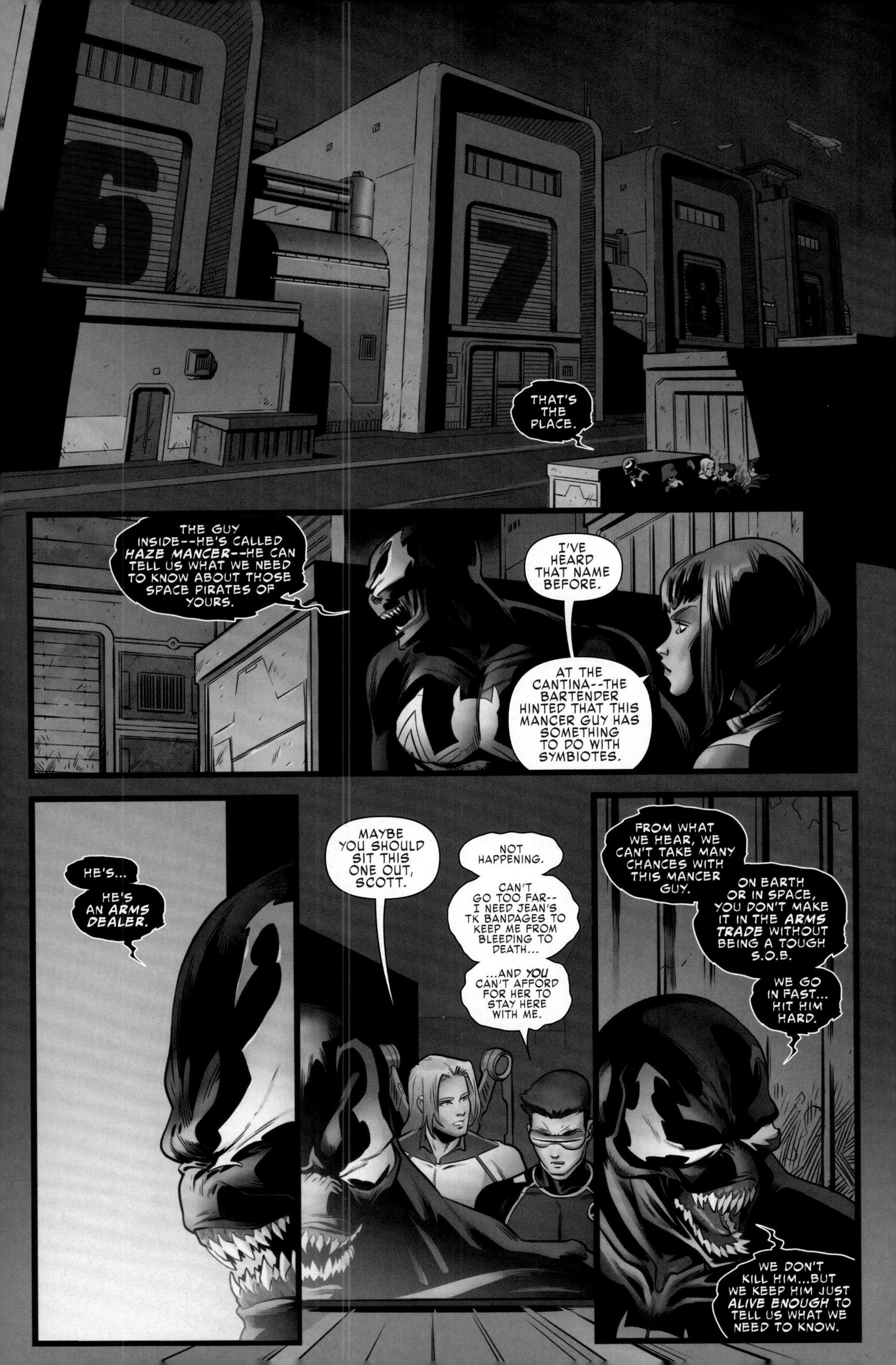
THAT'S THE PLACE.
THE GUY INSIDE--HE'S CALLED HAZE MANCER--HE CAN TELL US WHAT WE NEED TO KNOW ABOUT THOSE SPACE PIRATES OF YOURS.
I'VE HEARD THAT NAME BEFORE.
AT THE CANTINA--THE BARTENDER HINTED THAT THIS MANCER GUY HAS SOMETHING TO DO WITH SYMBIOTES.
HE'S...
HE'S AN ARMS DEALER.
MAYBE YOU SHOULD SIT THIS ONE OUT, SCOTT.
NOT HAPPENING.
CAN'T GO TOO FAR--I NEED JEAN'S TK BANDAGES TO KEEP ME FROM BLEEDING TO DEATH...
...AND YOU CAN'T AFFORD FOR HER TO STAY HERE WITH ME.
FROM WHAT WE HEAR, WE CAN'T TAKE MANY CHANCES WITH THIS MANCER GUY.
ON EARTH OR IN SPACE, YOU DON'T MAKE IT IN THE ARMS TRADE WITHOUT BEING A TOUGH S.O.B.
WE GO IN FAST... HIT HIM HARD.
WE DON'T KILL HIM...BUT WE KEEP HIM JUST ALIVE ENOUGH TO TELL US WHAT WE NEED TO KNOW.

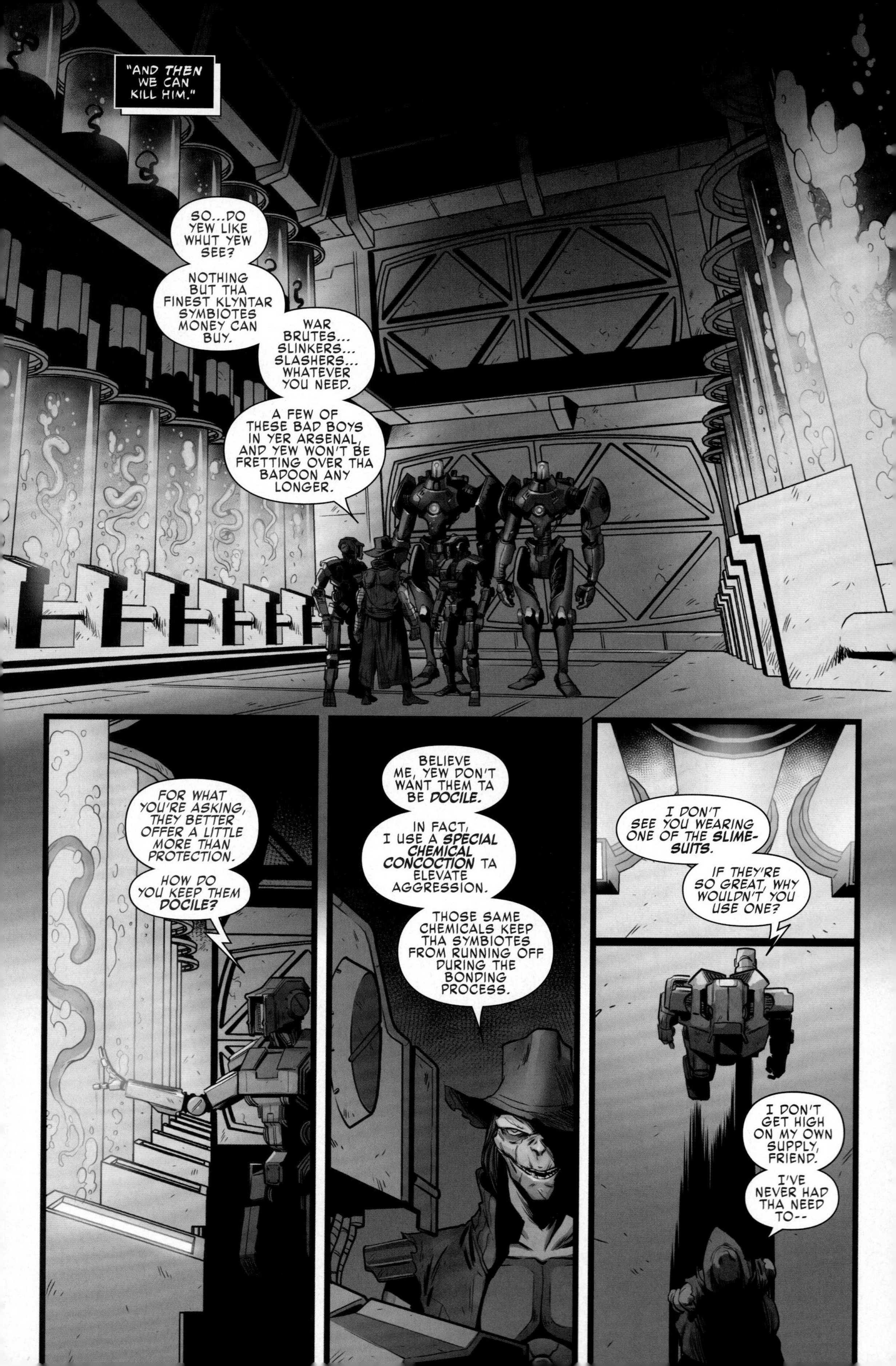
"AND THEN WE CAN KILL HIM."
SO...DO YEW LIKE WHUT YEW SEE?
NOTHING BUT THA FINEST KLYNTAR SYMBIOTES MONEY CAN BUY.
WAR BRUTES... SLINKERS... SLASHERS... WHATEVER YOU NEED.
A FEW OF THESE BAD BOYS IN YER ARSENAL, AND YEW WON'T BE FRETTING OVER THA BADOON ANY LONGER.
FOR WHAT YOU'RE ASKING, THEY BETTER OFFER A LITTLE MORE THAN PROTECTION.
HOW DO YOU KEEP THEM DOCILE?
BELIEVE ME, YEW DON'T WANT THEM TA BE DOCILE.
IN FACT, I USE A SPECIAL CHEMICAL CONCOCTION TA ELEVATE AGGRESSION.
THOSE SAME CHEMICALS KEEP THA SYMBIOTES FROM RUNNING OFF DURING THE BONDING PROCESS.
I DON'T SEE YOU WEARING ONE OF THE SLIME-SUITS.
IF THEY'RE SO GREAT, WHY WOULDN'T YOU USE ONE?
I DON'T GET HIGH ON MY OWN SUPPLY, FRIEND.
I'VE NEVER HAD THA NEED TO--

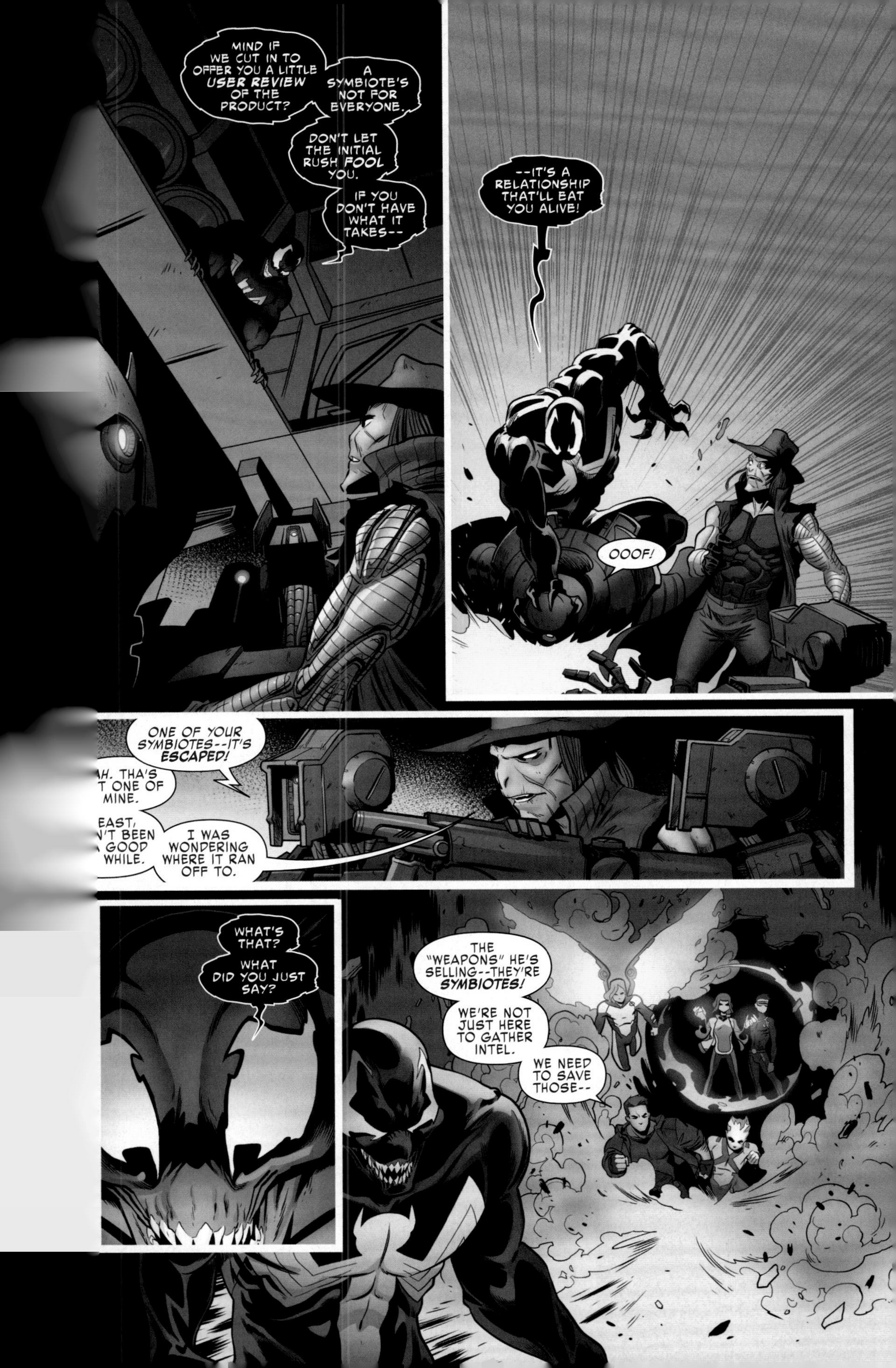
MIND IF WE CUT IN TO OFFER YOU A LITTLE USER REVIEW OF THE PRODUCT?
A SYMBIOTE'S NOT FOR EVERYONE.
DON'T LET THE INITIAL RUSH FOOL YOU.
IF YOU DON'T HAVE WHAT IT TAKES--
--IT'S A RELATIONSHIP THAT'LL EAT YOU ALIVE!
OOOF!
ONE OF YOUR SYMBIOTES--IT'S ESCAPED!
AH. THA'S T ONE OF MINE.
EAST, N'T BEEN A GOOD WHILE.
I WAS WONDERING WHERE IT RAN OFF TO.
WHAT'S THAT?
WHAT DID YOU JUST SAY?
THE "WEAPONS" HE'S SELLING--THEY'RE SYMBIOTES!
WE'RE NOT JUST HERE TO GATHER INTEL.
WE NEED TO SAVE THOSE--

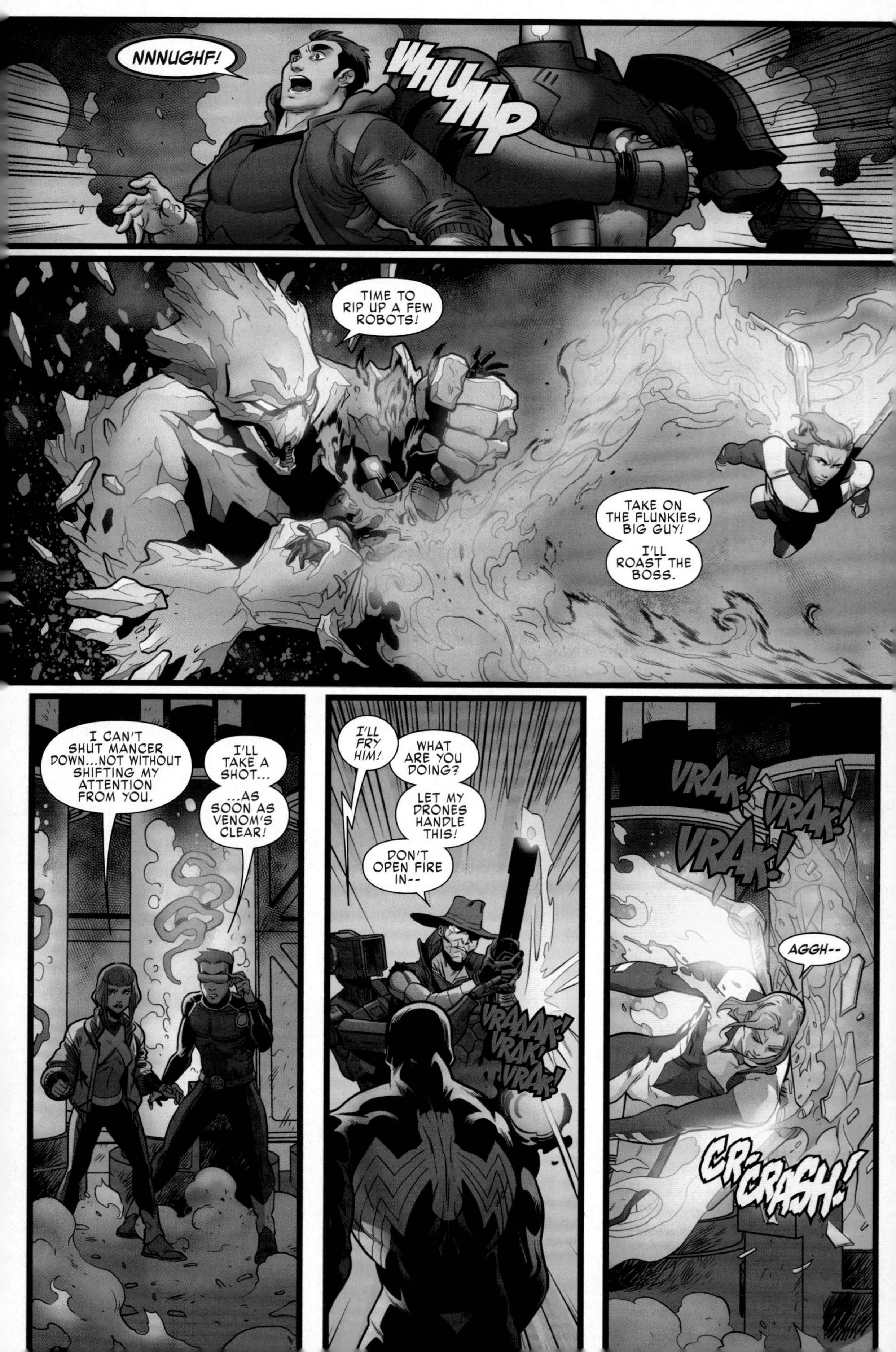
NNNUGHF!
WHUMP
TIME TO RIP UP A FEW ROBOTS!
TAKE ON THE FLUNKIES, BIG GUY!
I'LL ROAST THE BOSS.
I CAN'T SHUT MANCER DOWN...NOT WITHOUT SHIFTING MY ATTENTION FROM YOU.
I'LL TAKE A SHOT...
...AS SOON AS VENOM'S CLEAR!
I'LL FRY HIM!
WHAT ARE YOU DOING?
LET MY DRONES HANDLE THIS!
DON'T OPEN FIRE IN--
VRAAAK! VRAK! VRAK!
VRAK! VRAK! VRAK!
AGGH--
CR-CRASH!

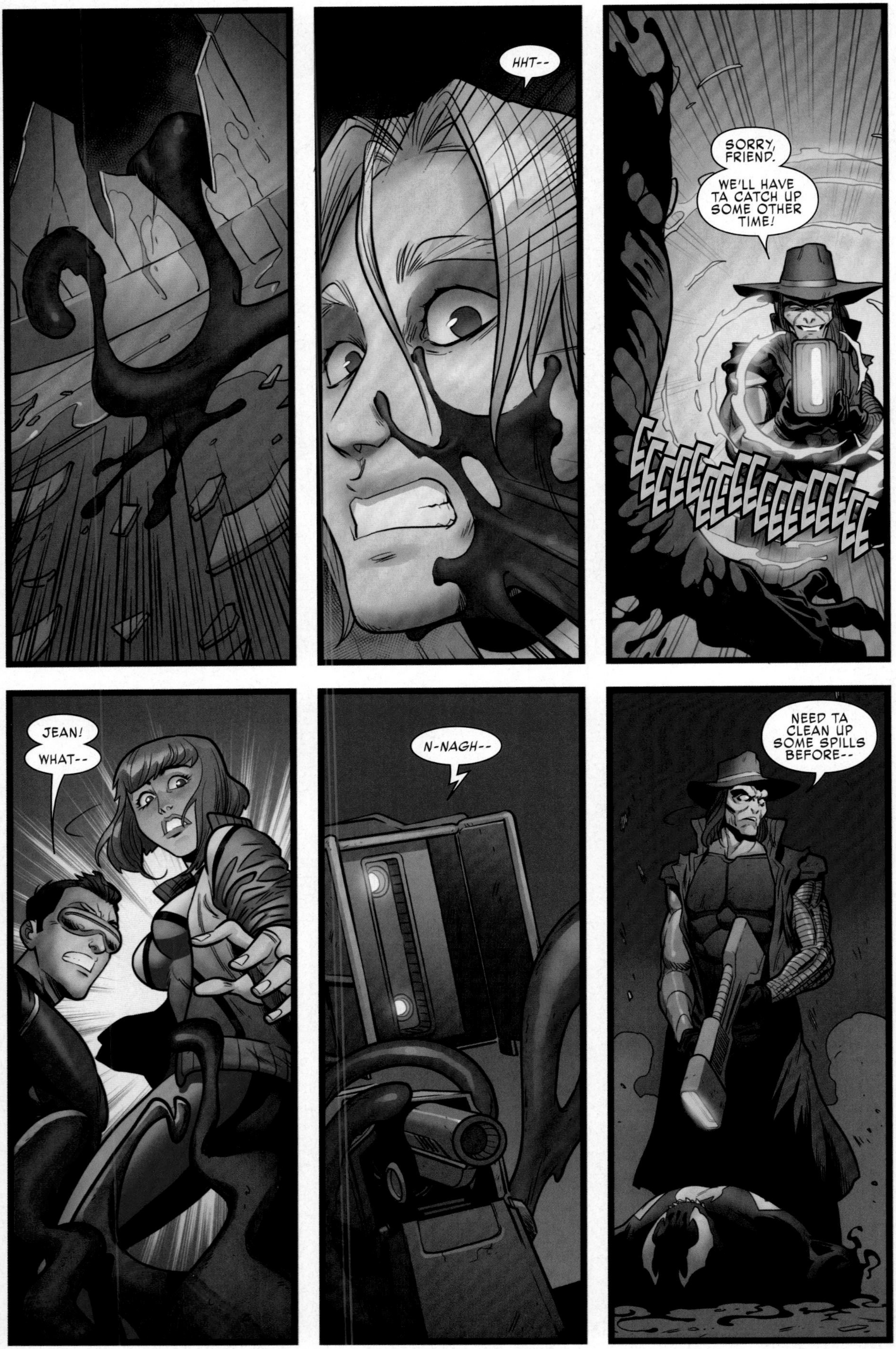
HHT--
SORRY, FRIEND.
WE'LL HAVE TA CATCH UP SOME OTHER TIME!
EEEEEEEEEEEEEEEEE
JEAN!
WHAT--
N-NAGH--
NEED TA CLEAN UP SOME SPILLS BEFORE--

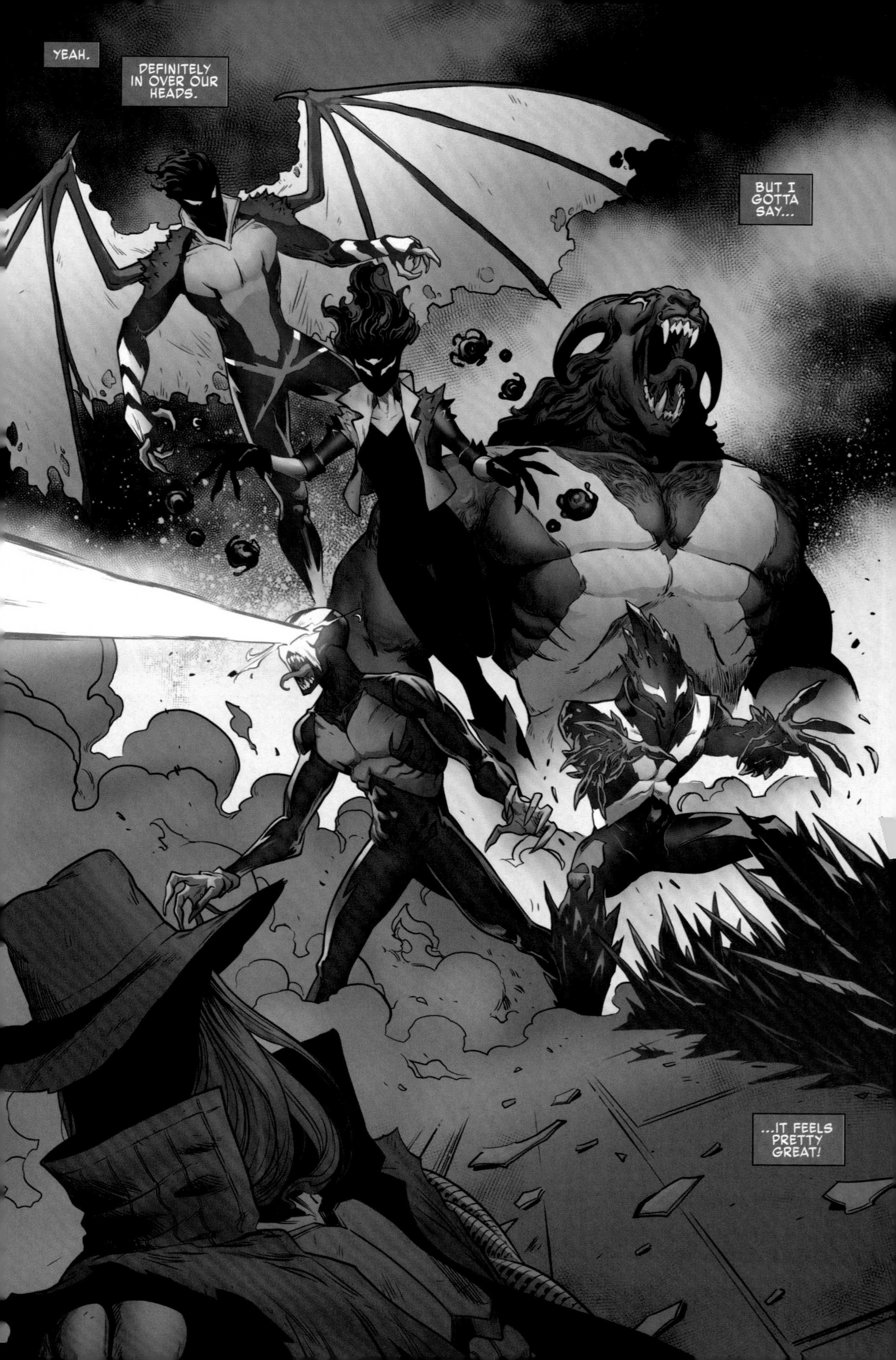
YEAH.
DEFINITELY IN OVER OUR HEADS.
BUT I GOTTA SAY...
...IT FEELS PRETTY GREAT!

VENOM 162

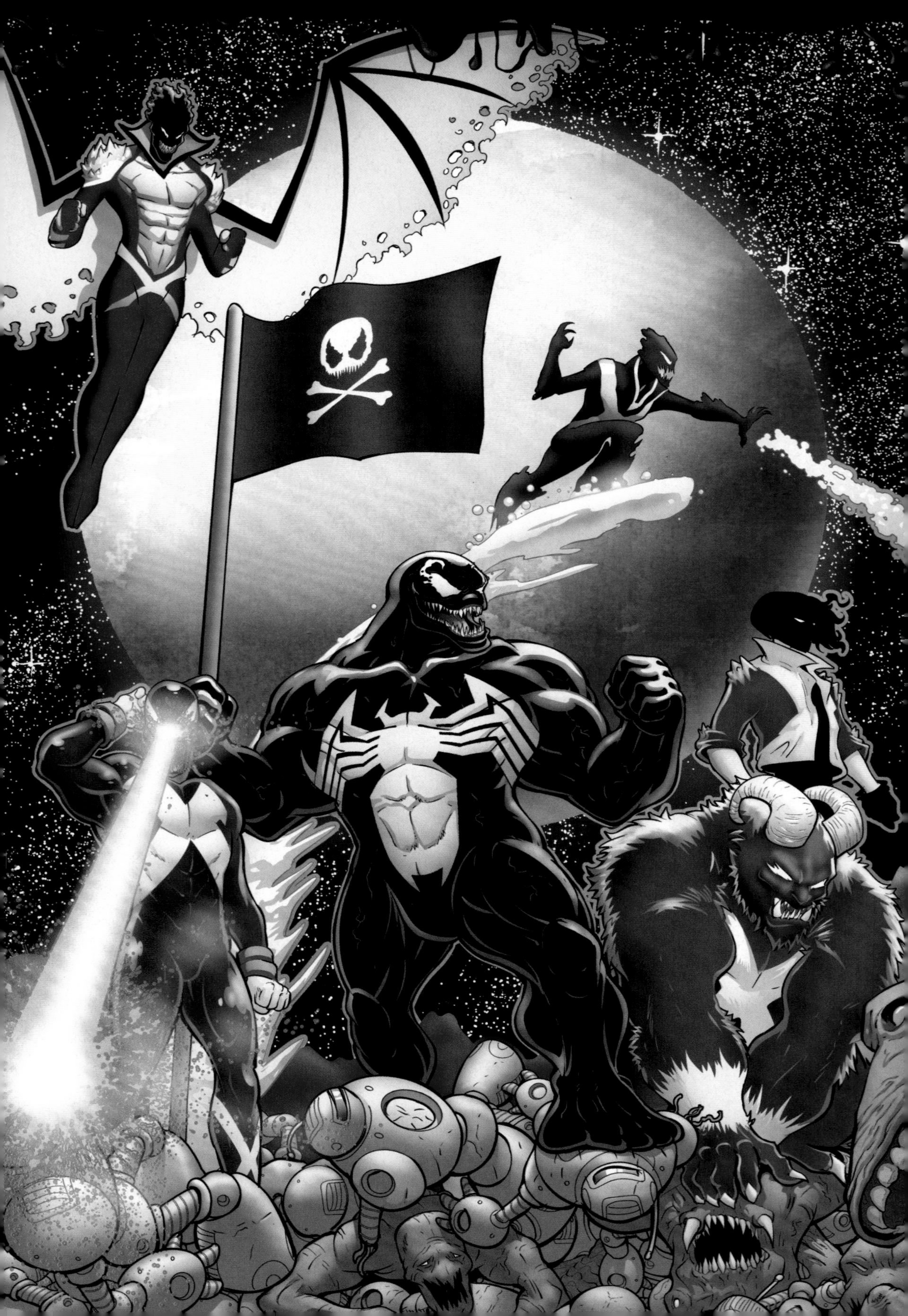

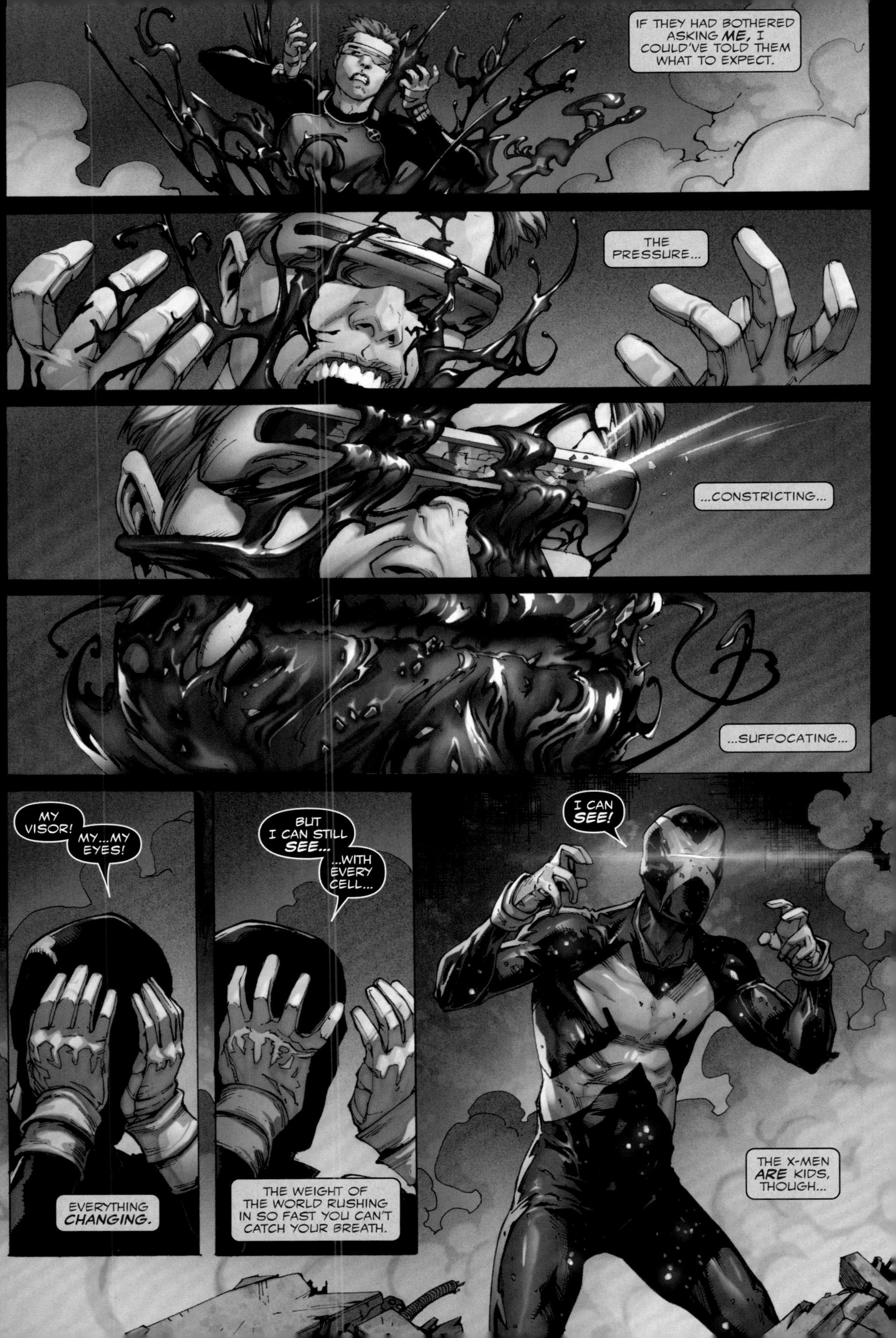
IF THEY HAD BOTHERED ASKING ME, I COULD'VE TOLD THEM WHAT TO EXPECT.
THE PRESSURE...
...CONSTRICTING...
...SUFFOCATING...
MY VISOR!
MY...MY EYES!
EVERYTHING CHANGING.
BUT I CAN STILL SEE...
...WITH EVERY CELL...
THE WEIGHT OF THE WORLD RUSHING IN SO FAST YOU CAN'T CATCH YOUR BREATH.
I CAN SEE!
THE X-MEN ARE KIDS, THOUGH...

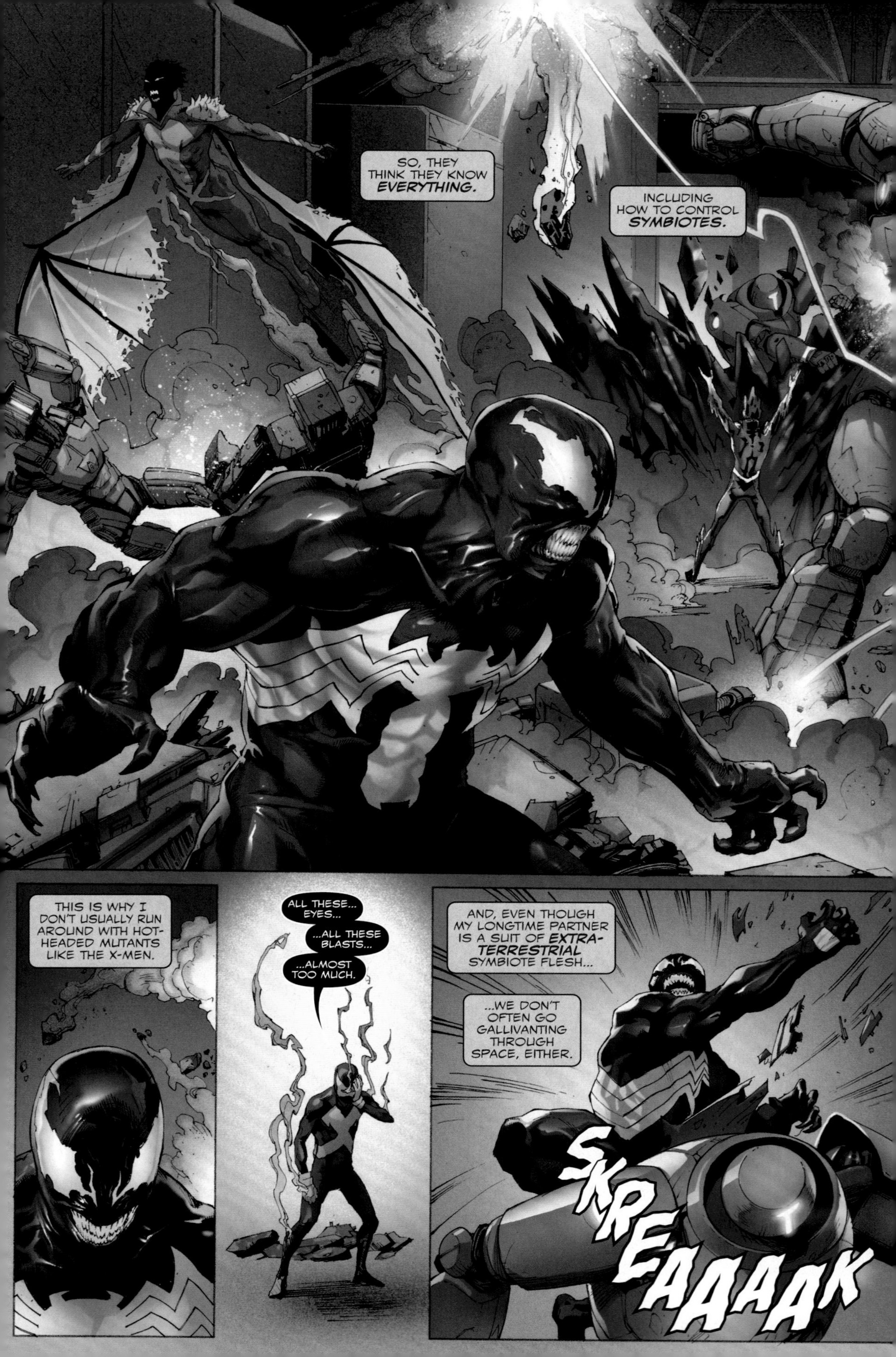
SO, THEY THINK THEY KNOW EVERYTHING.
INCLUDING HOW TO CONTROL SYMBIOTES.
THIS IS WHY I DON'T USUALLY RUN AROUND WITH HOT-HEADED MUTANTS LIKE THE X-MEN.
ALL THESE... EYES...
...ALL THESE BLASTS...
...ALMOST TOO MUCH.
AND, EVEN THOUGH MY LONGTIME PARTNER IS A SUIT OF EXTRA-TERRESTRIAL SYMBIOTE FLESH...
...WE DON'T OFTEN GO GALLIVANTING THROUGH SPACE, EITHER.
SKREAAAAK

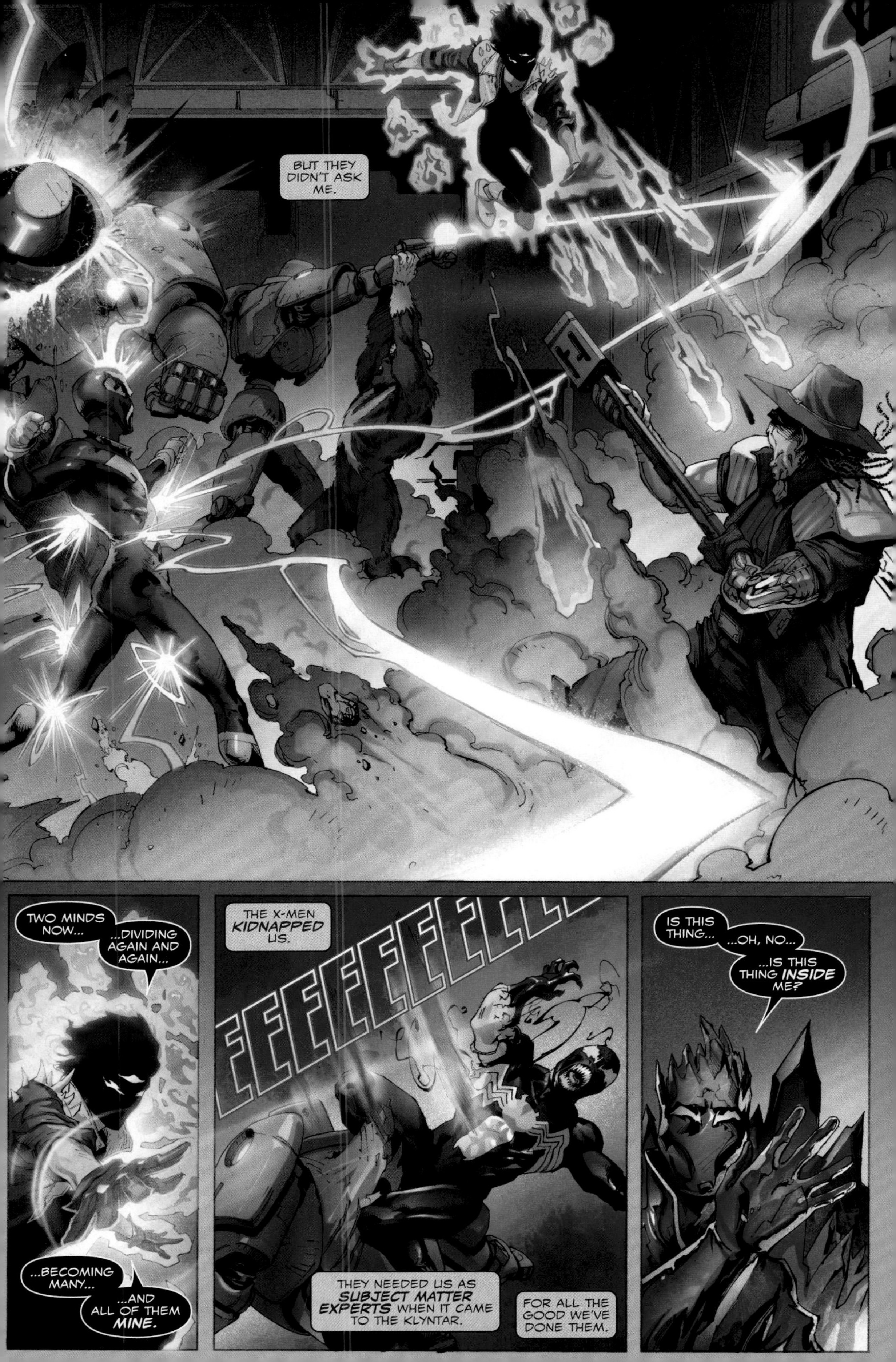
BUT THEY DIDN'T ASK ME.
TWO MINDS NOW...
...DIVIDING AGAIN AND AGAIN...
...BECOMING MANY...
...AND ALL OF THEM MINE.
THE X-MEN KIDNAPPED US.
EEEEEEEEEEE
THEY NEEDED US AS SUBJECT MATTER EXPERTS WHEN IT CAME TO THE KLYNTAR.
FOR ALL THE GOOD WE'VE DONE THEM.
IS THIS THING...
...OH, NO...
...IS THIS THING INSIDE ME?

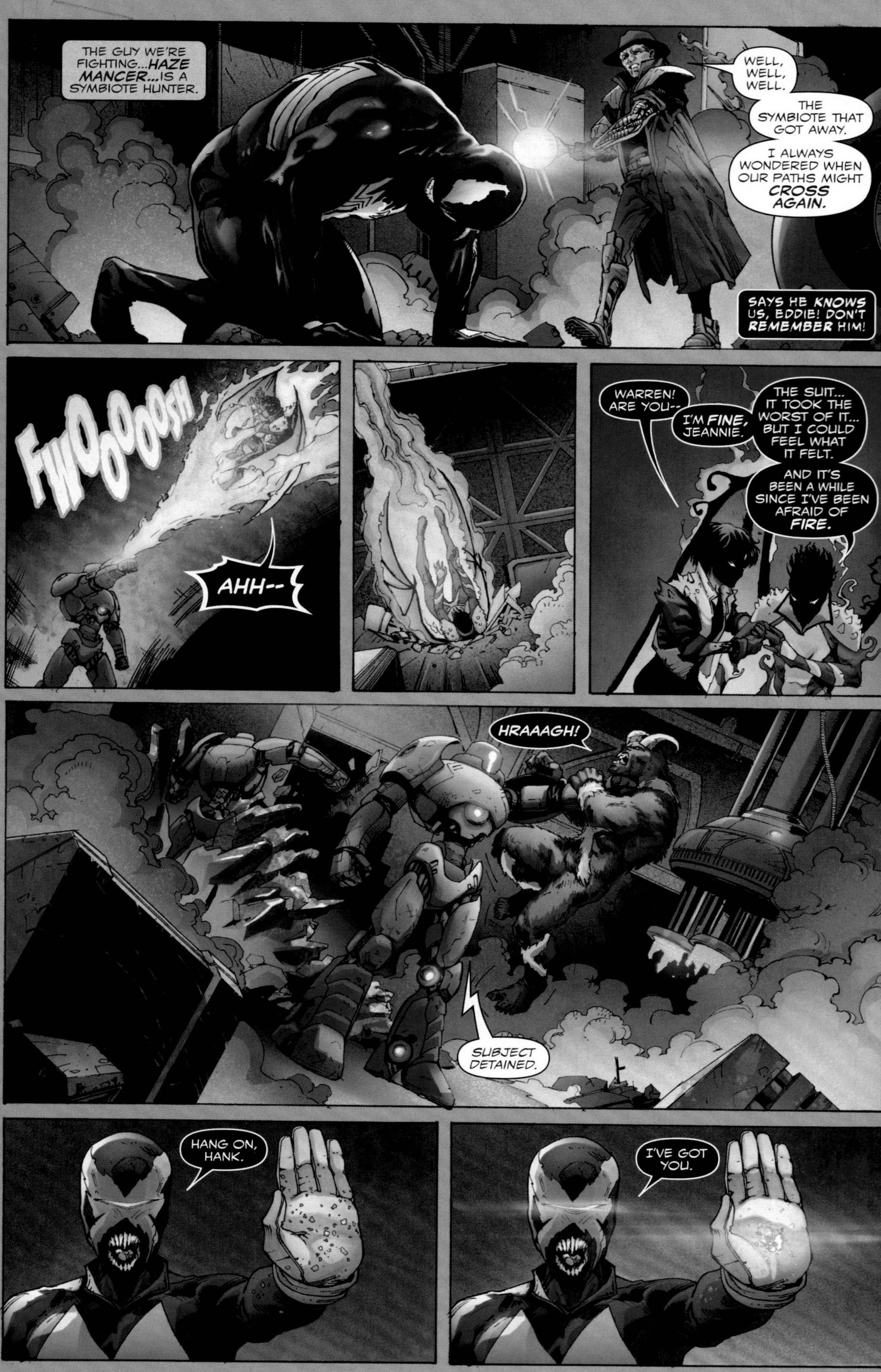
THE GUY WE'RE FIGHTING...HAZE MANCER...IS A SYMBIOTE HUNTER.
WELL, WELL, WELL.
THE SYMBIOTE THAT GOT AWAY.
I ALWAYS WONDERED WHEN OUR PATHS MIGHT CROSS AGAIN.
SAYS HE KNOWS US, EDDIE! DON'T REMEMBER HIM!
FWOOOOOSH
AHH--
WARREN! ARE YOU--
I'M FINE, JEANNIE.
THE SUIT... IT TOOK THE WORST OF IT... BUT I COULD FEEL WHAT IT FELT.
AND IT'S BEEN A WHILE SINCE I'VE BEEN AFRAID OF FIRE.
HRAAAGH!
SUBJECT DETAINED.
HANG ON, HANK.
I'VE GOT YOU.

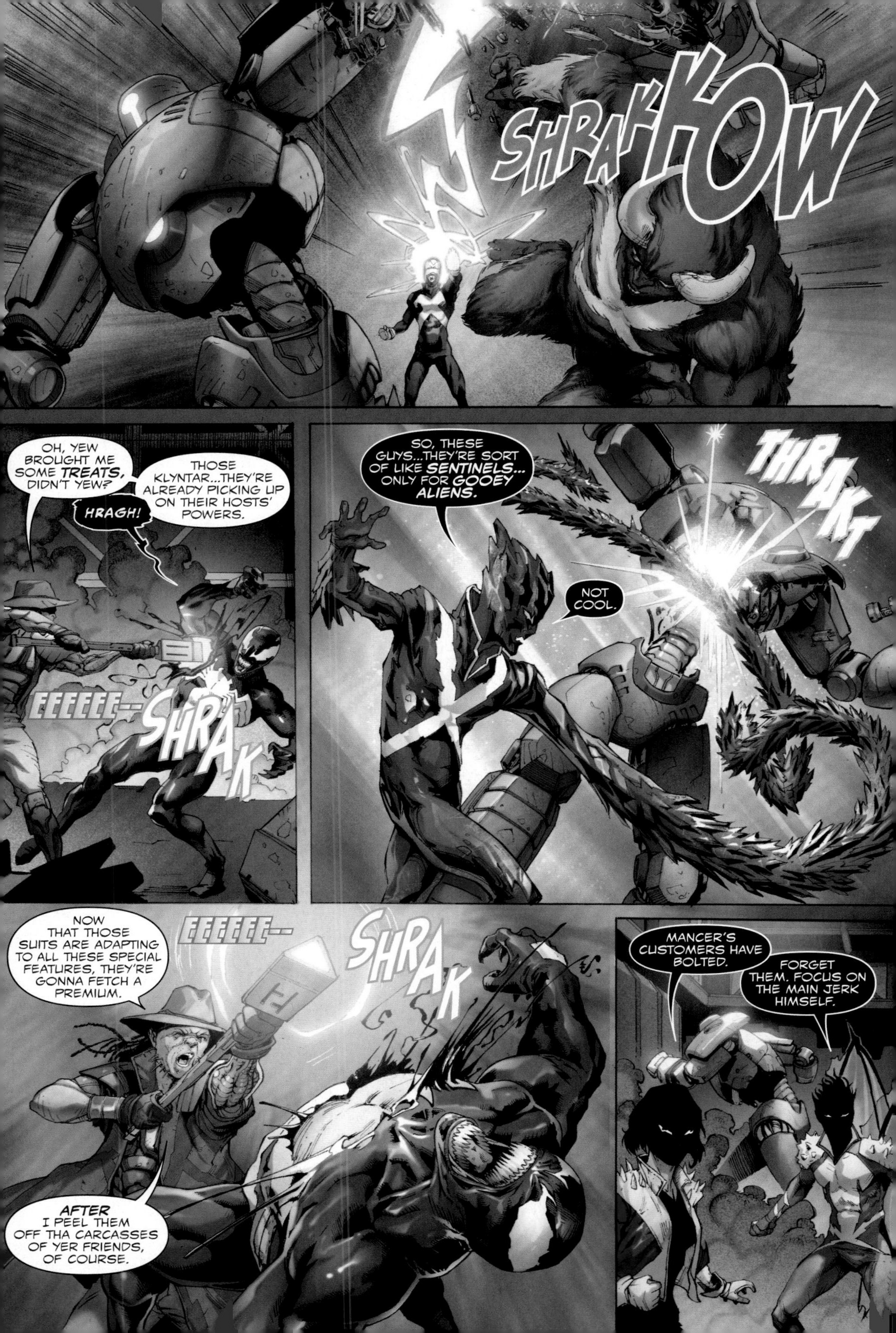
SHRAKKOW
OH, YEW BROUGHT ME SOME TREATS, DIDN'T YEW?
HRAGH!
THOSE KLYNTAR...THEY'RE ALREADY PICKING UP ON THEIR HOSTS' POWERS.
EEEEEE--SHRAK
SO, THESE GUYS...THEY'RE SORT OF LIKE SENTINELS... ONLY FOR GOOEY ALIENS.
THRAKT
NOT COOL.
NOW THAT THOSE SUITS ARE ADAPTING TO ALL THESE SPECIAL FEATURES, THEY'RE GONNA FETCH A PREMIUM.
EEEEEE--SHRAK
AFTER I PEEL THEM OFF THA CARCASSES OF YER FRIENDS, OF COURSE.
MANCER'S CUSTOMERS HAVE BOLTED.
FORGET THEM. FOCUS ON THE MAIN JERK HIMSELF.

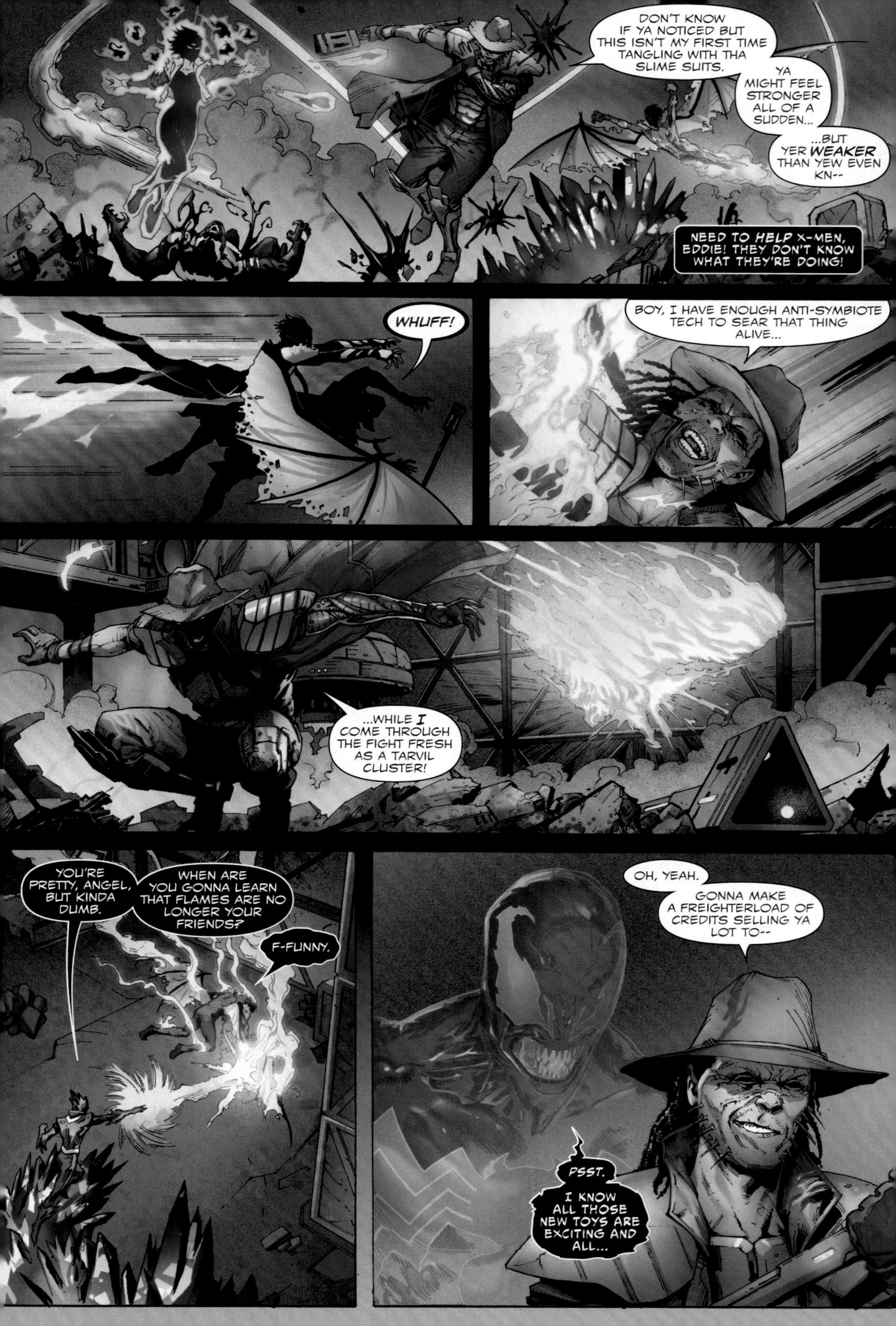

DON'T KNOW IF YA NOTICED BUT THIS ISN'T MY FIRST TIME TANGLING WITH THA SLIME SUITS.
YA MIGHT FEEL STRONGER ALL OF A SUDDEN...
...BUT YER WEAKER THAN YEW EVEN KN--
NEED TO HELP X-MEN, EDDIE! THEY DON'T KNOW WHAT THEY'RE DOING!
WHUFF!
BOY, I HAVE ENOUGH ANTI-SYMBIOTE TECH TO SEAR THAT THING ALIVE...
...WHILE I COME THROUGH THE FIGHT FRESH AS A TARVIL CLUSTER!
YOU'RE PRETTY, ANGEL, BUT KINDA DUMB.
WHEN ARE YOU GONNA LEARN THAT FLAMES ARE NO LONGER YOUR FRIENDS?
F-FUNNY.
OH, YEAH.
GONNA MAKE A FREIGHTERLOAD OF CREDITS SELLING YA LOT TO--
PSST.
I KNOW ALL THOSE NEW TOYS ARE EXCITING AND ALL...

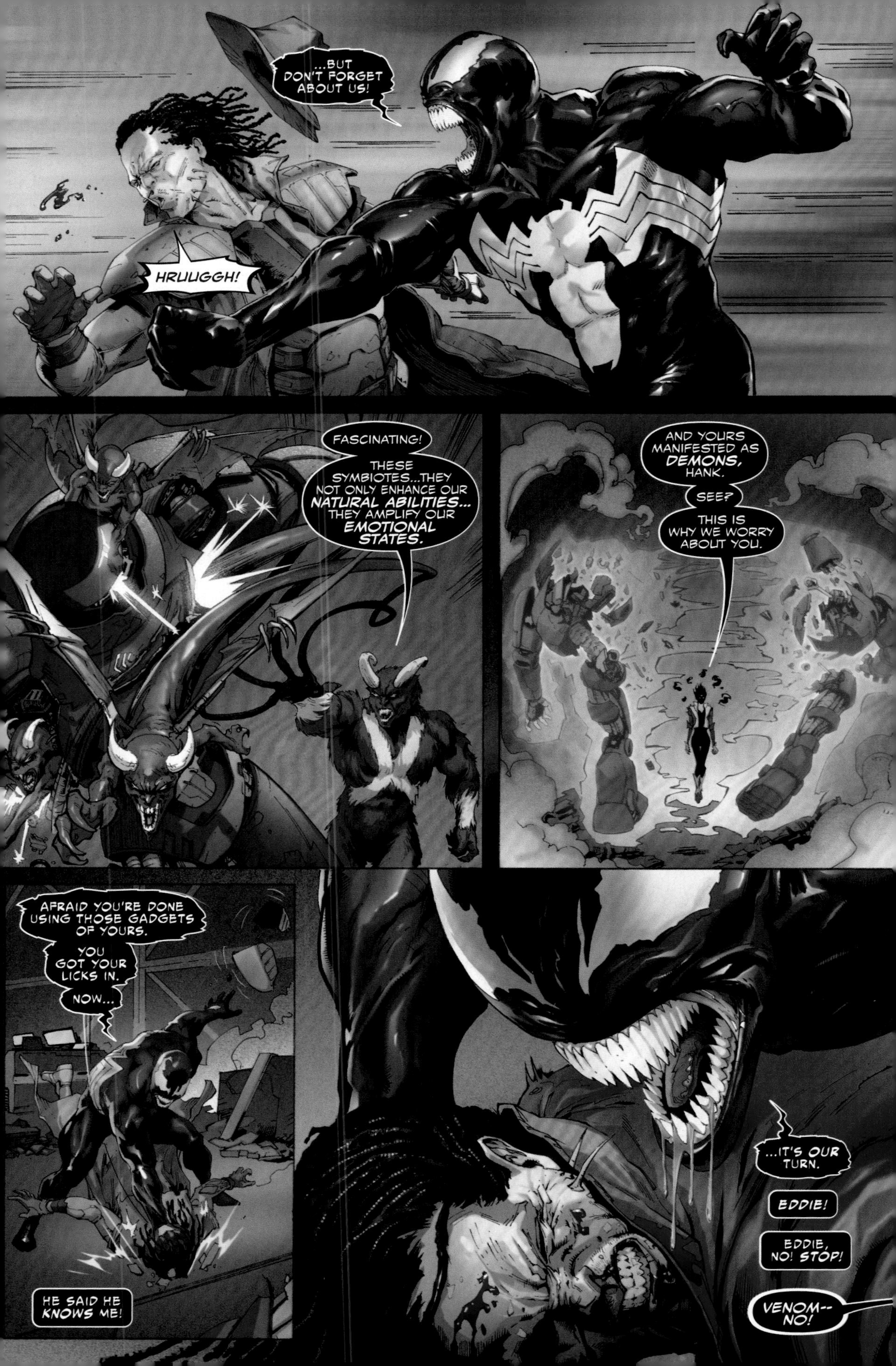
...BUT DON'T FORGET ABOUT US!
HRUUGGH!
FASCINATING!
THESE SYMBIOTES...THEY NOT ONLY ENHANCE OUR NATURAL ABILITIES... THEY AMPLIFY OUR EMOTIONAL STATES.
AND YOURS MANIFESTED AS DEMONS, HANK.
SEE?
THIS IS WHY WE WORRY ABOUT YOU.
AFRAID YOU'RE DONE USING THOSE GADGETS OF YOURS.
YOU GOT YOUR LICKS IN.
NOW...
HE SAID HE KNOWS ME!
...IT'S OUR TURN.
EDDIE!
EDDIE, NO! STOP!
VENOM-- NO!

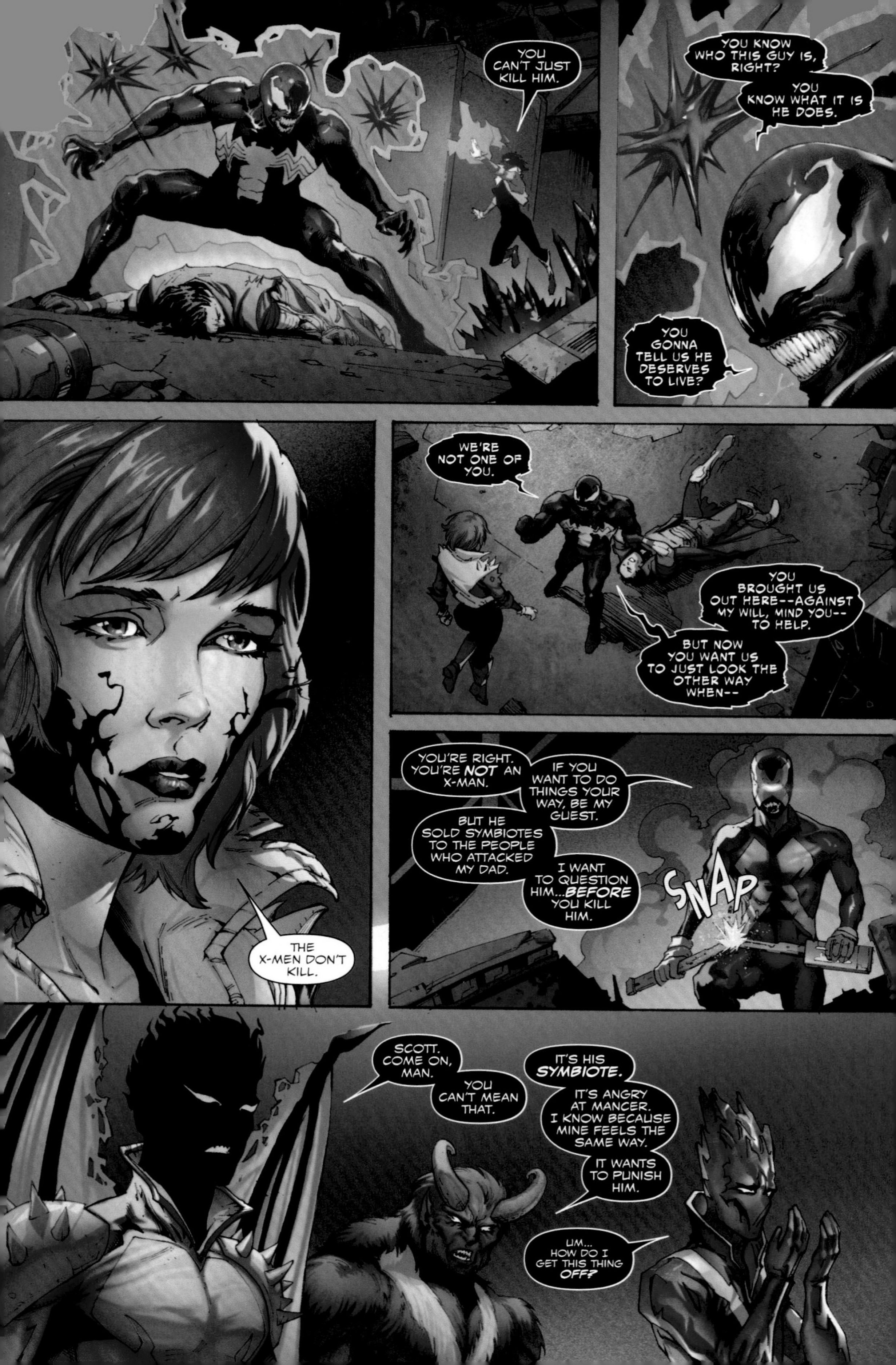

YOU CAN'T JUST KILL HIM.
YOU KNOW WHO THIS GUY IS, RIGHT?
YOU KNOW WHAT IT IS HE DOES.
YOU GONNA TELL US HE DESERVES TO LIVE?
THE X-MEN DON'T KILL.
WE'RE NOT ONE OF YOU.
YOU BROUGHT US OUT HERE--AGAINST MY WILL, MIND YOU--TO HELP.
BUT NOW YOU WANT US TO JUST LOOK THE OTHER WAY WHEN--
YOU'RE RIGHT. YOU'RE NOT AN X-MAN.
IF YOU WANT TO DO THINGS YOUR WAY, BE MY GUEST.
BUT HE SOLD SYMBIOTES TO THE PEOPLE WHO ATTACKED MY DAD.
I WANT TO QUESTION HIM...BEFORE YOU KILL HIM.
SNAP
SCOTT. COME ON, MAN.
YOU CAN'T MEAN THAT.
IT'S HIS SYMBIOTE.
IT'S ANGRY AT MANCER. I KNOW BECAUSE MINE FEELS THE SAME WAY.
IT WANTS TO PUNISH HIM.
UM... HOW DO I GET THIS THING OFF?

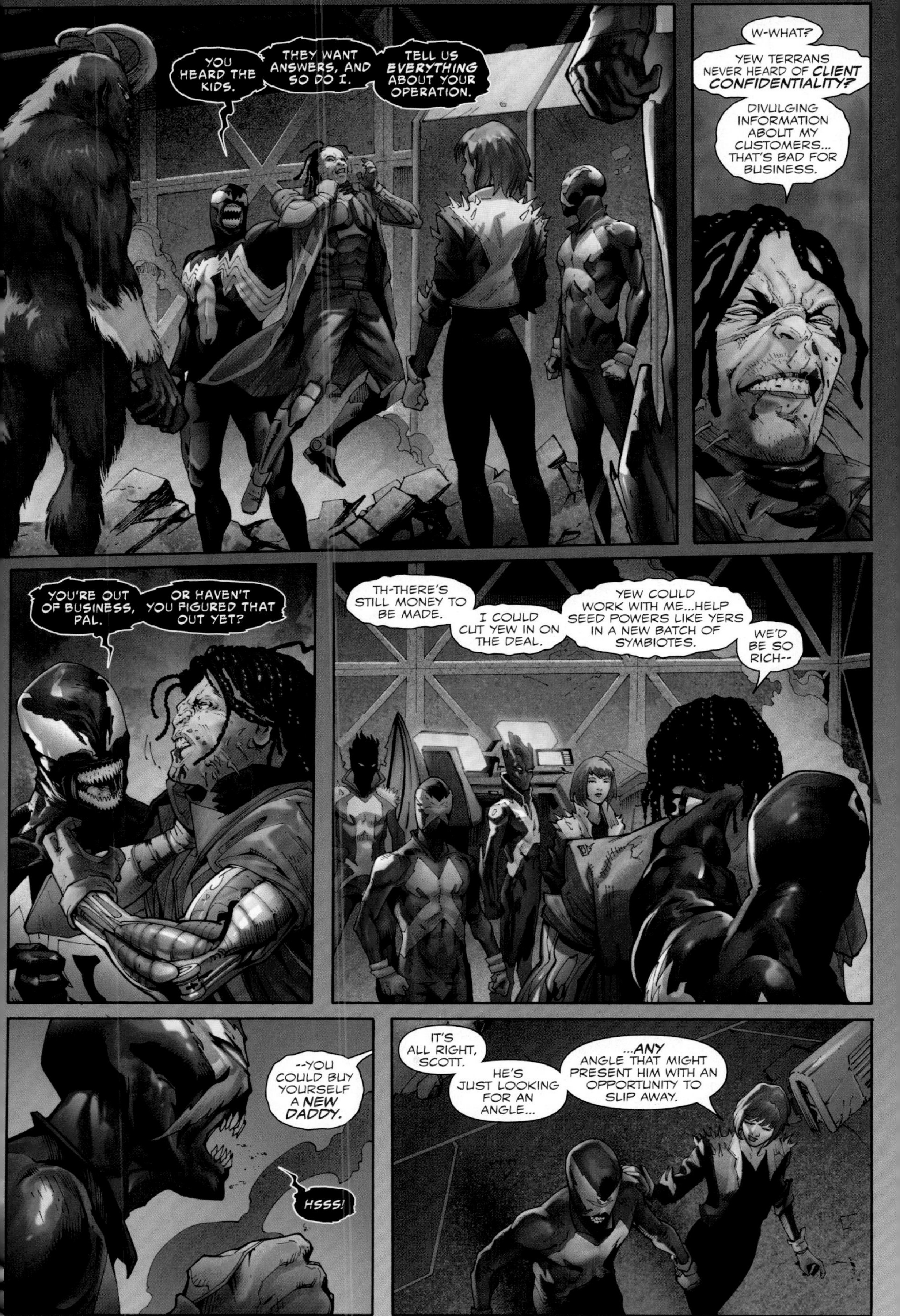
YOU HEARD THE KIDS.
THEY WANT ANSWERS, AND SO DO I.
TELL US EVERYTHING ABOUT YOUR OPERATION.
W-WHAT?
YEW TERRANS NEVER HEARD OF CLIENT CONFIDENTIALITY?
DIVULGING INFORMATION ABOUT MY CUSTOMERS... THAT'S BAD FOR BUSINESS.
YOU'RE OUT OF BUSINESS, PAL.
OR HAVEN'T YOU FIGURED THAT OUT YET?
TH-THERE'S STILL MONEY TO BE MADE.
I COULD CUT YEW IN ON THE DEAL.
YEW COULD WORK WITH ME...HELP SEED POWERS LIKE YERS IN A NEW BATCH OF SYMBIOTES.
WE'D BE SO RICH--
--YOU COULD BUY YOURSELF A NEW DADDY.
HSSS!
IT'S ALL RIGHT, SCOTT.
HE'S JUST LOOKING FOR AN ANGLE...
...ANY ANGLE THAT MIGHT PRESENT HIM WITH AN OPPORTUNITY TO SLIP AWAY.

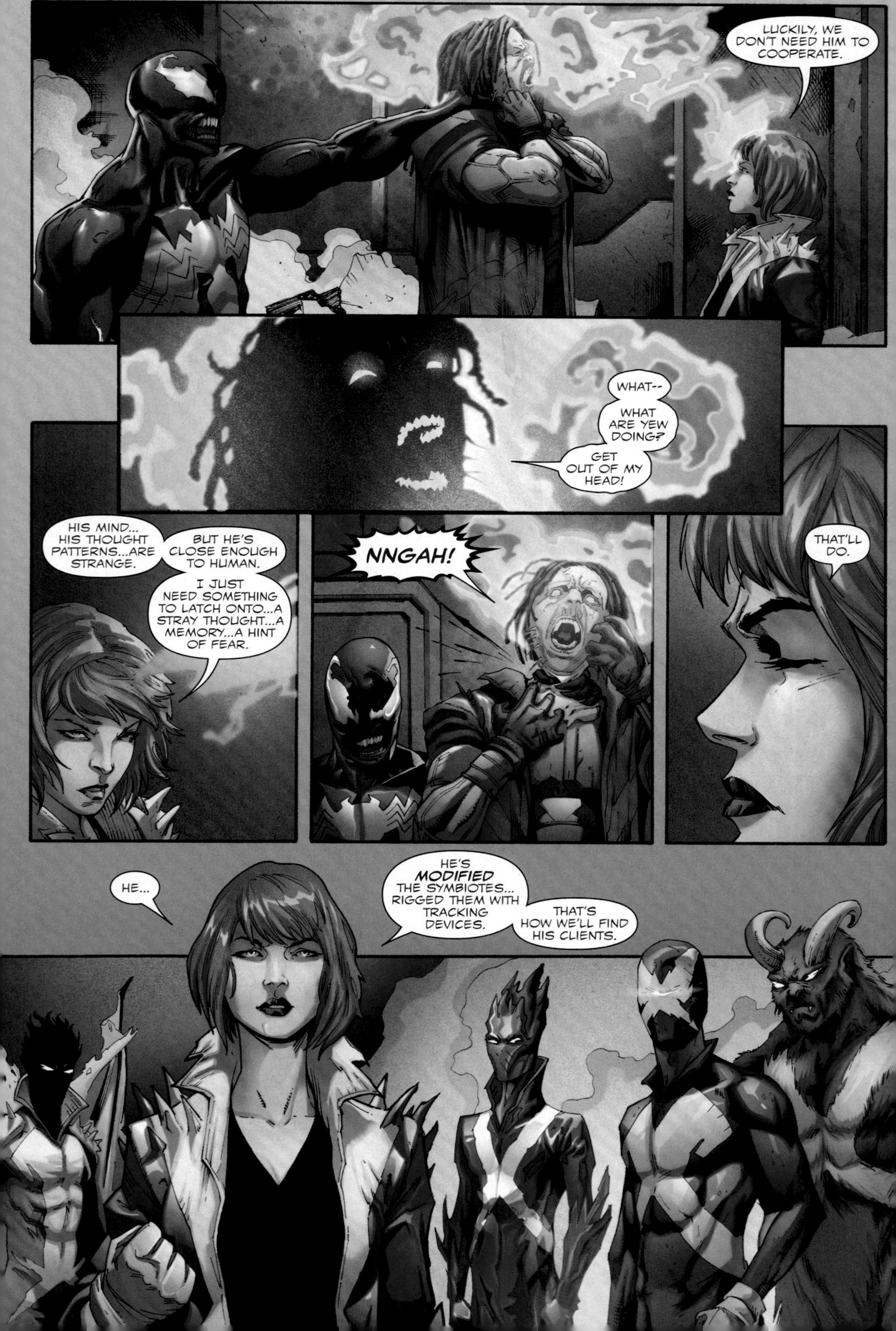

LUCKILY, WE DON'T NEED HIM TO COOPERATE.
WHAT--
WHAT ARE YEW DOING?
GET OUT OF MY HEAD!
HIS MIND... HIS THOUGHT PATTERNS...ARE STRANGE.
BUT HE'S CLOSE ENOUGH TO HUMAN.
I JUST NEED SOMETHING TO LATCH ONTO...A STRAY THOUGHT...A MEMORY...A HINT OF FEAR.
NNGAH!
THAT'LL DO.
HE...
HE'S MODIFIED THE SYMBIOTES... RIGGED THEM WITH TRACKING DEVICES.
THAT'S HOW WE'LL FIND HIS CLIENTS.

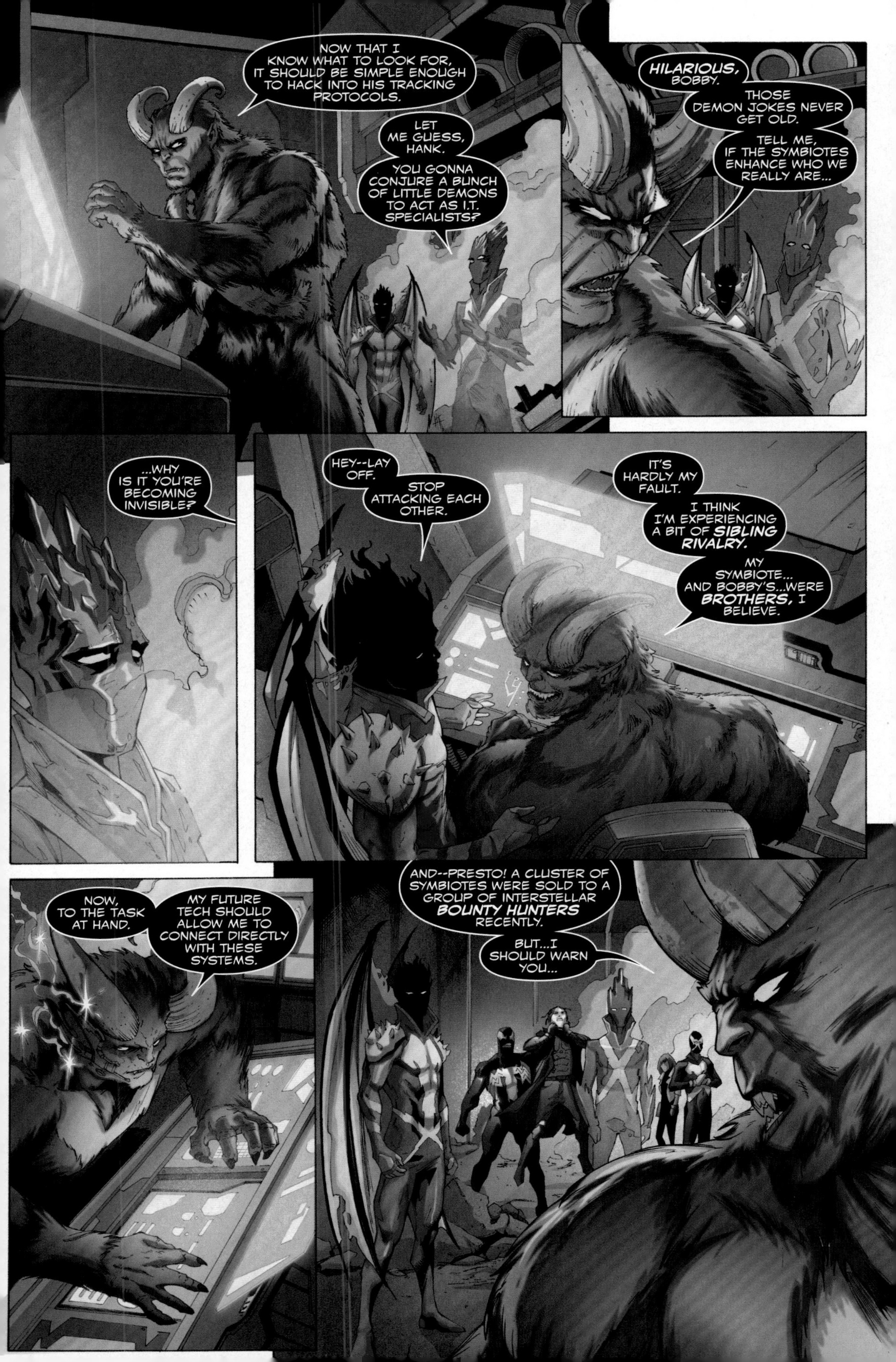
NOW THAT I KNOW WHAT TO LOOK FOR, IT SHOULD BE SIMPLE ENOUGH TO HACK INTO HIS TRACKING PROTOCOLS.
LET ME GUESS, HANK.
YOU GONNA CONJURE A BUNCH OF LITTLE DEMONS TO ACT AS I.T. SPECIALISTS?
HILARIOUS, BOBBY.
THOSE DEMON JOKES NEVER GET OLD.
TELL ME, IF THE SYMBIOTES ENHANCE WHO WE REALLY ARE...
...WHY IS IT YOU'RE BECOMING INVISIBLE?
HEY--LAY OFF.
STOP ATTACKING EACH OTHER.
IT'S HARDLY MY FAULT.
I THINK I'M EXPERIENCING A BIT OF SIBLING RIVALRY.
MY SYMBIOTE... AND BOBBY'S...WERE BROTHERS, I BELIEVE.
NOW, TO THE TASK AT HAND.
MY FUTURE TECH SHOULD ALLOW ME TO CONNECT DIRECTLY WITH THESE SYSTEMS.
AND--PRESTO! A CLUSTER OF SYMBIOTES WERE SOLD TO A GROUP OF INTERSTELLAR BOUNTY HUNTERS RECENTLY.
BUT...I SHOULD WARN YOU...

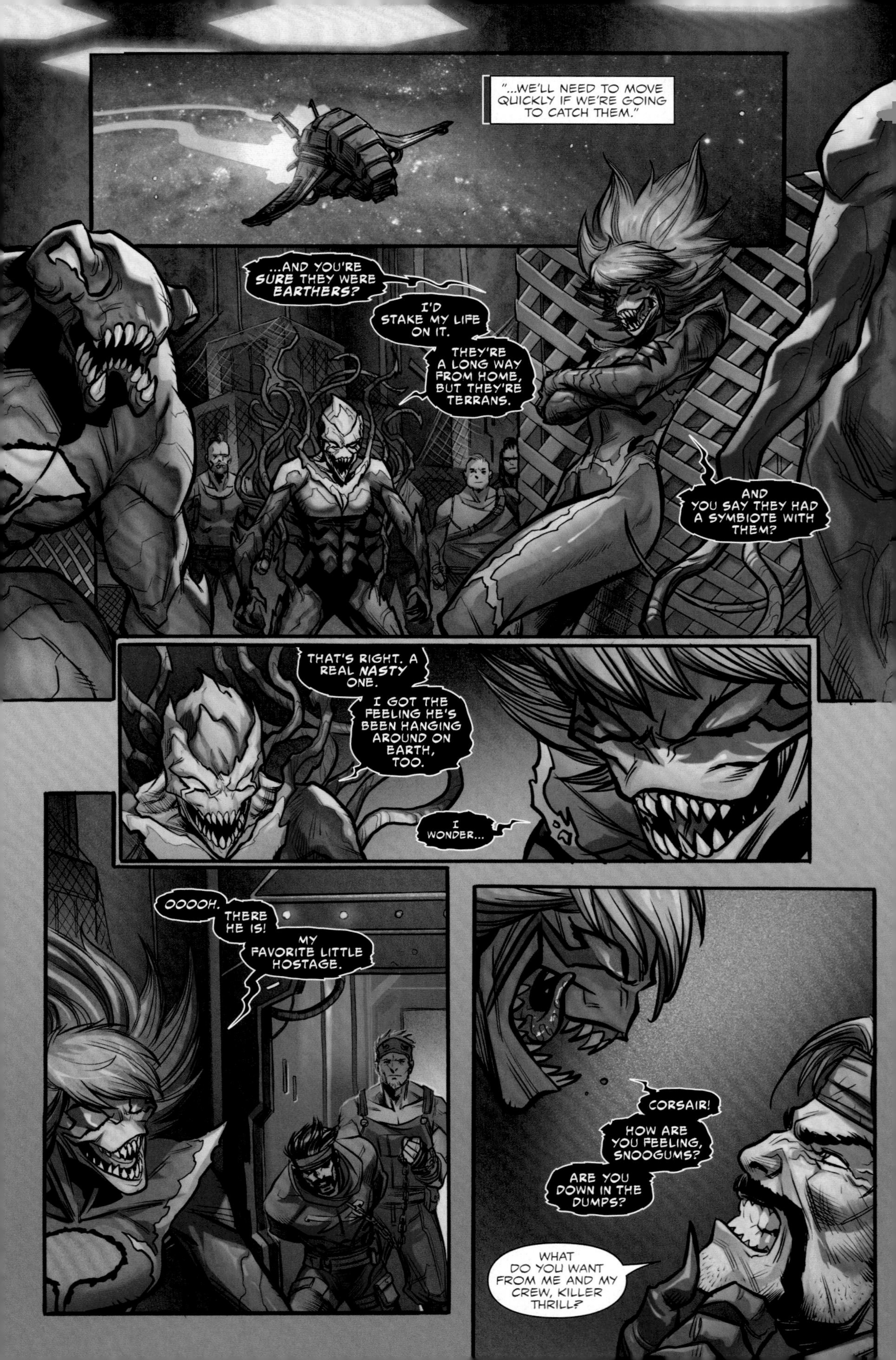
"...WE'LL NEED TO MOVE QUICKLY IF WE'RE GOING TO CATCH THEM."
...AND YOU'RE SURE THEY WERE EARTHERS?
I'D STAKE MY LIFE ON IT.
THEY'RE A LONG WAY FROM HOME, BUT THEY'RE TERRANS.
AND YOU SAY THEY HAD A SYMBIOTE WITH THEM?
THAT'S RIGHT. A REAL NASTY ONE.
I GOT THE FEELING HE'S BEEN HANGING AROUND ON EARTH, TOO.
I WONDER...
OOOOH.
THERE HE IS!
MY FAVORITE LITTLE HOSTAGE.
CORSAIR!
HOW ARE YOU FEELING, SNOOGUMS?
ARE YOU DOWN IN THE DUMPS?
WHAT DO YOU WANT FROM ME AND MY CREW, KILLER THRILL?

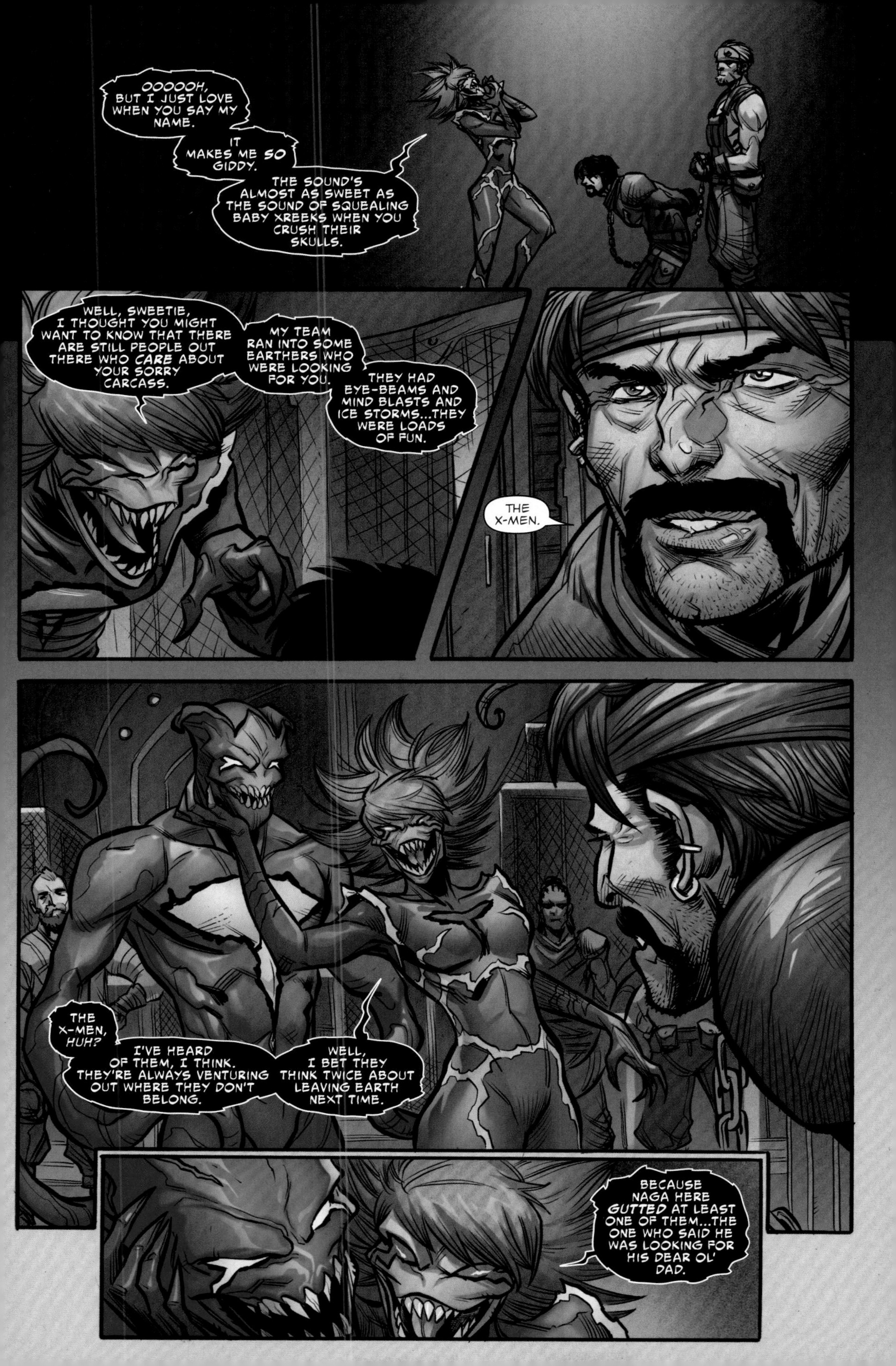
OOOOOH, BUT I JUST LOVE WHEN YOU SAY MY NAME.
IT MAKES ME SO GIDDY.
THE SOUND'S ALMOST AS SWEET AS THE SOUND OF SQUEALING BABY XREEKS WHEN YOU CRUSH THEIR SKULLS.
WELL, SWEETIE, I THOUGHT YOU MIGHT WANT TO KNOW THAT THERE ARE STILL PEOPLE OUT THERE WHO CARE ABOUT YOUR SORRY CARCASS.
MY TEAM RAN INTO SOME EARTHERS WHO WERE LOOKING FOR YOU.
THEY HAD EYE-BEAMS AND MIND BLASTS AND ICE STORMS...THEY WERE LOADS OF FUN.
THE X-MEN.
THE X-MEN, HUH?
I'VE HEARD OF THEM, I THINK. THEY'RE ALWAYS VENTURING OUT WHERE THEY DON'T BELONG.
WELL, I BET THEY THINK TWICE ABOUT LEAVING EARTH NEXT TIME.
BECAUSE NAGA HERE GUTTED AT LEAST ONE OF THEM...THE ONE WHO SAID HE WAS LOOKING FOR HIS DEAR OL' DAD.

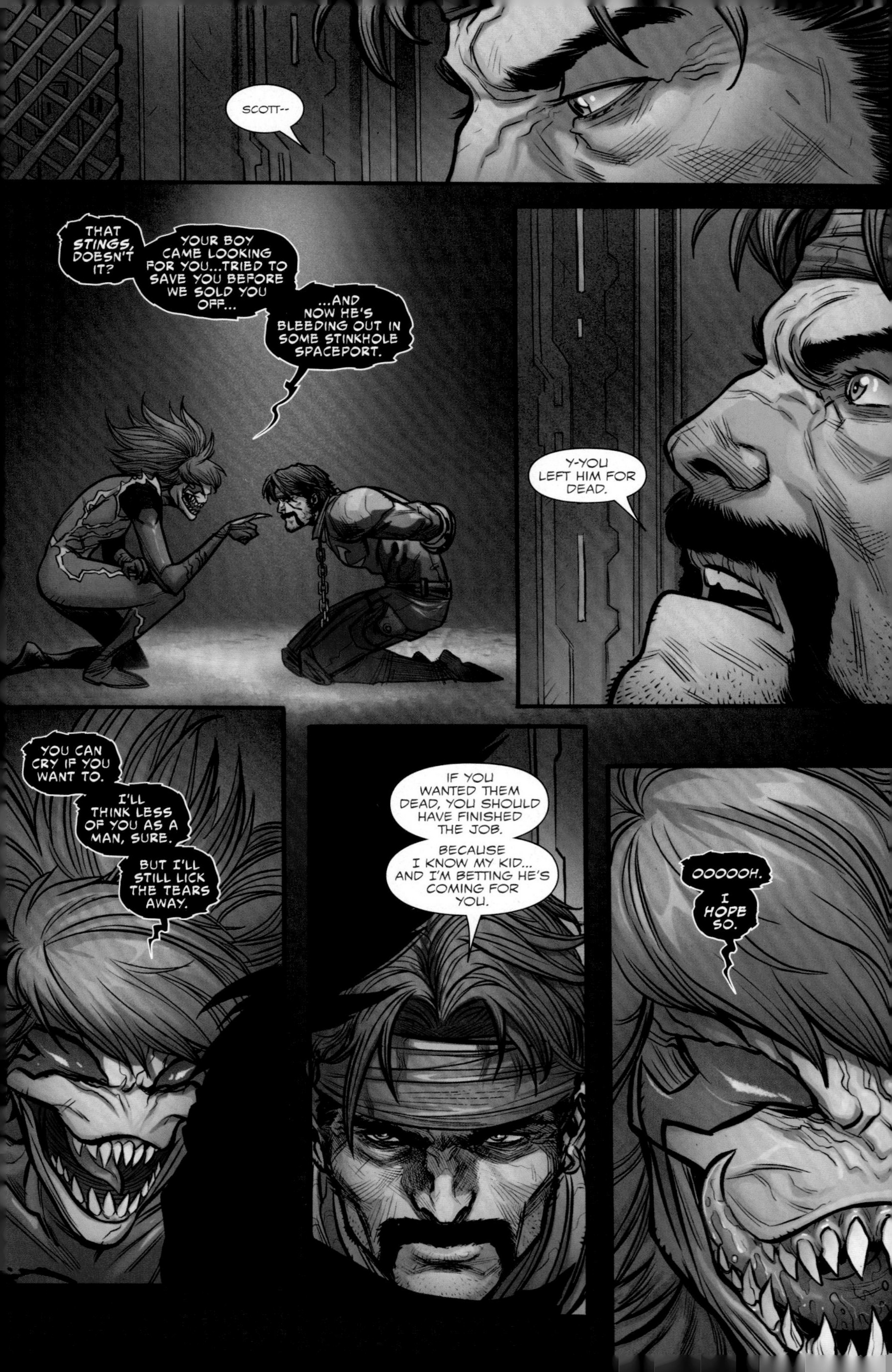
SCOTT--
THAT STINGS, DOESN'T IT?
YOUR BOY CAME LOOKING FOR YOU...TRIED TO SAVE YOU BEFORE WE SOLD YOU OFF...
...AND NOW HE'S BLEEDING OUT IN SOME STINKHOLE SPACEPORT.
Y-YOU LEFT HIM FOR DEAD.
YOU CAN CRY IF YOU WANT TO.
I'LL THINK LESS OF YOU AS A MAN, SURE.
BUT I'LL STILL LICK THE TEARS AWAY.
IF YOU WANTED THEM DEAD, YOU SHOULD HAVE FINISHED THE JOB.
BECAUSE I KNOW MY KID... AND I'M BETTING HE'S COMING FOR YOU.
OOOOOH.
I HOPE SO.

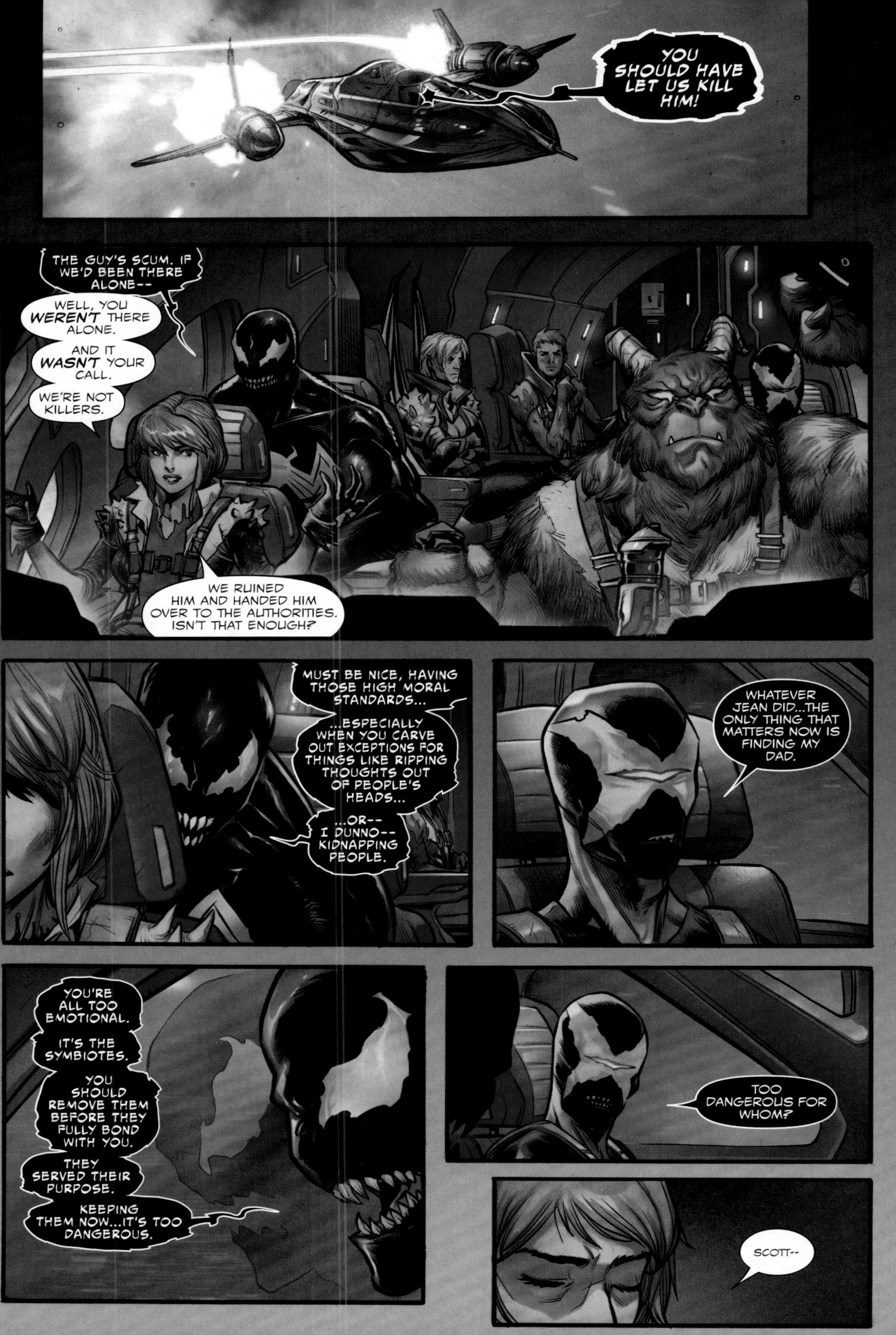

YOU SHOULD HAVE LET US KILL HIM!
THE GUY'S SCUM. IF WE'D BEEN THERE ALONE--
WELL, YOU WEREN'T THERE ALONE.
AND IT WASN'T YOUR CALL.
WE'RE NOT KILLERS.
WE RUINED HIM AND HANDED HIM OVER TO THE AUTHORITIES. ISN'T THAT ENOUGH?
MUST BE NICE, HAVING THOSE HIGH MORAL STANDARDS...
...ESPECIALLY WHEN YOU CARVE OUT EXCEPTIONS FOR THINGS LIKE RIPPING THOUGHTS OUT OF PEOPLE'S HEADS...
...OR-- I DUNNO-- KIDNAPPING PEOPLE.
WHATEVER JEAN DID...THE ONLY THING THAT MATTERS NOW IS FINDING MY DAD.
YOU'RE ALL TOO EMOTIONAL.
IT'S THE SYMBIOTES.
YOU SHOULD REMOVE THEM BEFORE THEY FULLY BOND WITH YOU.
THEY SERVED THEIR PURPOSE.
KEEPING THEM NOW...IT'S TOO DANGEROUS.
TOO DANGEROUS FOR WHOM?
SCOTT--

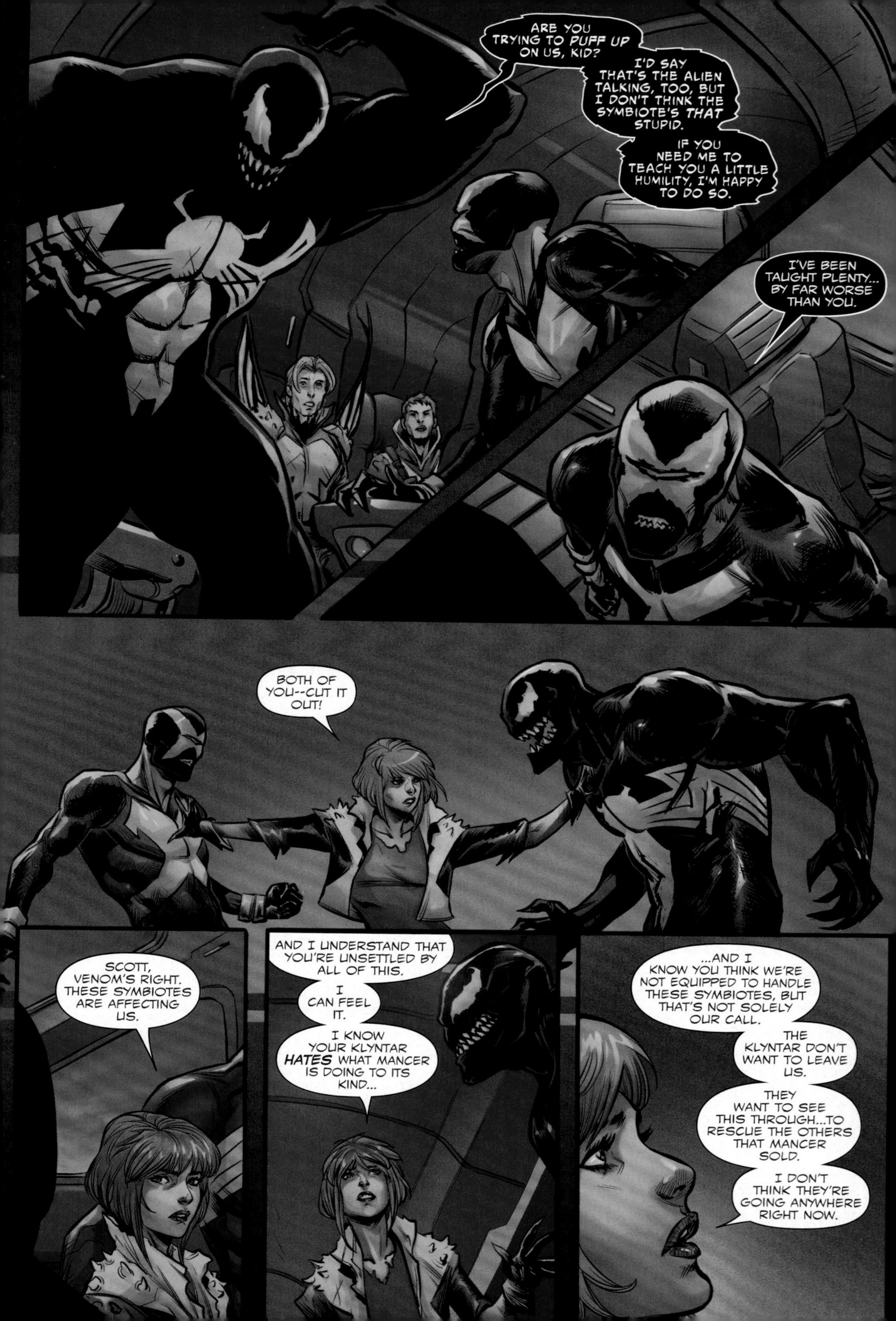

ARE YOU TRYING TO PUFF UP ON US, KID?
I'D SAY THAT'S THE ALIEN TALKING, TOO, BUT I DON'T THINK THE SYMBIOTE'S THAT STUPID.
IF YOU NEED ME TO TEACH YOU A LITTLE HUMILITY, I'M HAPPY TO DO SO.
I'VE BEEN TAUGHT PLENTY... BY FAR WORSE THAN YOU.
BOTH OF YOU--CUT IT OUT!
SCOTT, VENOM'S RIGHT. THESE SYMBIOTES ARE AFFECTING US.
AND I UNDERSTAND THAT YOU'RE UNSETTLED BY ALL OF THIS.
I CAN FEEL IT.
I KNOW YOUR KLYNTAR HATES WHAT MANCER IS DOING TO ITS KIND...
...AND I KNOW YOU THINK WE'RE NOT EQUIPPED TO HANDLE THESE SYMBIOTES, BUT THAT'S NOT SOLELY OUR CALL.
THE KLYNTAR DON'T WANT TO LEAVE US.
THEY WANT TO SEE THIS THROUGH...TO RESCUE THE OTHERS THAT MANCER SOLD.
I DON'T THINK THEY'RE GOING ANYWHERE RIGHT NOW.

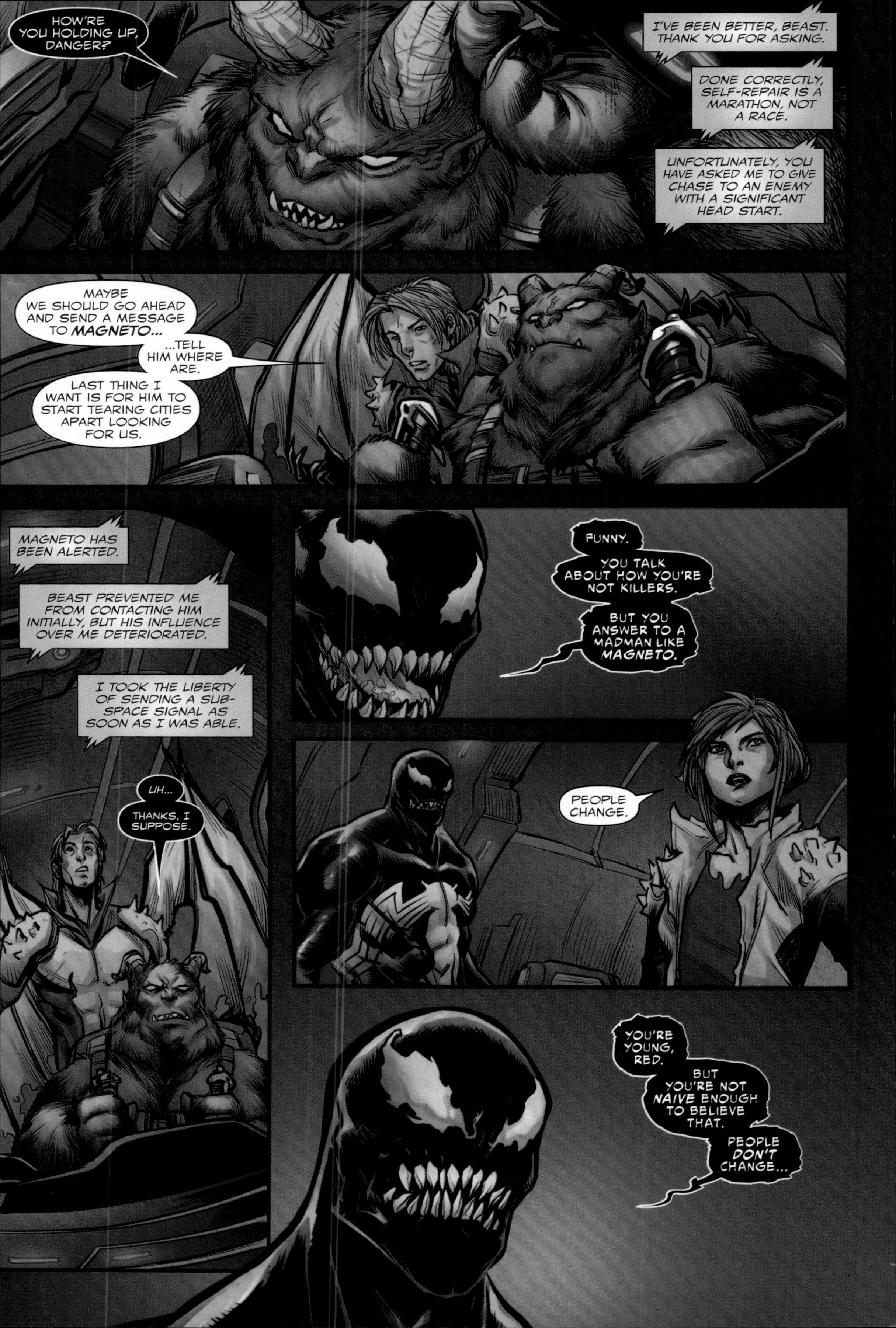

HOW'RE YOU HOLDING UP, DANGER?
I'VE BEEN BETTER, BEAST. THANK YOU FOR ASKING.
DONE CORRECTLY, SELF-REPAIR IS A MARATHON, NOT A RACE.
UNFORTUNATELY, YOU HAVE ASKED ME TO GIVE CHASE TO AN ENEMY WITH A SIGNIFICANT HEAD START.
MAYBE WE SHOULD GO AHEAD AND SEND A MESSAGE TO MAGNETO...
...TELL HIM WHERE ARE.
LAST THING I WANT IS FOR HIM TO START TEARING CITIES APART LOOKING FOR US.
MAGNETO HAS BEEN ALERTED.
BEAST PREVENTED ME FROM CONTACTING HIM INITIALLY, BUT HIS INFLUENCE OVER ME DETERIORATED.
I TOOK THE LIBERTY OF SENDING A SUB-SPACE SIGNAL AS SOON AS I WAS ABLE.
UH...
THANKS, I SUPPOSE.
FUNNY.
YOU TALK ABOUT HOW YOU'RE NOT KILLERS.
BUT YOU ANSWER TO A MADMAN LIKE MAGNETO.
PEOPLE CHANGE.
YOU'RE YOUNG, RED.
BUT YOU'RE NOT NAIVE ENOUGH TO BELIEVE THAT.
PEOPLE DON'T CHANGE...

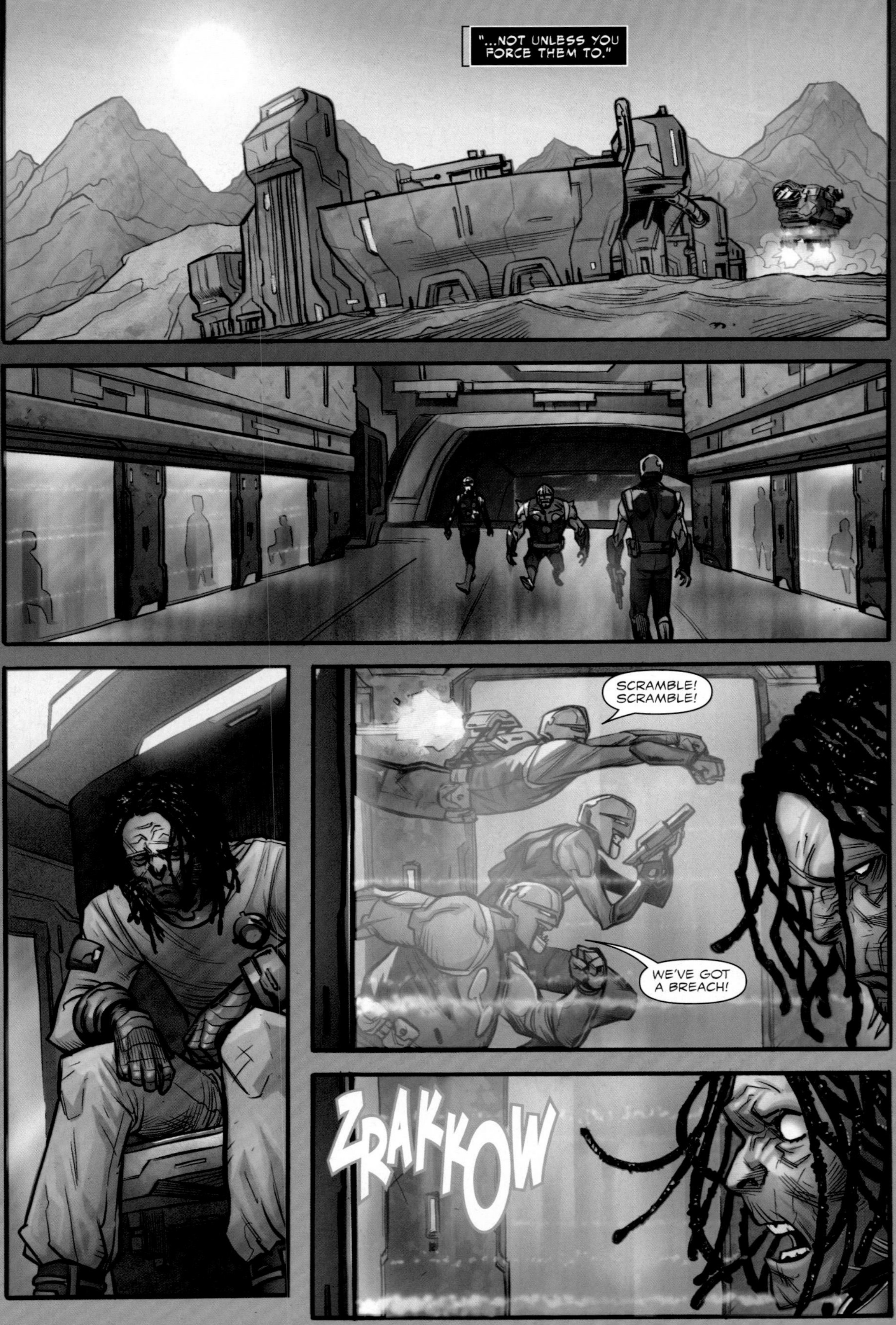
"...NOT UNLESS YOU FORCE THEM TO."
SCRAMBLE! SCRAMBLE!
WE'VE GOT A BREACH!
ZRAKKOW

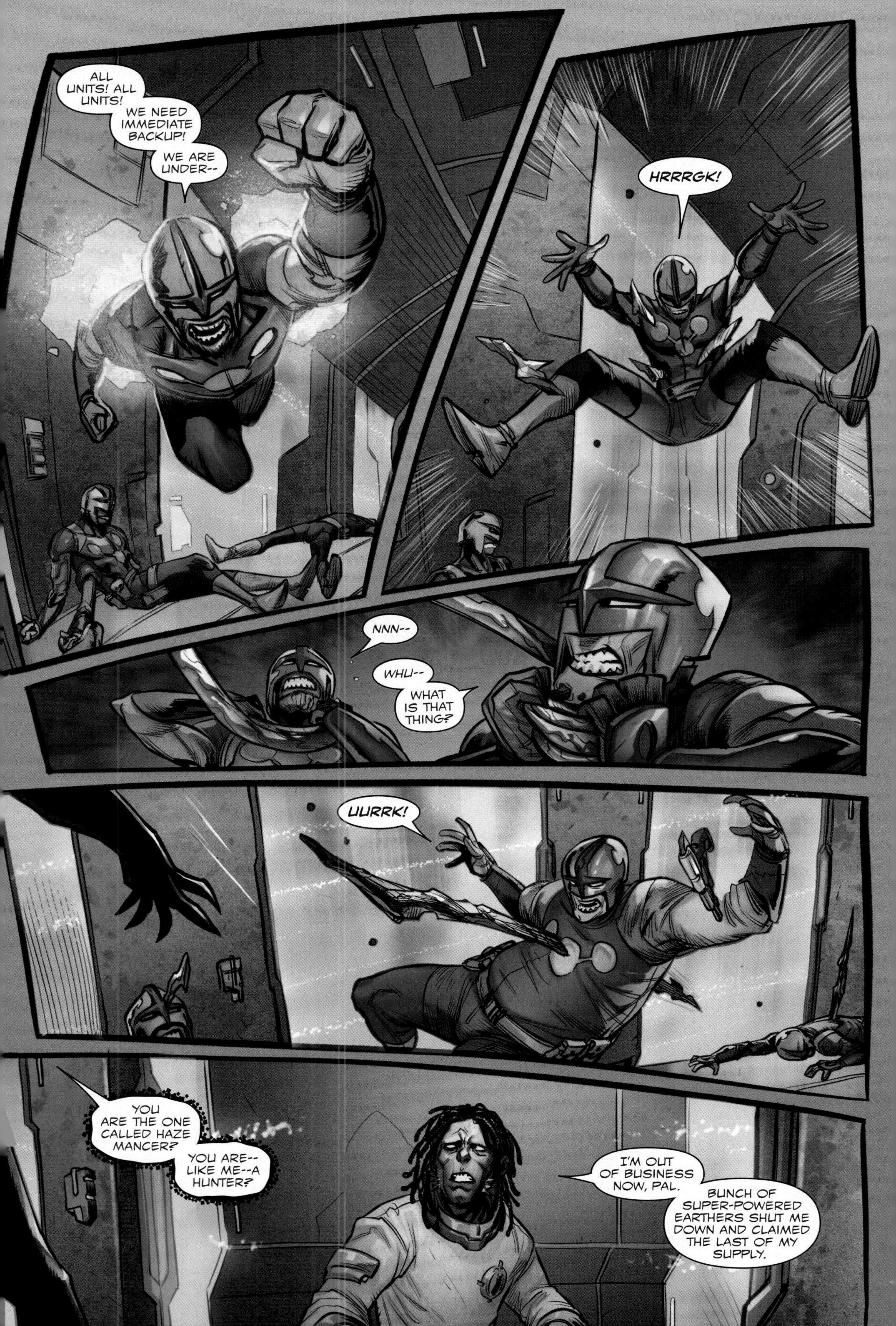
ALL UNITS! ALL UNITS!
WE NEED IMMEDIATE BACKUP!
WE ARE UNDER--
HRRRGK!
NNN--
WHU--
WHAT IS THAT THING?
UURRK!
YOU ARE THE ONE CALLED HAZE MANCER?
YOU ARE--LIKE ME--A HUNTER?
I'M OUT OF BUSINESS NOW, PAL.
BUNCH OF SUPER-POWERED EARTHERS SHUT ME DOWN AND CLAIMED THE LAST OF MY SUPPLY.

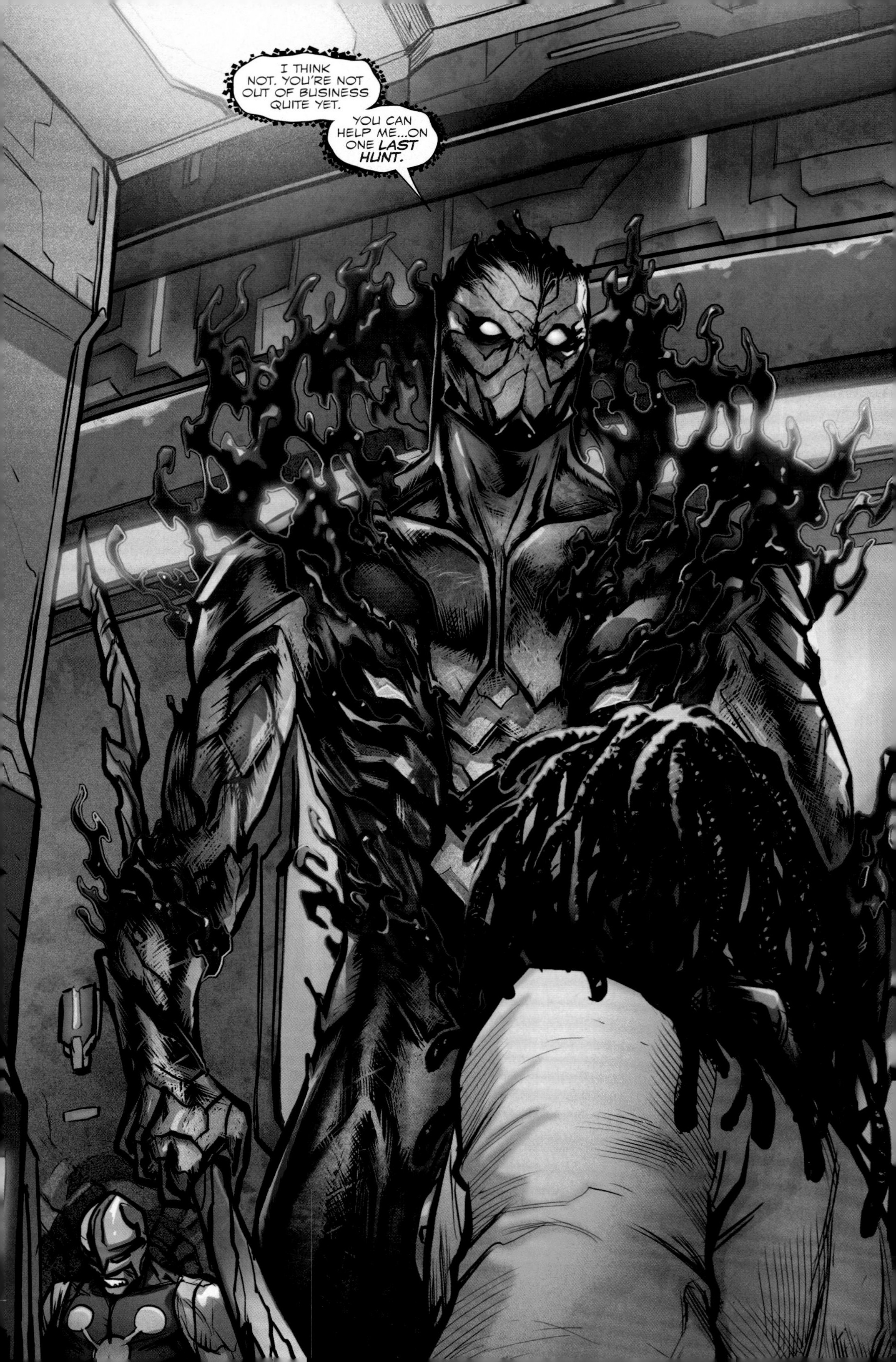
I THINK NOT. YOU'RE NOT OUT OF BUSINESS QUITE YET.
YOU CAN HELP ME...ON ONE ***LAST HUNT.***

X-MEN BLUE 22

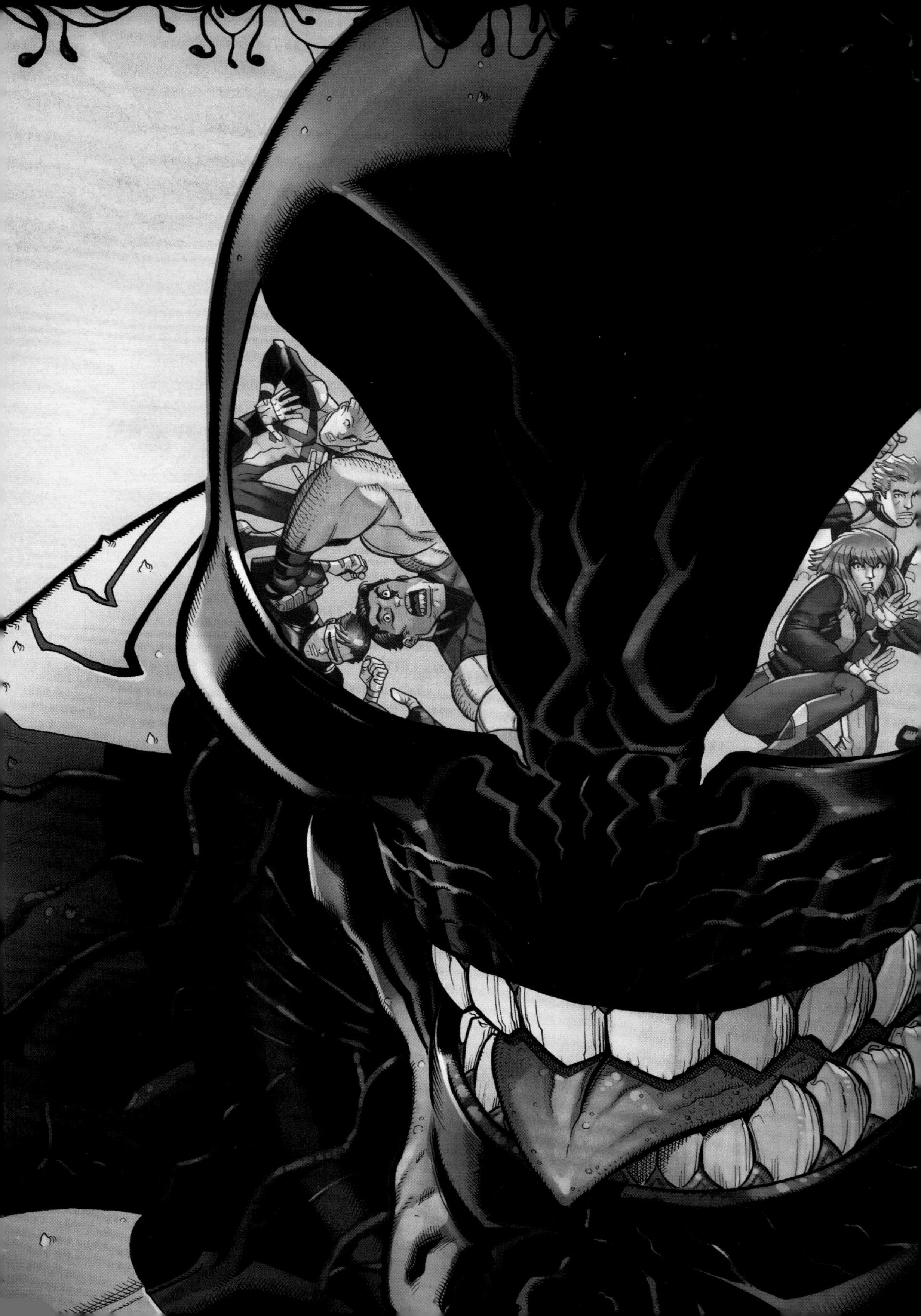

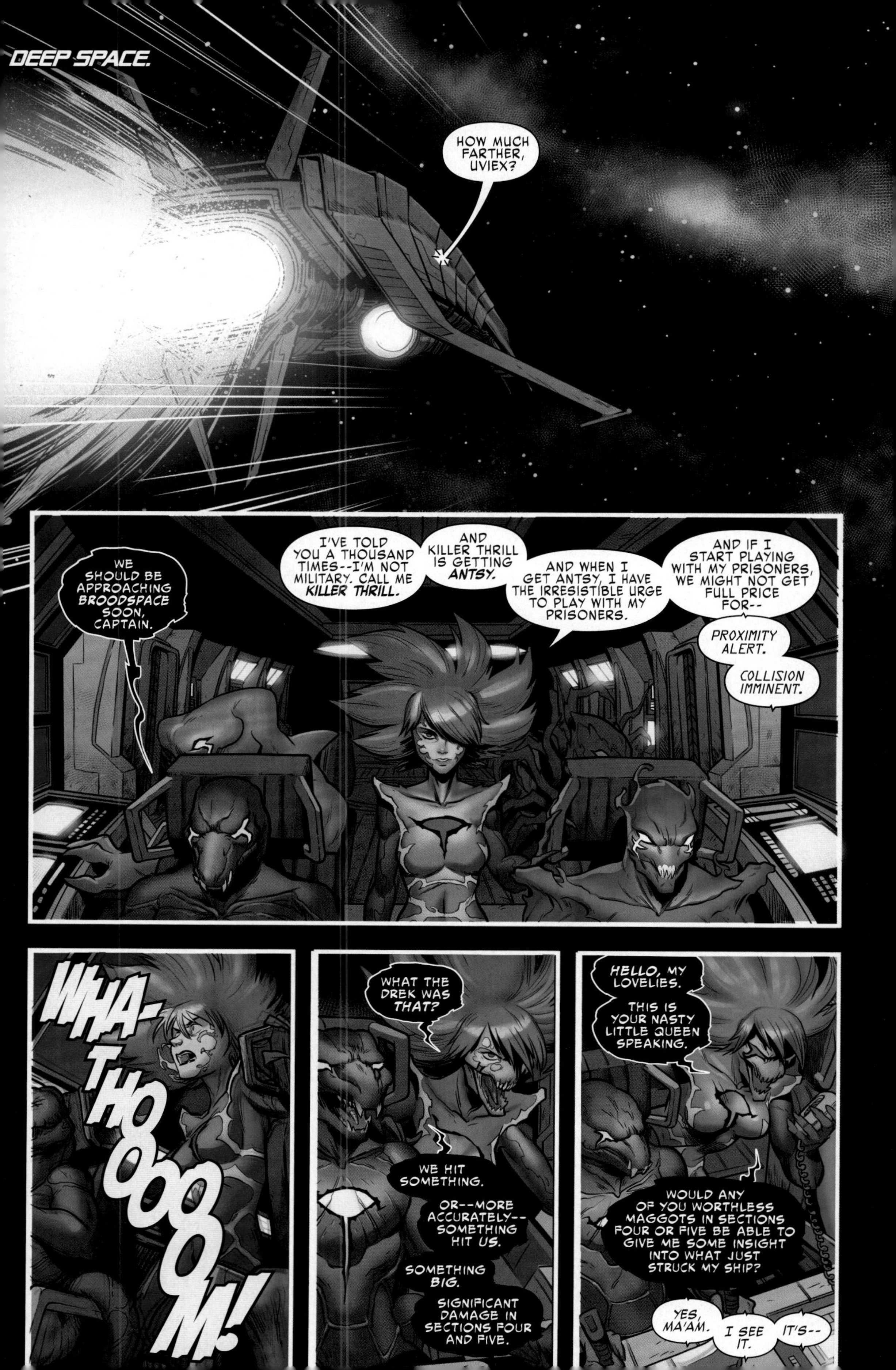

DEEP SPACE.
HOW MUCH FARTHER, UVIEX?
WE SHOULD BE APPROACHING BROODSPACE SOON, CAPTAIN.
I'VE TOLD YOU A THOUSAND TIMES--I'M NOT MILITARY. CALL ME KILLER THRILL.
AND KILLER THRILL IS GETTING ANTSY.
AND WHEN I GET ANTSY, I HAVE THE IRRESISTIBLE URGE TO PLAY WITH MY PRISONERS.
AND IF I START PLAYING WITH MY PRISONERS, WE MIGHT NOT GET FULL PRICE FOR--
PROXIMITY ALERT.
COLLISION IMMINENT.
WHA-THOOOOOM!
WHAT THE DREK WAS THAT?
WE HIT SOMETHING.
OR--MORE ACCURATELY--SOMETHING HIT US.
SOMETHING BIG.
SIGNIFICANT DAMAGE IN SECTIONS FOUR AND FIVE.
HELLO, MY LOVELIES.
THIS IS YOUR NASTY LITTLE QUEEN SPEAKING.
WOULD ANY OF YOU WORTHLESS MAGGOTS IN SECTIONS FOUR OR FIVE BE ABLE TO GIVE ME SOME INSIGHT INTO WHAT JUST STRUCK MY SHIP?
YES, MA'AM.
I SEE IT.
IT'S--

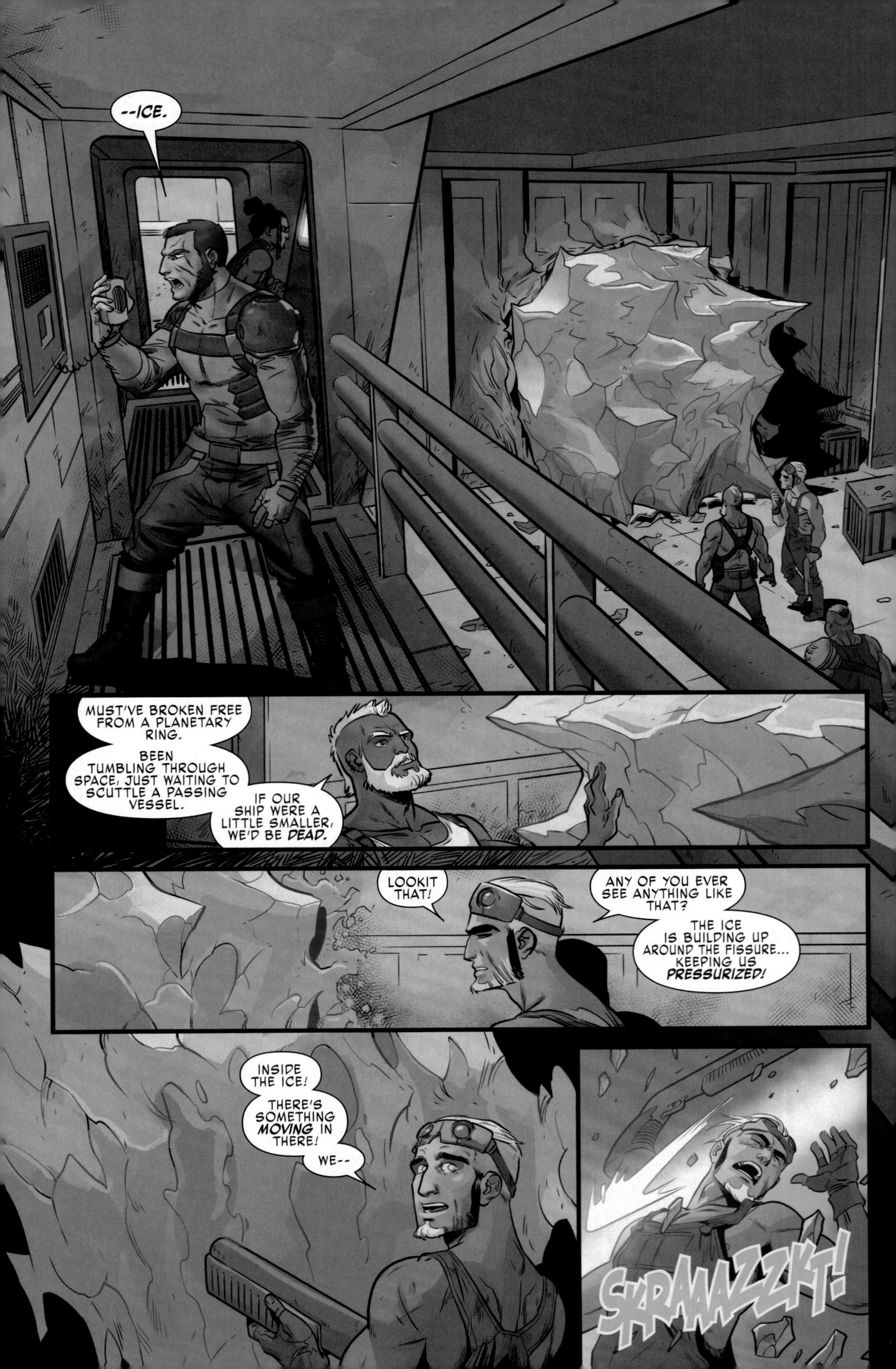
--ICE.
MUST'VE BROKEN FREE FROM A PLANETARY RING.
BEEN TUMBLING THROUGH SPACE, JUST WAITING TO SCUTTLE A PASSING VESSEL.
IF OUR SHIP WERE A LITTLE SMALLER, WE'D BE *DEAD.*
LOOKIT THAT!
ANY OF YOU EVER SEE ANYTHING LIKE THAT?
THE ICE IS BUILDING UP AROUND THE FISSURE... KEEPING US *PRESSURIZED!*
INSIDE THE ICE!
THERE'S SOMETHING *MOVING* IN THERE!
WE--
SKRAAAZZKT!

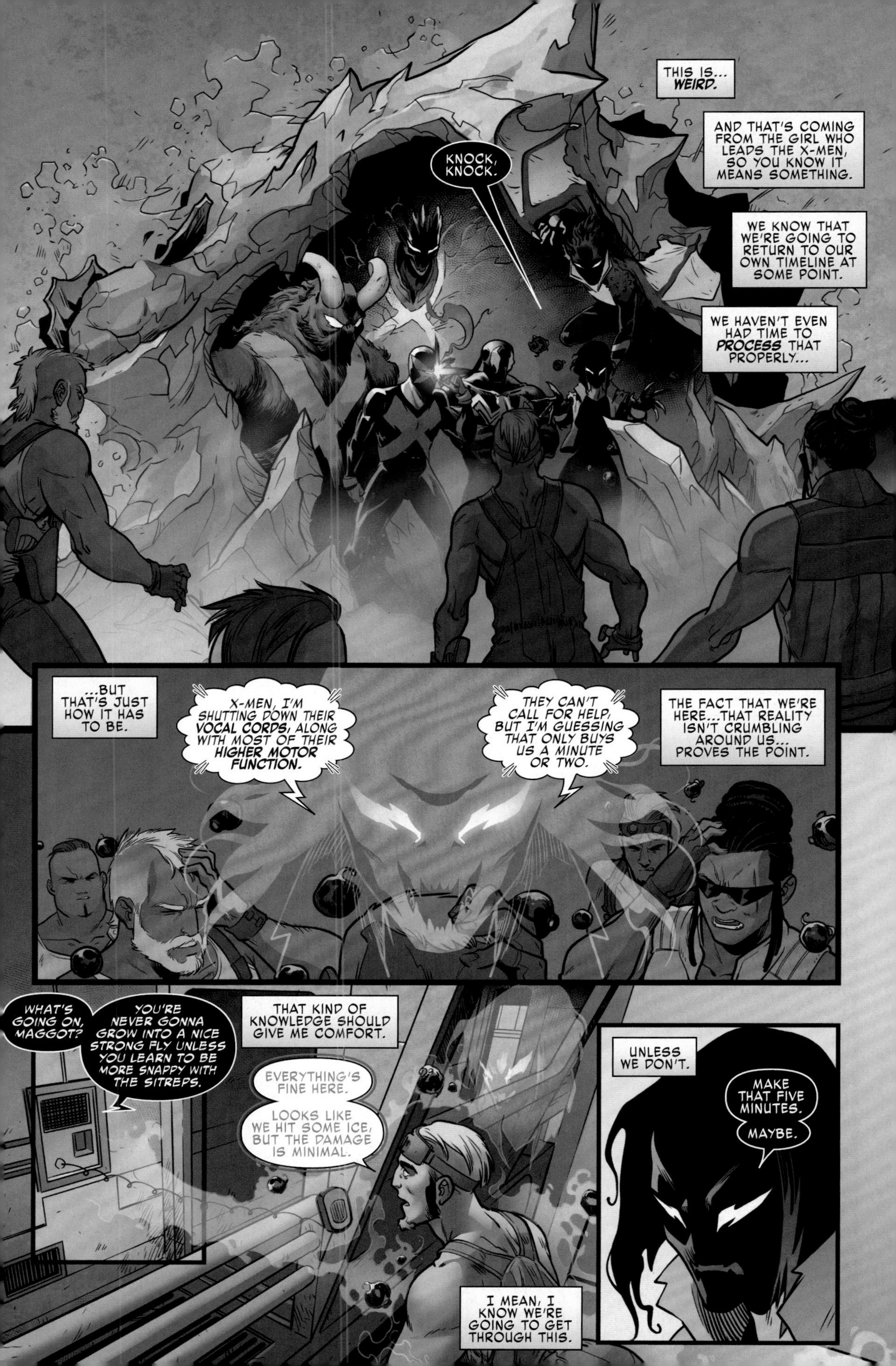
THIS IS... WEIRD.
AND THAT'S COMING FROM THE GIRL WHO LEADS THE X-MEN, SO YOU KNOW IT MEANS SOMETHING.
KNOCK, KNOCK.
WE KNOW THAT WE'RE GOING TO RETURN TO OUR OWN TIMELINE AT SOME POINT.
WE HAVEN'T EVEN HAD TIME TO PROCESS THAT PROPERLY...
...BUT THAT'S JUST HOW IT HAS TO BE.
X-MEN, I'M SHUTTING DOWN THEIR VOCAL CORDS, ALONG WITH MOST OF THEIR HIGHER MOTOR FUNCTION.
THEY CAN'T CALL FOR HELP, BUT I'M GUESSING THAT ONLY BUYS US A MINUTE OR TWO.
THE FACT THAT WE'RE HERE...THAT REALITY ISN'T CRUMBLING AROUND US... PROVES THE POINT.
WHAT'S GOING ON, MAGGOT?
YOU'RE NEVER GONNA GROW INTO A NICE STRONG FLY UNLESS YOU LEARN TO BE MORE SNAPPY WITH THE SITREPS.
THAT KIND OF KNOWLEDGE SHOULD GIVE ME COMFORT.
EVERYTHING'S FINE HERE.
LOOKS LIKE WE HIT SOME ICE, BUT THE DAMAGE IS MINIMAL.
I MEAN, I KNOW WE'RE GOING TO GET THROUGH THIS.
UNLESS WE DON'T.
MAKE THAT FIVE MINUTES.
MAYBE.

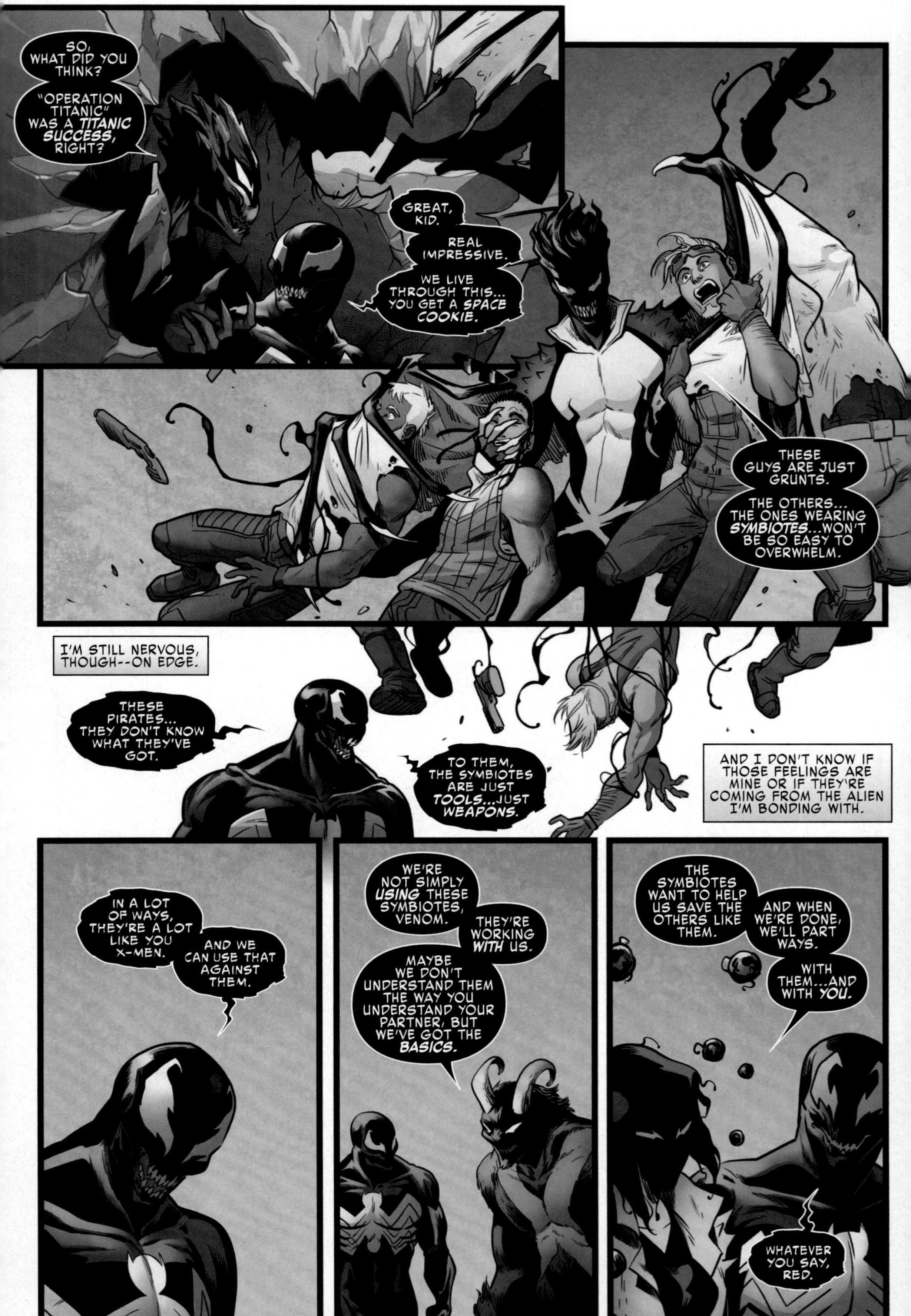
SO, WHAT DID YOU THINK?
"OPERATION TITANIC" WAS A TITANIC SUCCESS, RIGHT?
GREAT, KID.
REAL IMPRESSIVE.
WE LIVE THROUGH THIS... YOU GET A SPACE COOKIE.
THESE GUYS ARE JUST GRUNTS.
THE OTHERS... THE ONES WEARING SYMBIOTES...WON'T BE SO EASY TO OVERWHELM.
I'M STILL NERVOUS, THOUGH--ON EDGE.
THESE PIRATES... THEY DON'T KNOW WHAT THEY'VE GOT.
TO THEM, THE SYMBIOTES ARE JUST TOOLS...JUST WEAPONS.
AND I DON'T KNOW IF THOSE FEELINGS ARE MINE OR IF THEY'RE COMING FROM THE ALIEN I'M BONDING WITH.
IN A LOT OF WAYS, THEY'RE A LOT LIKE YOU X-MEN.
AND WE CAN USE THAT AGAINST THEM.
WE'RE NOT SIMPLY USING THESE SYMBIOTES, VENOM.
THEY'RE WORKING WITH US.
MAYBE WE DON'T UNDERSTAND THEM THE WAY YOU UNDERSTAND YOUR PARTNER, BUT WE'VE GOT THE BASICS.
THE SYMBIOTES WANT TO HELP US SAVE THE OTHERS LIKE THEM.
AND WHEN WE'RE DONE, WE'LL PART WAYS.
WITH THEM...AND WITH YOU.
WHATEVER YOU SAY, RED.

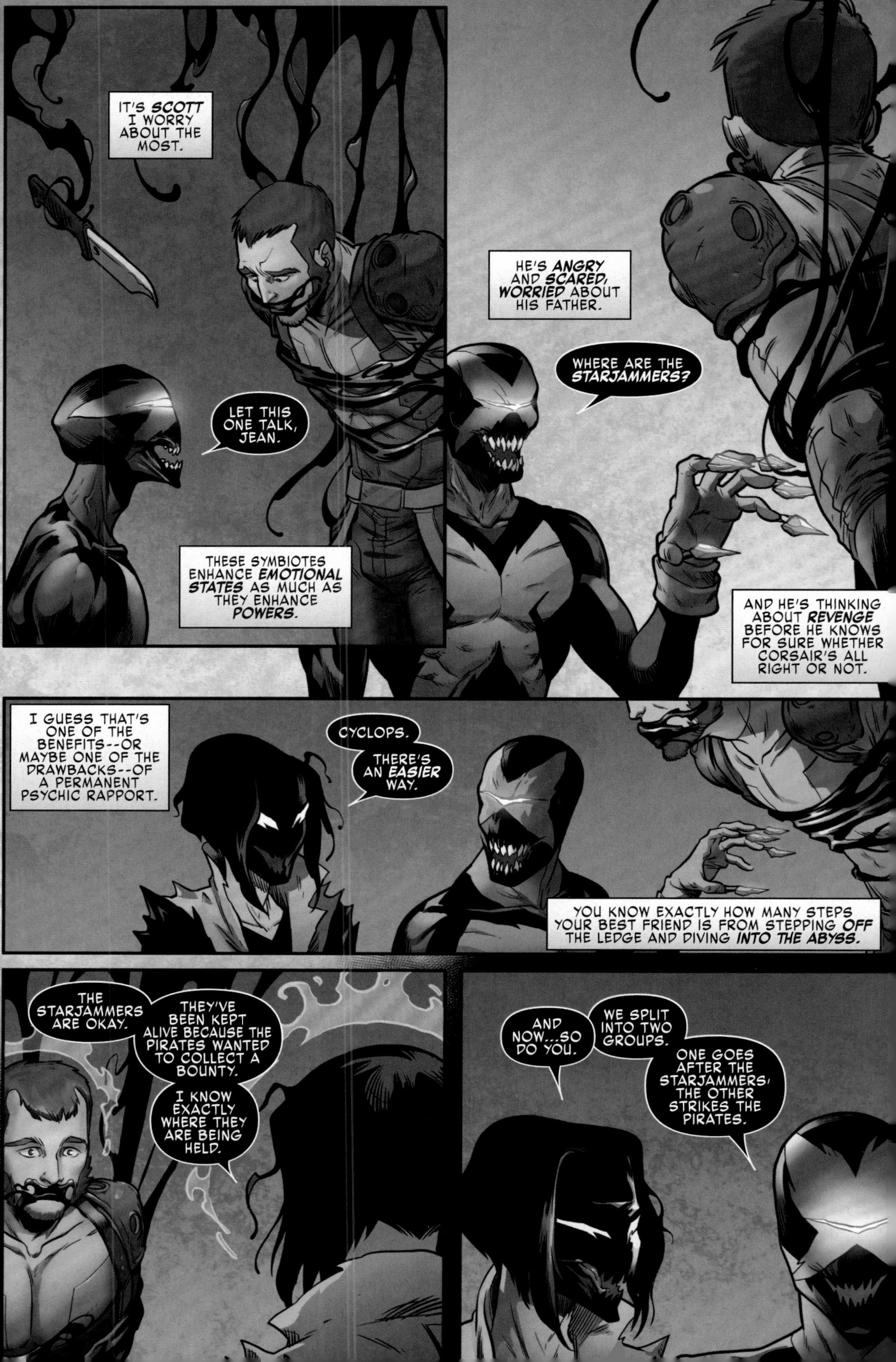
IT'S SCOTT I WORRY ABOUT THE MOST.
HE'S ANGRY AND SCARED, WORRIED ABOUT HIS FATHER.
LET THIS ONE TALK, JEAN.
WHERE ARE THE STARJAMMERS?
THESE SYMBIOTES ENHANCE EMOTIONAL STATES AS MUCH AS THEY ENHANCE POWERS.
AND HE'S THINKING ABOUT REVENGE BEFORE HE KNOWS FOR SURE WHETHER CORSAIR'S ALL RIGHT OR NOT.
I GUESS THAT'S ONE OF THE BENEFITS--OR MAYBE ONE OF THE DRAWBACKS--OF A PERMANENT PSYCHIC RAPPORT.
CYCLOPS.
THERE'S AN EASIER WAY.
YOU KNOW EXACTLY HOW MANY STEPS YOUR BEST FRIEND IS FROM STEPPING OFF THE LEDGE AND DIVING INTO THE ABYSS.
THE STARJAMMERS ARE OKAY.
THEY'VE BEEN KEPT ALIVE BECAUSE THE PIRATES WANTED TO COLLECT A BOUNTY.
I KNOW EXACTLY WHERE THEY ARE BEING HELD.
AND NOW...SO DO YOU.
WE SPLIT INTO TWO GROUPS.
ONE GOES AFTER THE STARJAMMERS, THE OTHER STRIKES THE PIRATES.

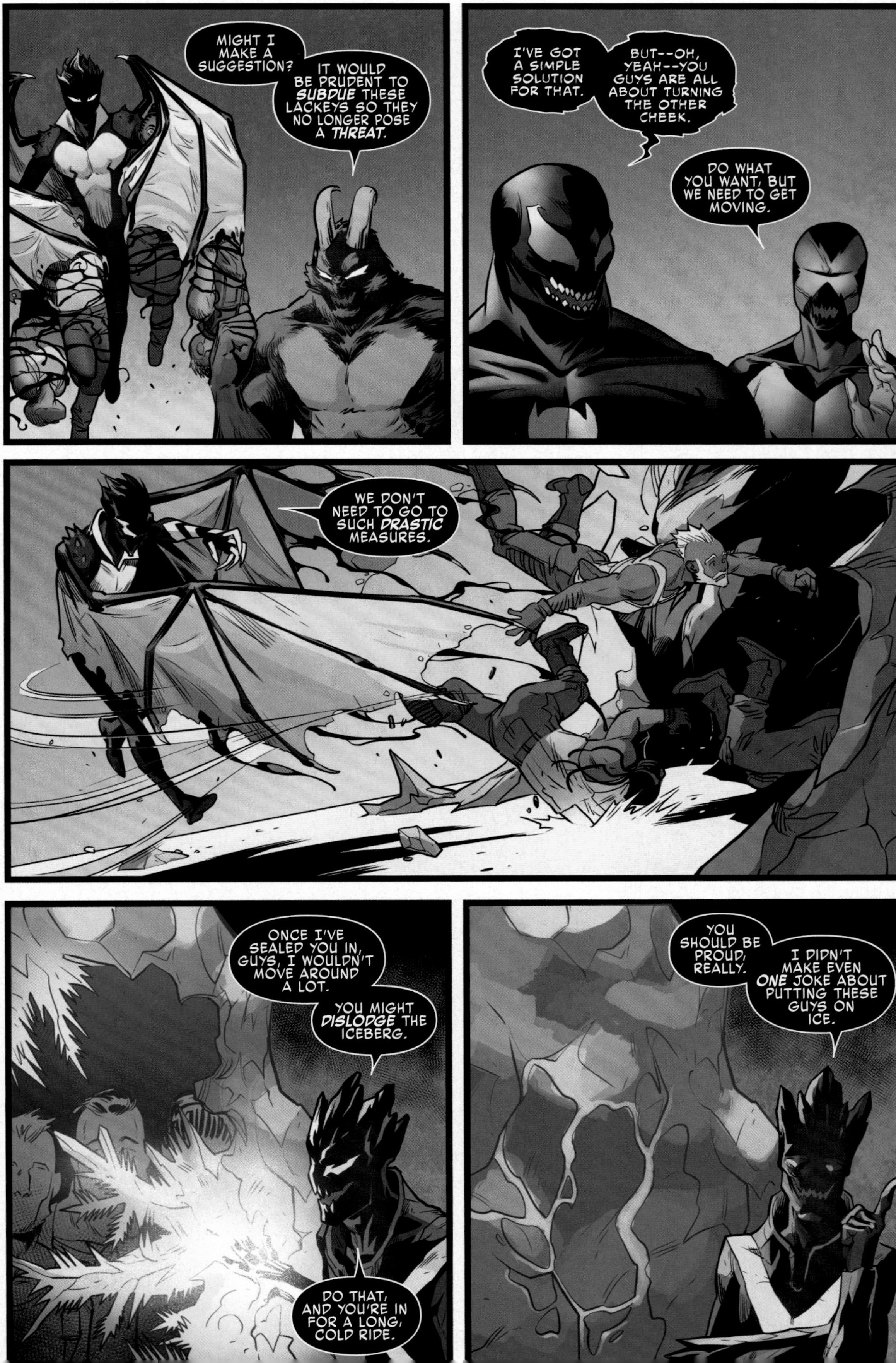
MIGHT I MAKE A SUGGESTION?
IT WOULD BE PRUDENT TO SUBDUE THESE LACKEYS SO THEY NO LONGER POSE A THREAT.
I'VE GOT A SIMPLE SOLUTION FOR THAT.
BUT--OH, YEAH--YOU GUYS ARE ALL ABOUT TURNING THE OTHER CHEEK.
DO WHAT YOU WANT, BUT WE NEED TO GET MOVING.
WE DON'T NEED TO GO TO SUCH DRASTIC MEASURES.
ONCE I'VE SEALED YOU IN, GUYS, I WOULDN'T MOVE AROUND A LOT.
YOU MIGHT DISLODGE THE ICEBERG.
DO THAT, AND YOU'RE IN FOR A LONG, COLD RIDE.
YOU SHOULD BE PROUD, REALLY.
I DIDN'T MAKE EVEN ONE JOKE ABOUT PUTTING THESE GUYS ON ICE.

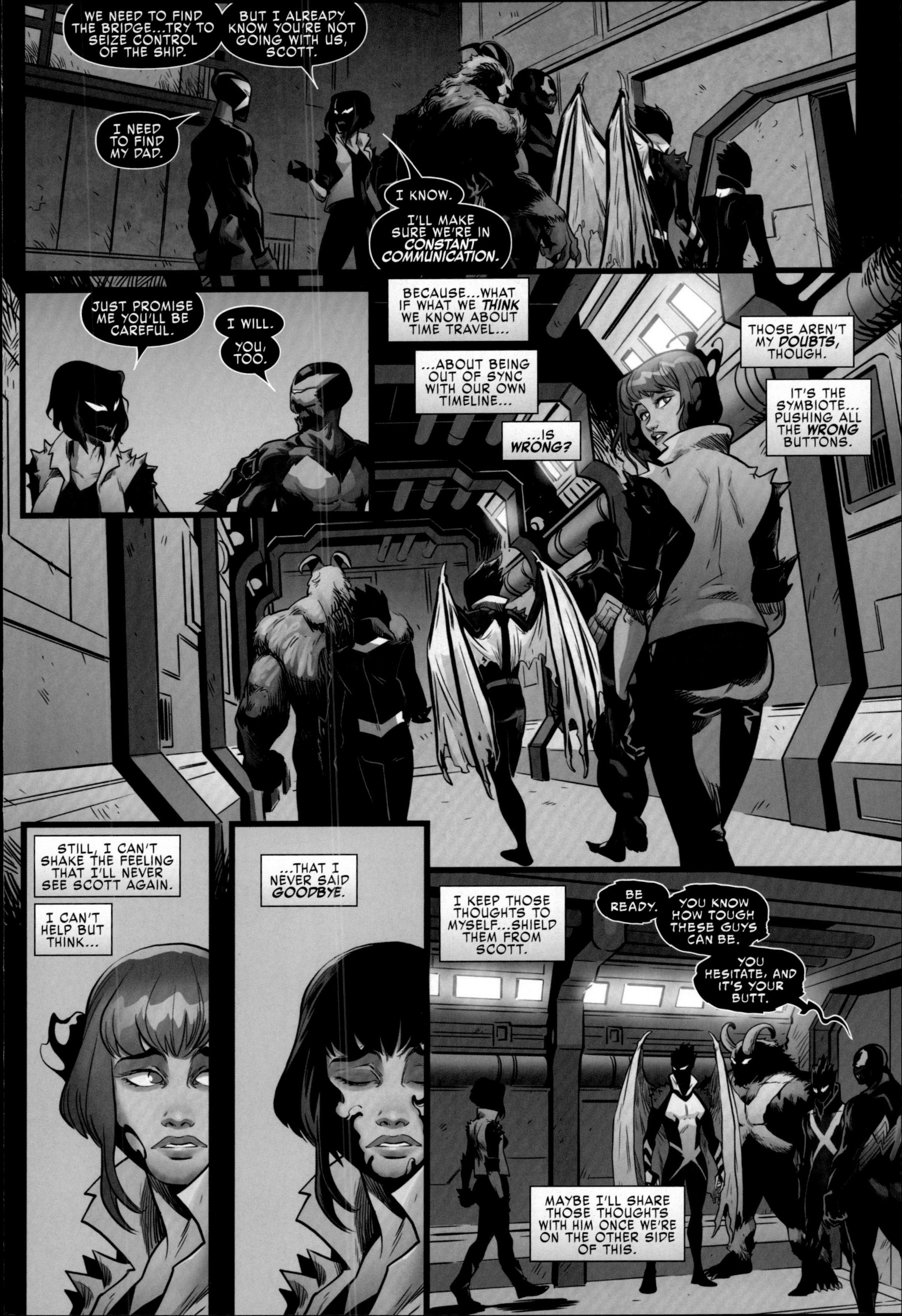
WE NEED TO FIND THE BRIDGE...TRY TO SEIZE CONTROL OF THE SHIP.
BUT I ALREADY KNOW YOU'RE NOT GOING WITH US, SCOTT.
I NEED TO FIND MY DAD.
I KNOW.
I'LL MAKE SURE WE'RE IN CONSTANT COMMUNICATION.
JUST PROMISE ME YOU'LL BE CAREFUL.
I WILL.
YOU, TOO.
BECAUSE...WHAT IF WHAT WE THINK WE KNOW ABOUT TIME TRAVEL...
...ABOUT BEING OUT OF SYNC WITH OUR OWN TIMELINE...
...IS WRONG?
THOSE AREN'T MY DOUBTS, THOUGH.
IT'S THE SYMBIOTE... PUSHING ALL THE WRONG BUTTONS.
STILL, I CAN'T SHAKE THE FEELING THAT I'LL NEVER SEE SCOTT AGAIN.
I CAN'T HELP BUT THINK...
...THAT I NEVER SAID GOODBYE.
I KEEP THOSE THOUGHTS TO MYSELF...SHIELD THEM FROM SCOTT.
BE READY.
YOU KNOW HOW TOUGH THESE GUYS CAN BE.
YOU HESITATE, AND IT'S YOUR BUTT.
MAYBE I'LL SHARE THOSE THOUGHTS WITH HIM ONCE WE'RE ON THE OTHER SIDE OF THIS.

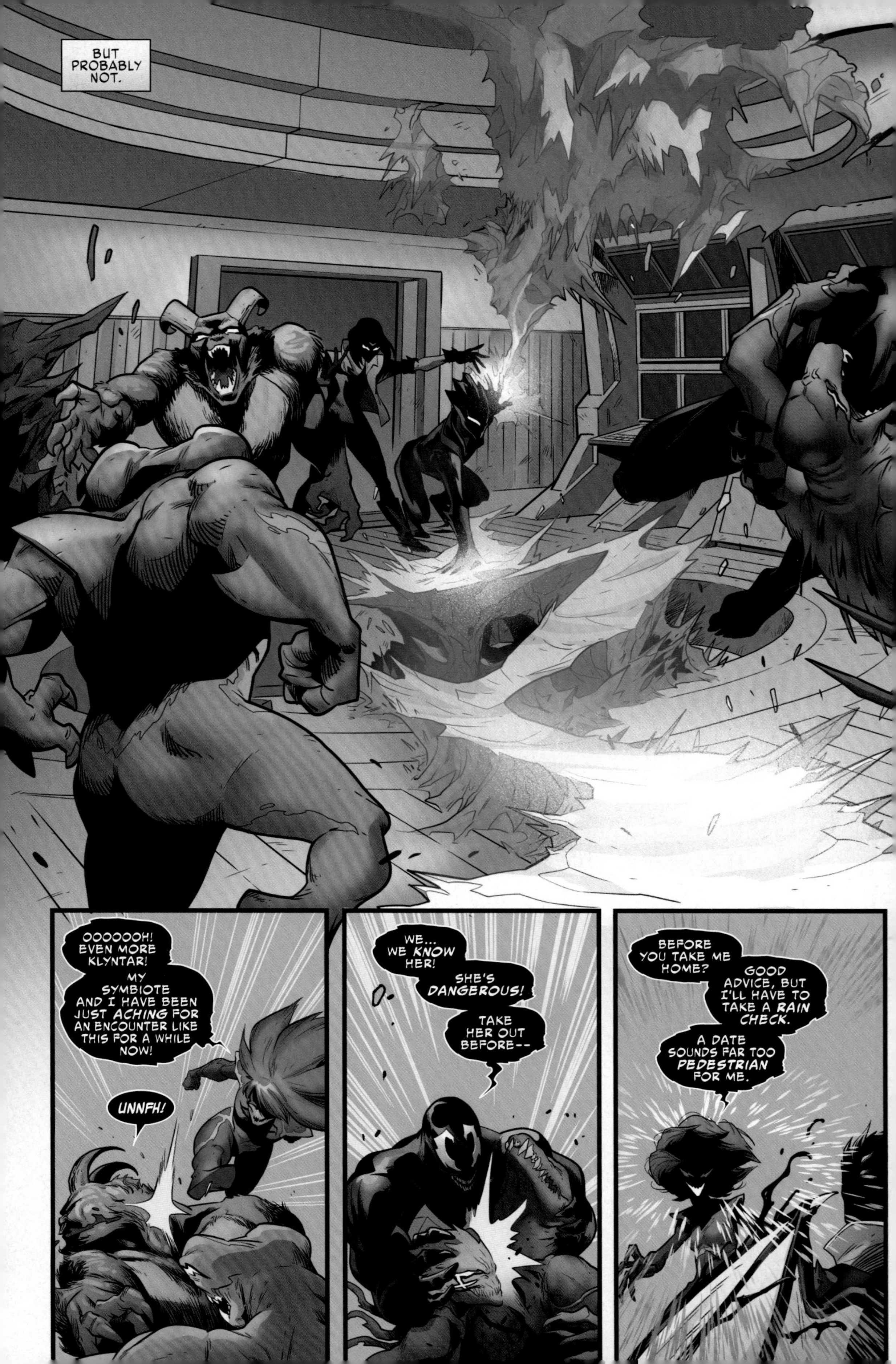
BUT PROBABLY NOT.
OOOOOOH! EVEN MORE KLYNTAR!
MY SYMBIOTE AND I HAVE BEEN JUST ACHING FOR AN ENCOUNTER LIKE THIS FOR A WHILE NOW!
UNNFH!
WE... WE KNOW HER!
SHE'S DANGEROUS!
TAKE HER OUT BEFORE--
BEFORE YOU TAKE ME HOME?
GOOD ADVICE, BUT I'LL HAVE TO TAKE A RAIN CHECK.
A DATE SOUNDS FAR TOO PEDESTRIAN FOR ME.

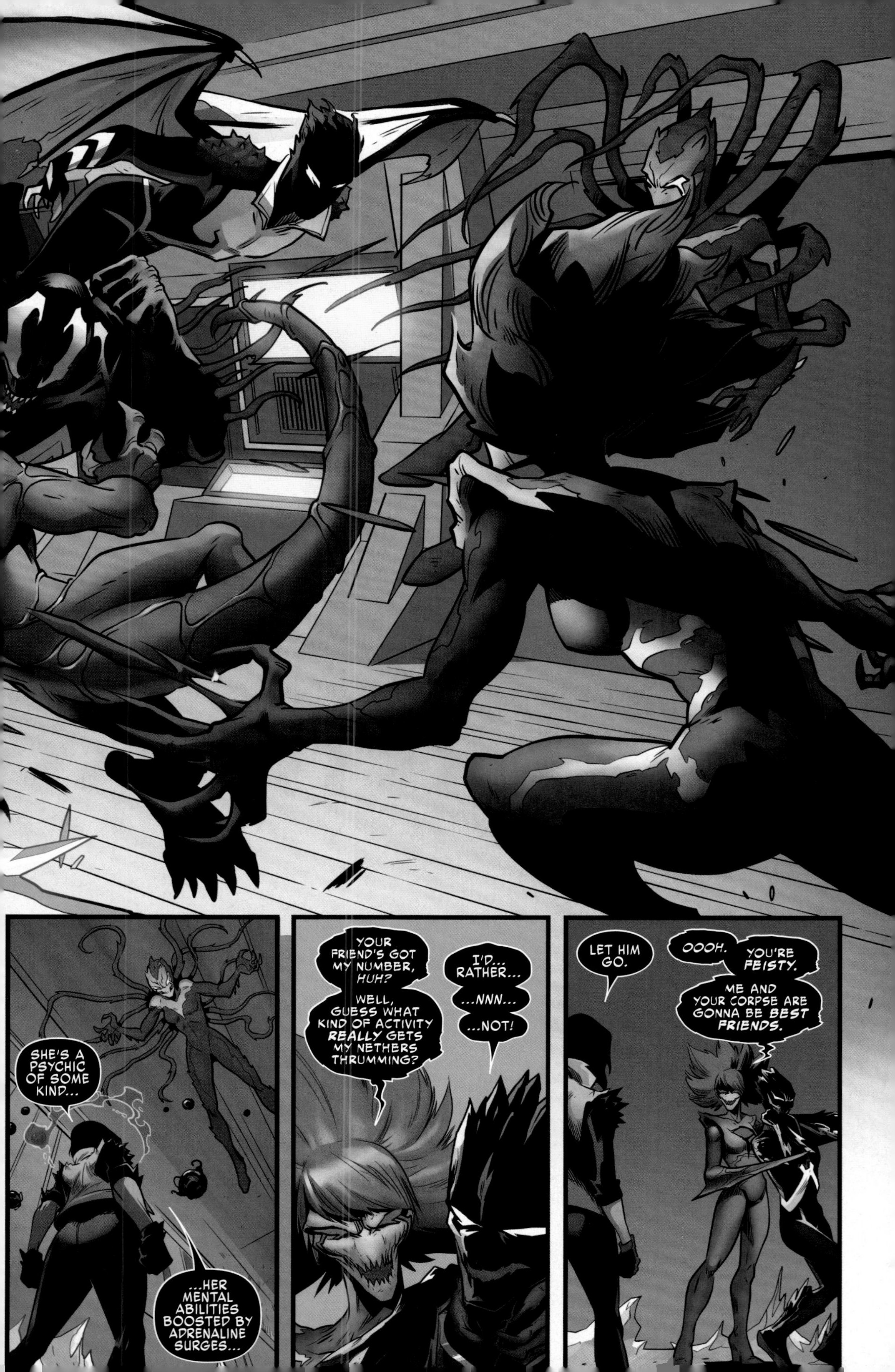
SHE'S A PSYCHIC OF SOME KIND...
...HER MENTAL ABILITIES BOOSTED BY ADRENALINE SURGES...
YOUR FRIEND'S GOT MY NUMBER, HUH?
WELL, GUESS WHAT KIND OF ACTIVITY REALLY GETS MY NETHERS THRUMMING?
I'D... RATHER...
...NNN...
...NOT!
LET HIM GO.
OOOH.
YOU'RE FEISTY.
ME AND YOUR CORPSE ARE GONNA BE BEST FRIENDS.

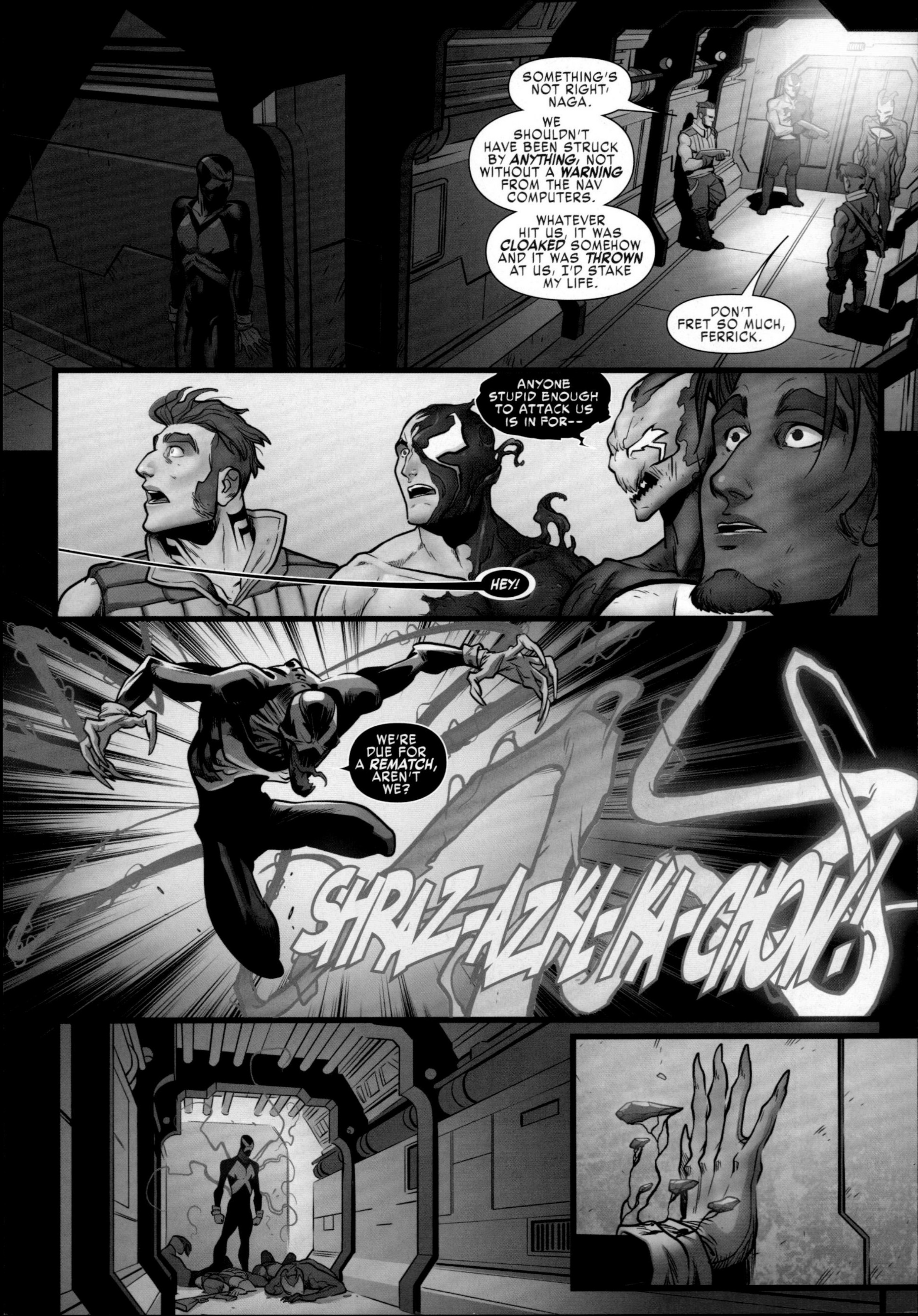
SOMETHING'S NOT RIGHT, NAGA.
WE SHOULDN'T HAVE BEEN STRUCK BY ANYTHING, NOT WITHOUT A WARNING FROM THE NAV COMPUTERS.
WHATEVER HIT US, IT WAS CLOAKED SOMEHOW AND IT WAS THROWN AT US, I'D STAKE MY LIFE.
DON'T FRET SO MUCH, FERRICK.
ANYONE STUPID ENOUGH TO ATTACK US IS IN FOR--
HEY!
WE'RE DUE FOR A REMATCH, AREN'T WE?
SHRAZ-AZAK-KA-CHOW!

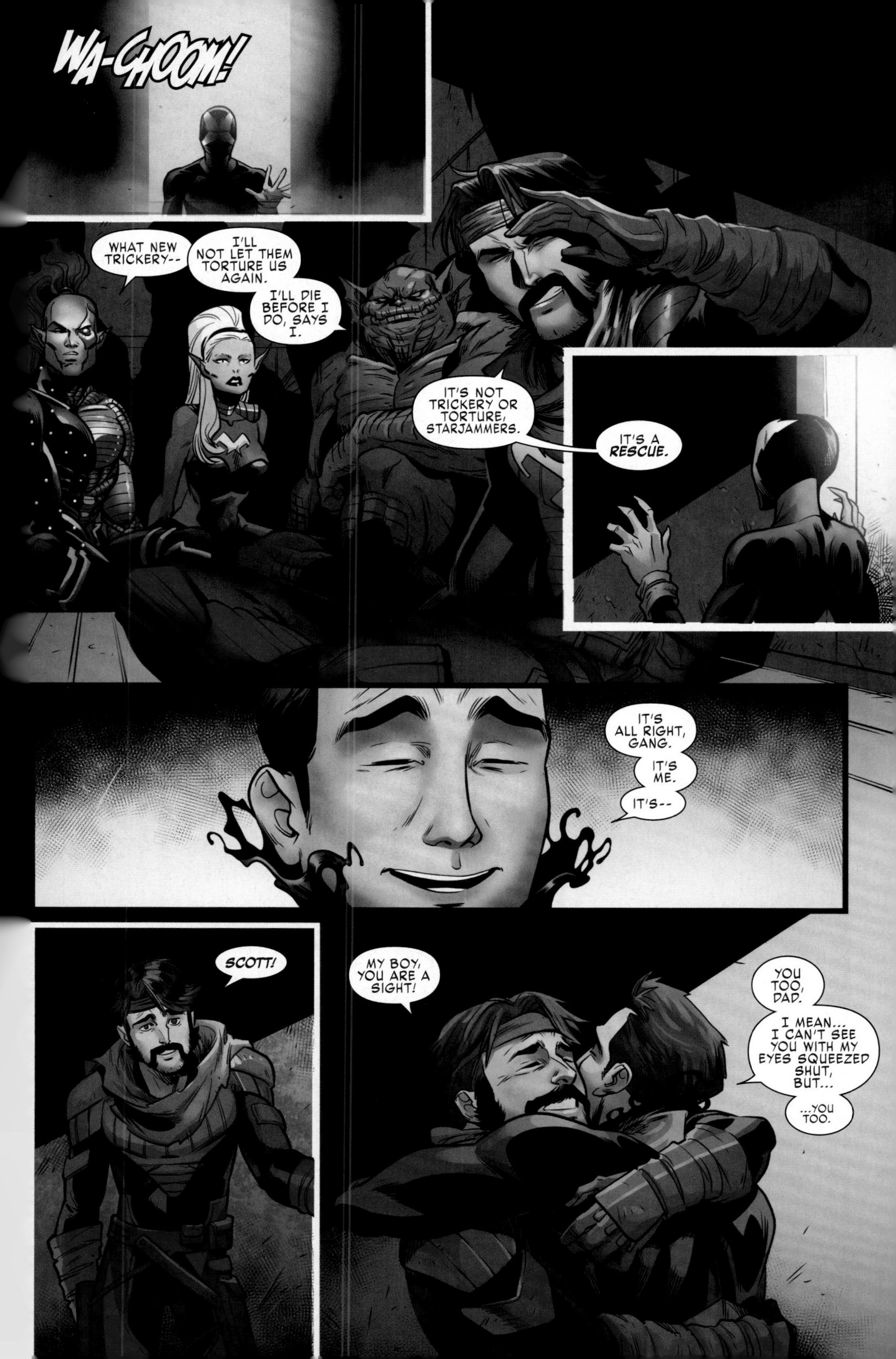
WA-CHOOM!
WHAT NEW TRICKERY--
I'LL NOT LET THEM TORTURE US AGAIN.
I'LL DIE BEFORE I DO, SAYS I.
IT'S NOT TRICKERY OR TORTURE, STARJAMMERS.
IT'S A RESCUE.
IT'S ALL RIGHT, GANG.
IT'S ME.
IT'S--
SCOTT!
MY BOY, YOU ARE A SIGHT!
YOU TOO, DAD.
I MEAN... I CAN'T SEE YOU WITH MY EYES SQUEEZED SHUT, BUT...
...YOU TOO.

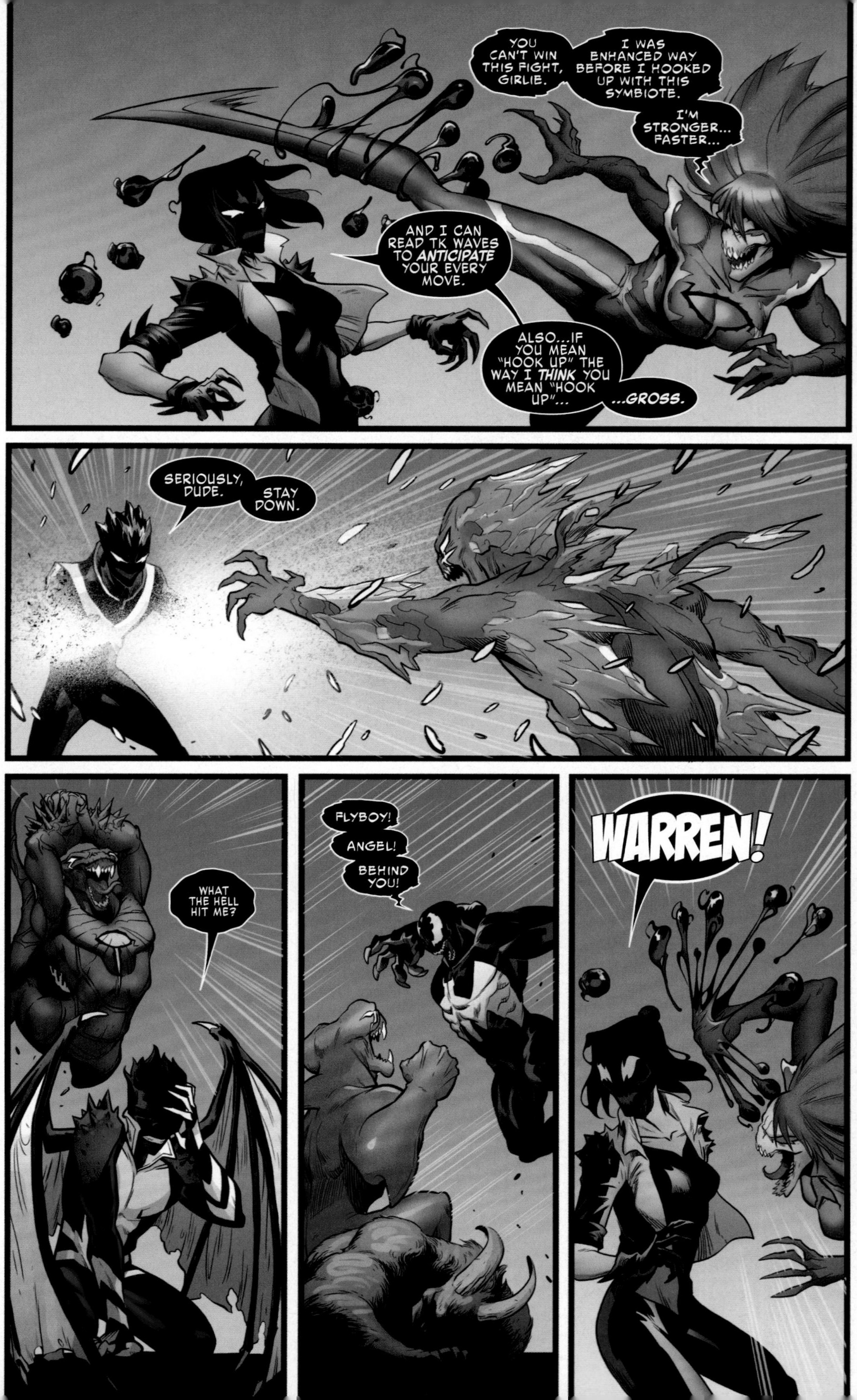
YOU CAN'T WIN THIS FIGHT, GIRLIE.
I WAS ENHANCED WAY BEFORE I HOOKED UP WITH THIS SYMBIOTE.
I'M STRONGER... FASTER...
AND I CAN READ TK WAVES TO ANTICIPATE YOUR EVERY MOVE.
ALSO...IF YOU MEAN "HOOK UP" THE WAY I THINK YOU MEAN "HOOK UP"...
...GROSS.
SERIOUSLY, DUDE.
STAY DOWN.
WHAT THE HELL HIT ME?
FLYBOY!
ANGEL!
BEHIND YOU!
WARREN!

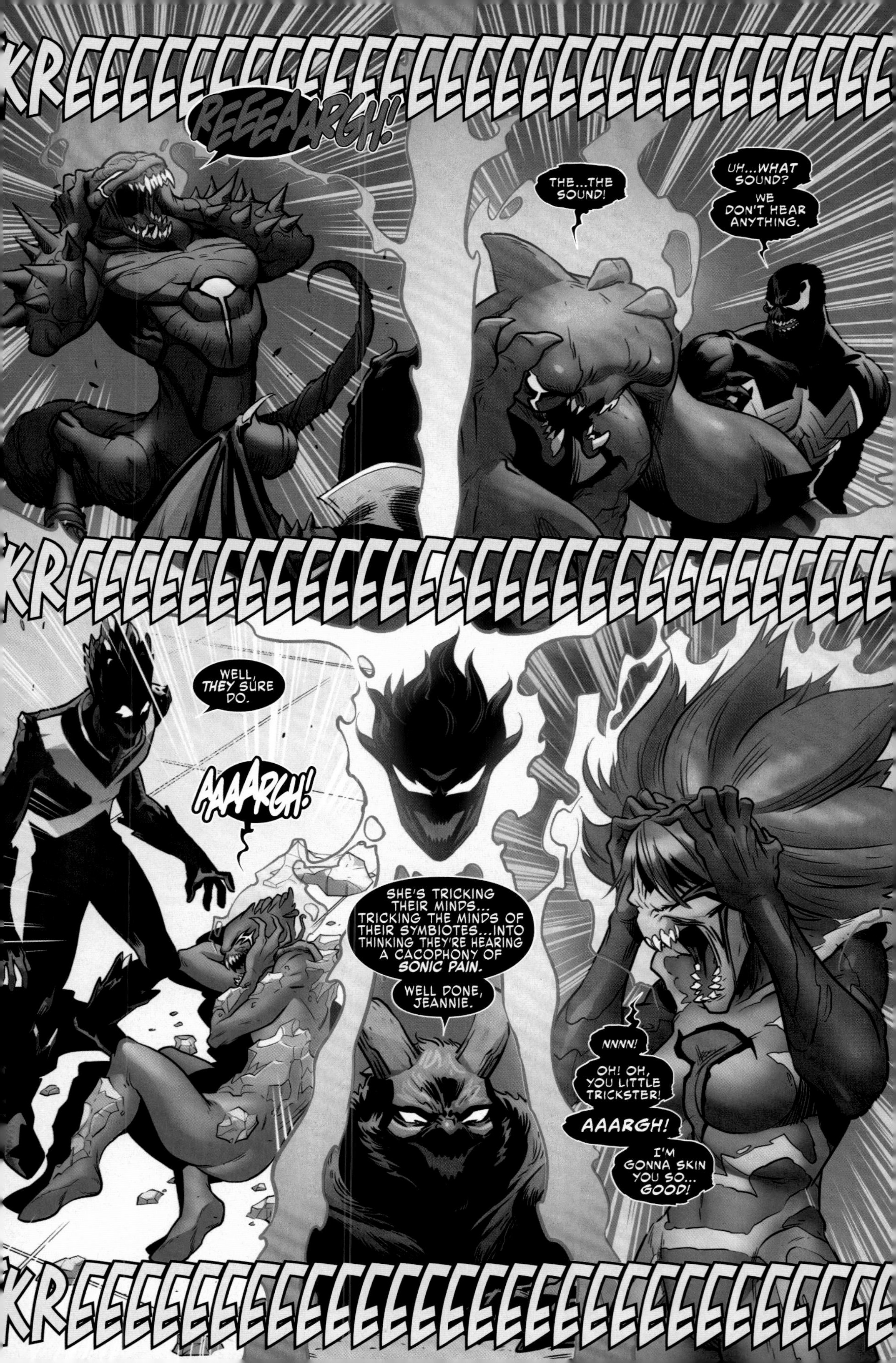
KREEEEEEEEEEEEEEEEEEEEEEEEEEE
REEEAARGH!
THE...THE SOUND!
UH...WHAT SOUND? WE DON'T HEAR ANYTHING.
KREEEEEEEEEEEEEEEEEEEEEEEEEEE
WELL, THEY SURE DO.
AAAARGH!
SHE'S TRICKING THEIR MINDS... TRICKING THE MINDS OF THEIR SYMBIOTES...INTO THINKING THEY'RE HEARING A CACOPHONY OF SONIC PAIN.
WELL DONE, JEANNIE.
NNNN!
OH! OH, YOU LITTLE TRICKSTER!
AAARGH!
I'M GONNA SKIN YOU SO... GOOD!
KREEEEEEEEEEEEEEEEEEEEEEEEEEE

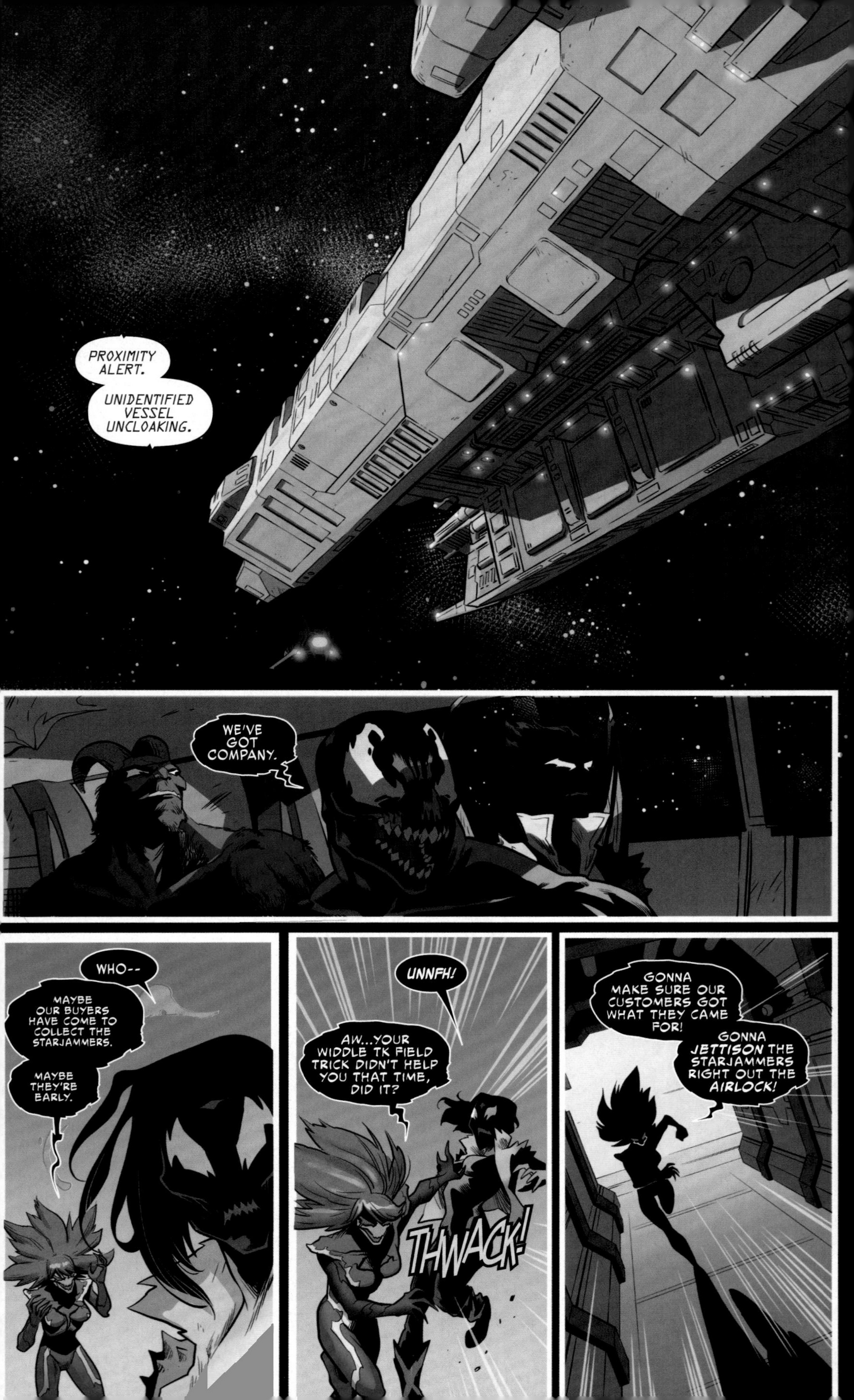
PROXIMITY ALERT.
UNIDENTIFIED VESSEL UNCLOAKING.
WE'VE GOT COMPANY.
WHO--
MAYBE OUR BUYERS HAVE COME TO COLLECT THE STARJAMMERS.
MAYBE THEY'RE EARLY.
UNNFH!
AW...YOUR WIDDLE TK FIELD TRICK DIDN'T HELP YOU THAT TIME, DID IT?
THWACK!
GONNA MAKE SURE OUR CUSTOMERS GOT WHAT THEY CAME FOR!
GONNA JETTISON THE STARJAMMERS RIGHT OUT THE AIRLOCK!

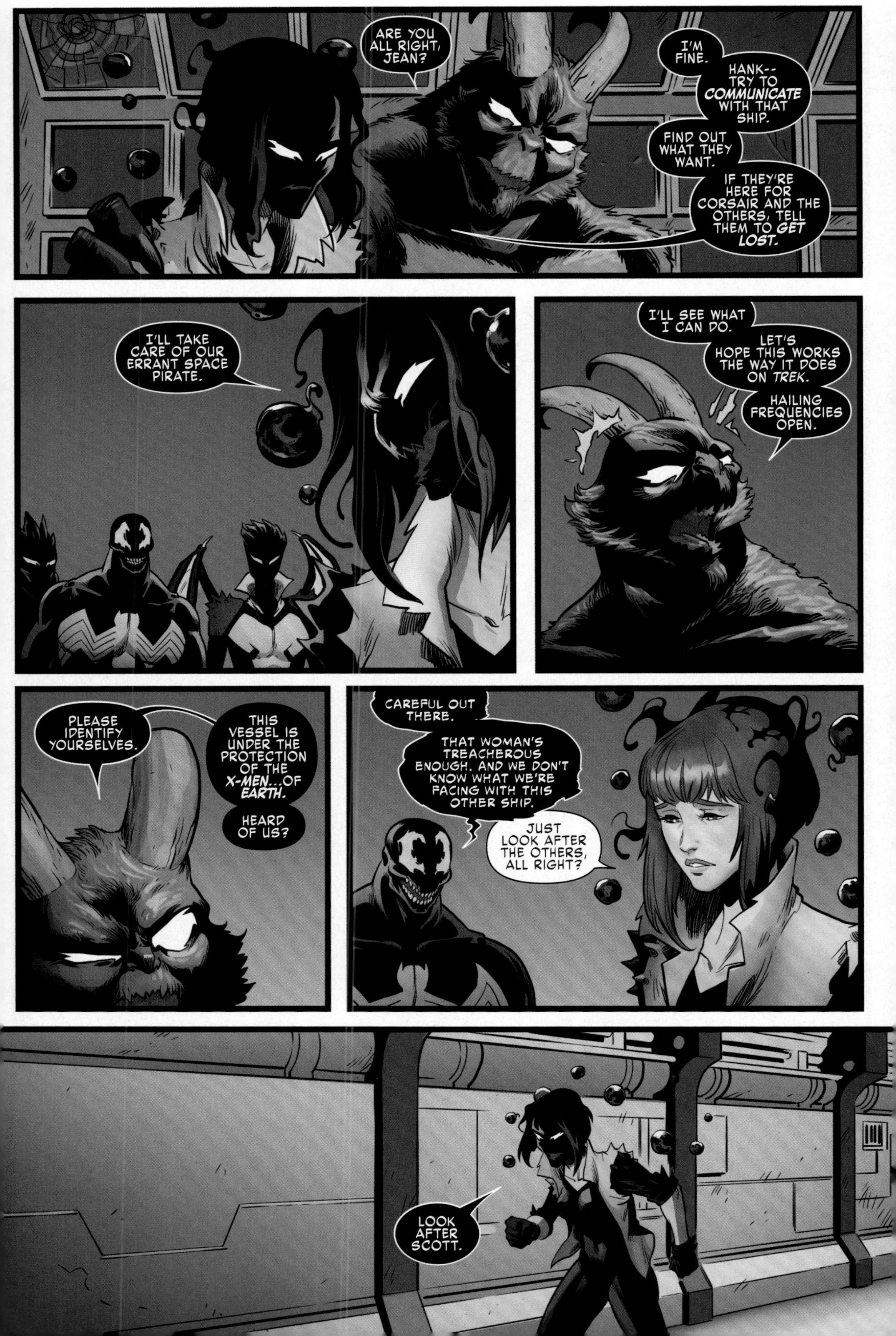
ARE YOU ALL RIGHT, JEAN?
I'M FINE.
HANK-- TRY TO COMMUNICATE WITH THAT SHIP.
FIND OUT WHAT THEY WANT.
IF THEY'RE HERE FOR CORSAIR AND THE OTHERS, TELL THEM TO GET LOST.
I'LL TAKE CARE OF OUR ERRANT SPACE PIRATE.
I'LL SEE WHAT I CAN DO.
LET'S HOPE THIS WORKS THE WAY IT DOES ON TREK.
HAILING FREQUENCIES OPEN.
PLEASE IDENTIFY YOURSELVES.
THIS VESSEL IS UNDER THE PROTECTION OF THE X-MEN...OF EARTH.
HEARD OF US?
CAREFUL OUT THERE.
THAT WOMAN'S TREACHEROUS ENOUGH. AND WE DON'T KNOW WHAT WE'RE FACING WITH THIS OTHER SHIP.
JUST LOOK AFTER THE OTHERS, ALL RIGHT?
LOOK AFTER SCOTT.

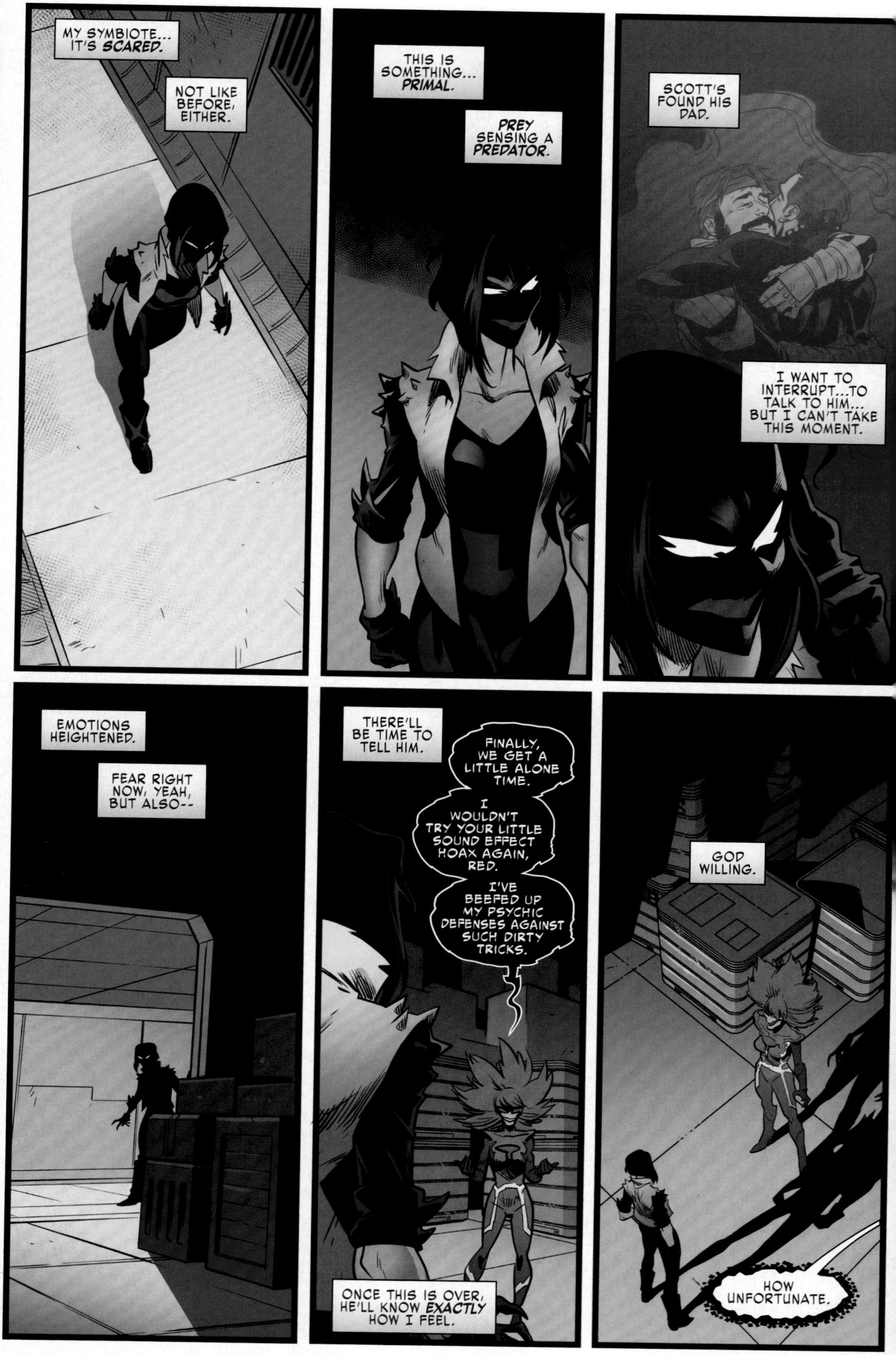
MY SYMBIOTE... IT'S SCARED.
NOT LIKE BEFORE, EITHER.
THIS IS SOMETHING... PRIMAL.
PREY SENSING A PREDATOR.
SCOTT'S FOUND HIS DAD.
I WANT TO INTERRUPT...TO TALK TO HIM... BUT I CAN'T TAKE THIS MOMENT.
EMOTIONS HEIGHTENED.
FEAR RIGHT NOW, YEAH, BUT ALSO--
THERE'LL BE TIME TO TELL HIM.
FINALLY, WE GET A LITTLE ALONE TIME.
I WOULDN'T TRY YOUR LITTLE SOUND EFFECT HOAX AGAIN, RED.
I'VE BEEFED UP MY PSYCHIC DEFENSES AGAINST SUCH DIRTY TRICKS.
ONCE THIS IS OVER, HE'LL KNOW EXACTLY HOW I FEEL.
GOD WILLING.
HOW UNFORTUNATE.

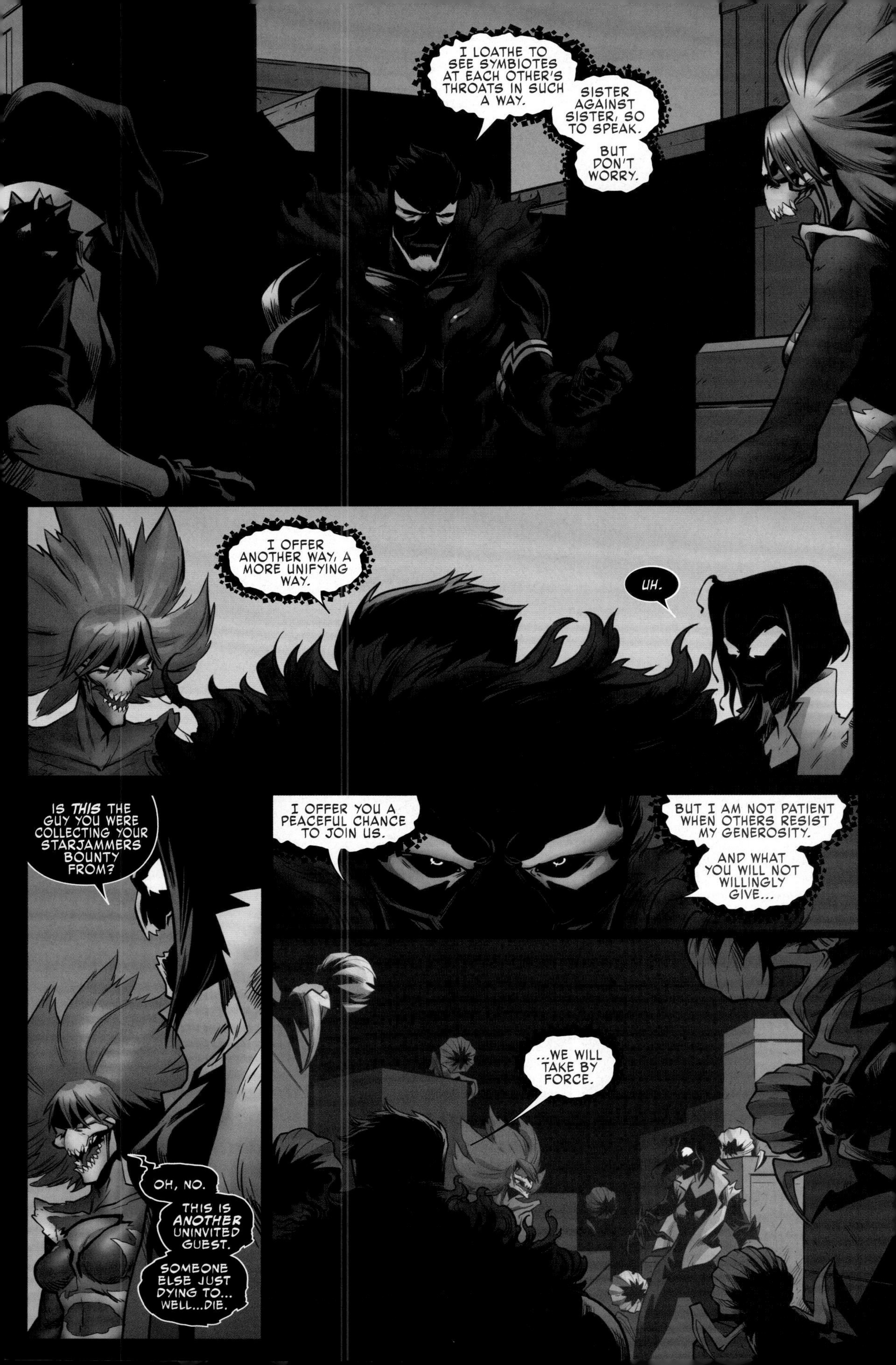
I LOATHE TO SEE SYMBIOTES AT EACH OTHER'S THROATS IN SUCH A WAY.
SISTER AGAINST SISTER, SO TO SPEAK.
BUT DON'T WORRY.
I OFFER ANOTHER WAY, A MORE UNIFYING WAY.
UH.
IS THIS THE GUY YOU WERE COLLECTING YOUR STARJAMMERS BOUNTY FROM?
I OFFER YOU A PEACEFUL CHANCE TO JOIN US.
BUT I AM NOT PATIENT WHEN OTHERS RESIST MY GENEROSITY.
AND WHAT YOU WILL NOT WILLINGLY GIVE...
...WE WILL TAKE BY FORCE.
OH, NO.
THIS IS ANOTHER UNINVITED GUEST.
SOMEONE ELSE JUST DYING TO... WELL...DIE.

YEEEEEEAAAARRGH!

SCOTT! SON!

WHAT IS IT?

WHAT'S WRONG?

IT...

IT WAS JEAN.

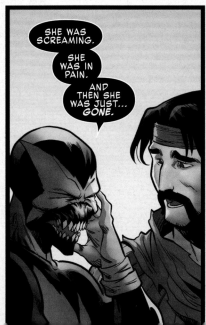

SHE WAS SCREAMING.

SHE WAS IN PAIN.

AND THEN SHE WAS JUST... GONE.

DAD-- I DON'T HEAR HER ANYMORE.

I DON'T FEEL HER PRESENCE.

SOMETHING... SOMETHING'S HAPPENED TO JEAN!

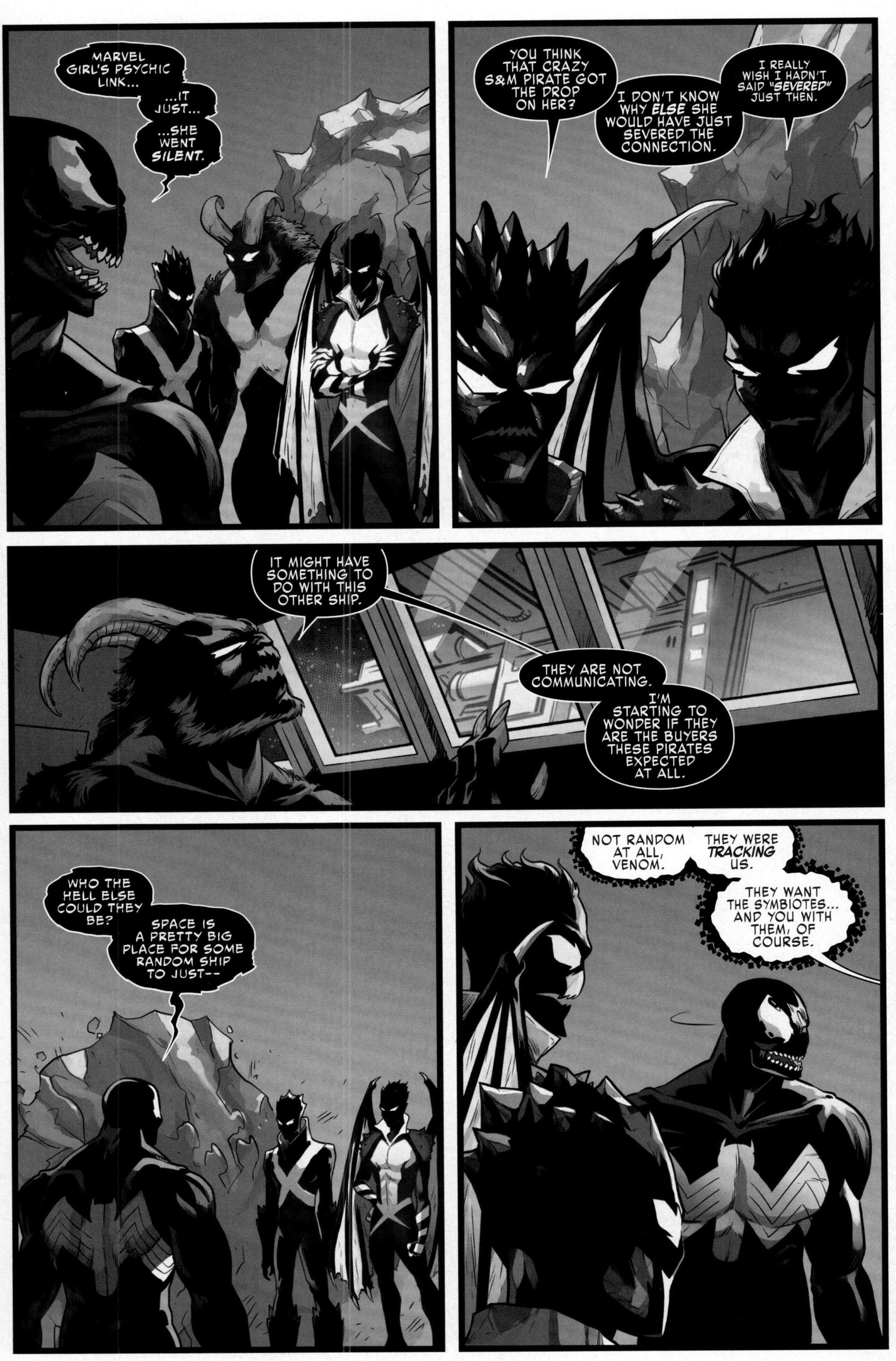
MARVEL GIRL'S PSYCHIC LINK...
...IT JUST...
...SHE WENT SILENT.
YOU THINK THAT CRAZY S&M PIRATE GOT THE DROP ON HER?
I DON'T KNOW WHY ELSE SHE WOULD HAVE JUST SEVERED THE CONNECTION.
I REALLY WISH I HADN'T SAID "SEVERED" JUST THEN.
IT MIGHT HAVE SOMETHING TO DO WITH THIS OTHER SHIP.
THEY ARE NOT COMMUNICATING.
I'M STARTING TO WONDER IF THEY ARE THE BUYERS THESE PIRATES EXPECTED AT ALL.
WHO THE HELL ELSE COULD THEY BE?
SPACE IS A PRETTY BIG PLACE FOR SOME RANDOM SHIP TO JUST--
NOT RANDOM AT ALL, VENOM.
THEY WERE TRACKING US.
THEY WANT THE SYMBIOTES... AND YOU WITH THEM, OF COURSE.

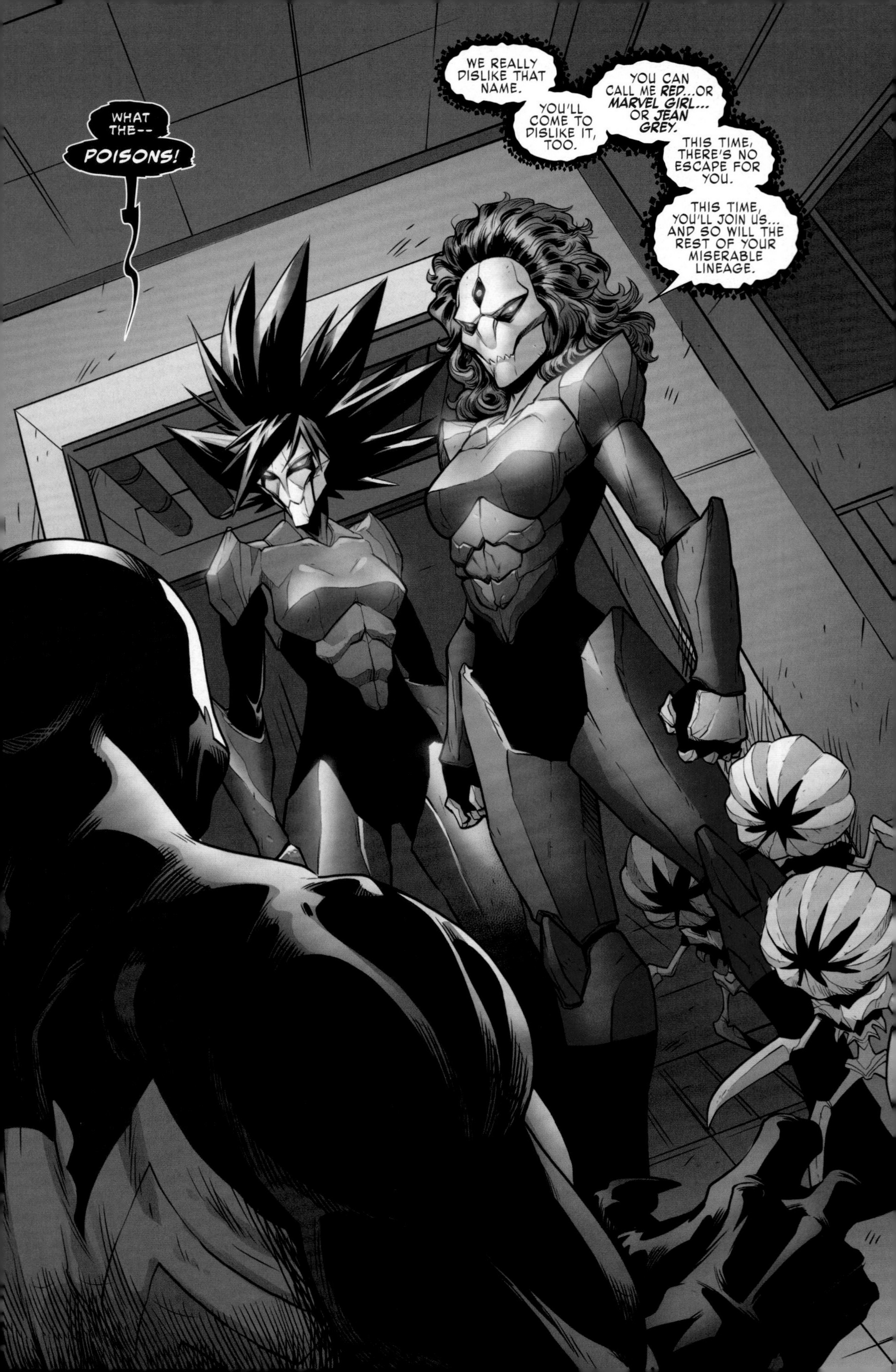
WHAT THE--
POISONS!
WE REALLY DISLIKE THAT NAME.
YOU'LL COME TO DISLIKE IT, TOO.
YOU CAN CALL ME RED...OR MARVEL GIRL... OR JEAN GREY.
THIS TIME, THERE'S NO ESCAPE FOR YOU.
THIS TIME, YOU'LL JOIN US... AND SO WILL THE REST OF YOUR MISERABLE LINEAGE.

VENOM 163

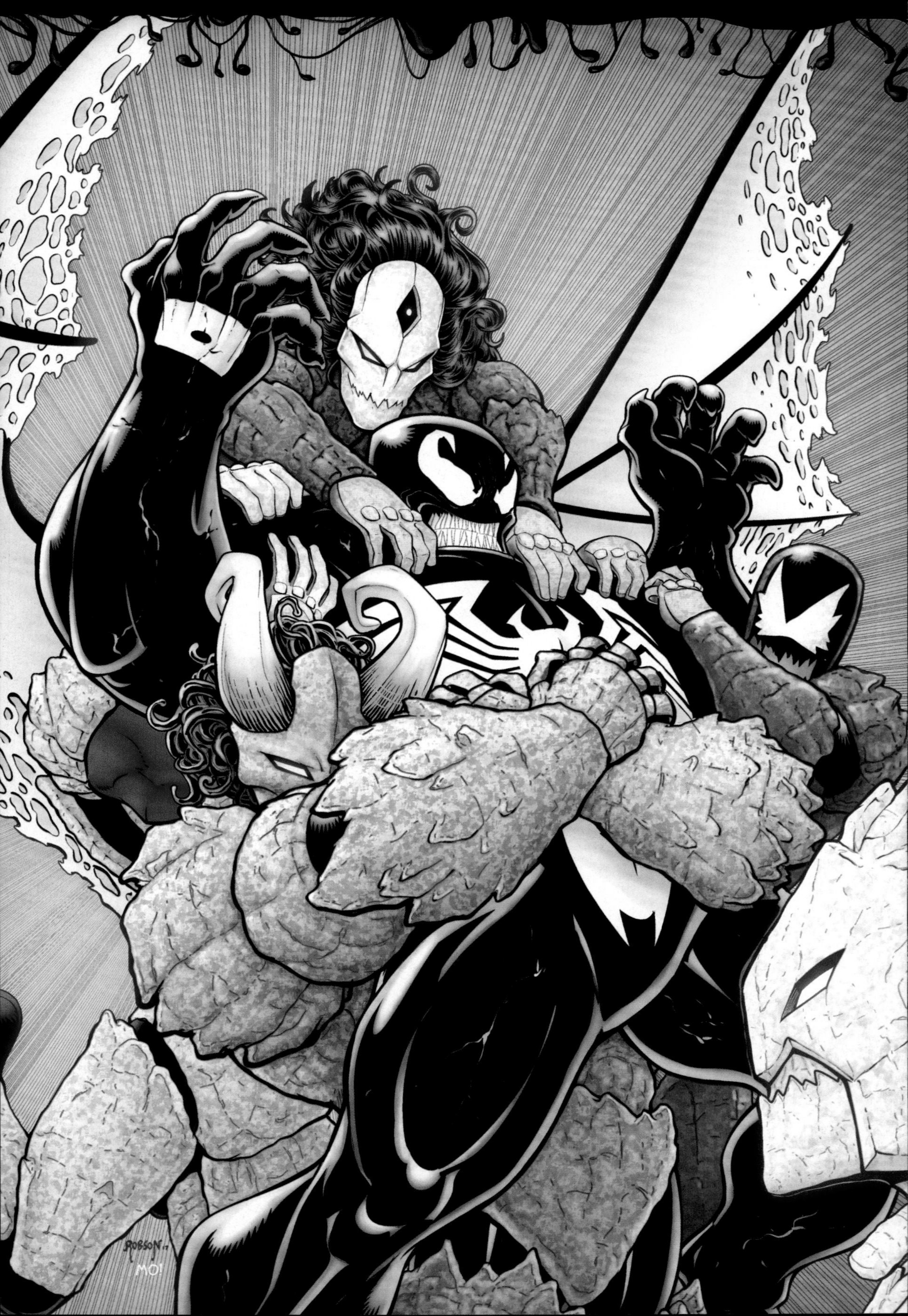

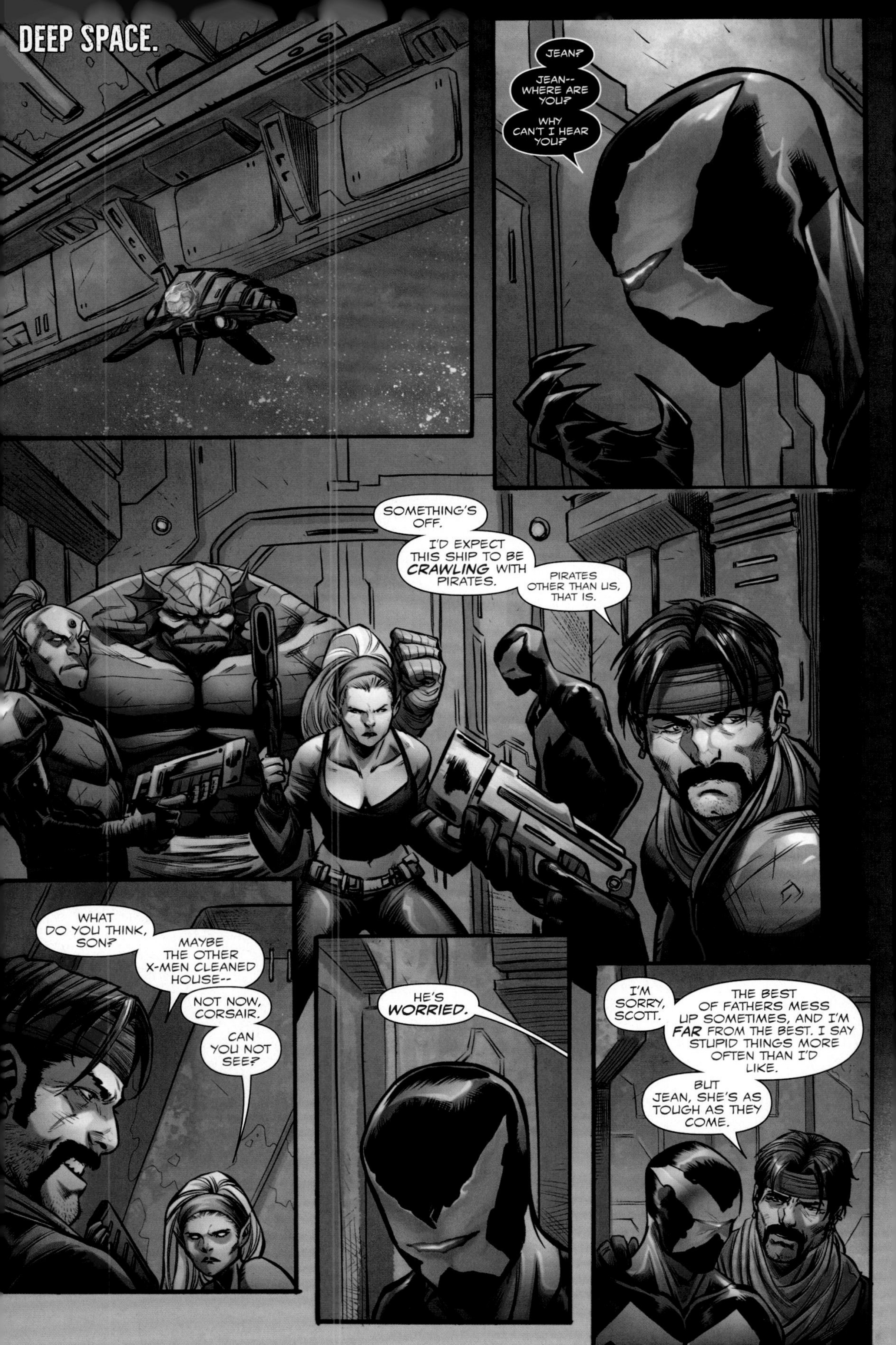

DEEP SPACE.
JEAN?
JEAN-- WHERE ARE YOU?
WHY CAN'T I HEAR YOU?
SOMETHING'S OFF.
I'D EXPECT THIS SHIP TO BE CRAWLING WITH PIRATES.
PIRATES OTHER THAN US, THAT IS.
WHAT DO YOU THINK, SON?
MAYBE THE OTHER X-MEN CLEANED HOUSE--
NOT NOW, CORSAIR.
CAN YOU NOT SEE?
HE'S WORRIED.
I'M SORRY, SCOTT.
THE BEST OF FATHERS MESS UP SOMETIMES, AND I'M FAR FROM THE BEST. I SAY STUPID THINGS MORE OFTEN THAN I'D LIKE.
BUT JEAN, SHE'S AS TOUGH AS THEY COME.

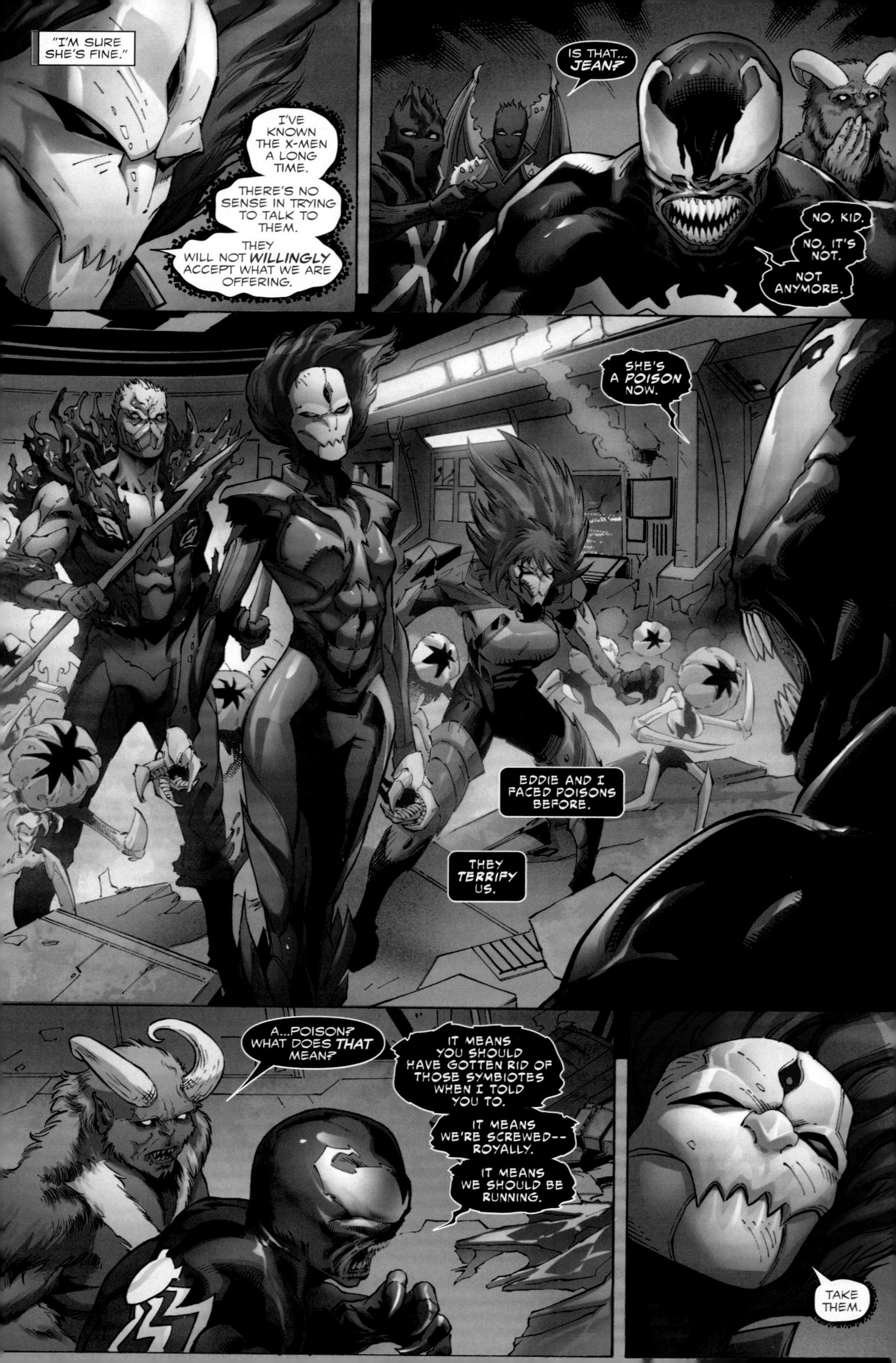
"I'M SURE SHE'S FINE."
I'VE KNOWN THE X-MEN A LONG TIME.
THERE'S NO SENSE IN TRYING TO TALK TO THEM.
THEY WILL NOT WILLINGLY ACCEPT WHAT WE ARE OFFERING.
IS THAT... JEAN?
NO, KID.
NO, IT'S NOT.
NOT ANYMORE.
SHE'S A POISON NOW.
EDDIE AND I FACED POISONS BEFORE.
THEY TERRIFY US.
A...POISON? WHAT DOES THAT MEAN?
IT MEANS YOU SHOULD HAVE GOTTEN RID OF THOSE SYMBIOTES WHEN I TOLD YOU TO.
IT MEANS WE'RE SCREWED--ROYALLY.
IT MEANS WE SHOULD BE RUNNING.
TAKE THEM.

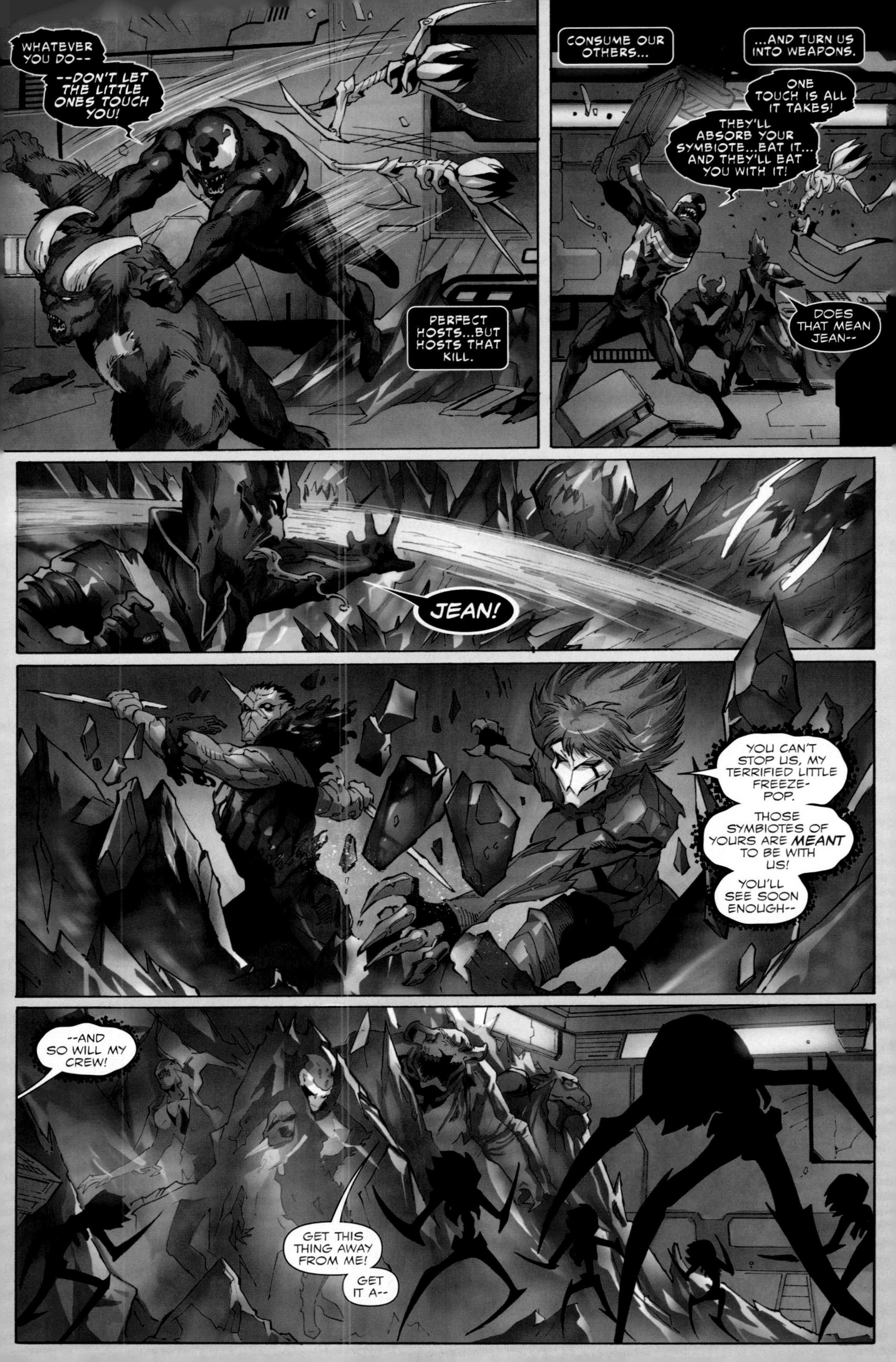
WHATEVER YOU DO--
--DON'T LET THE LITTLE ONES TOUCH YOU!
PERFECT HOSTS...BUT HOSTS THAT KILL.
CONSUME OUR OTHERS...
...AND TURN US INTO WEAPONS.
ONE TOUCH IS ALL IT TAKES!
THEY'LL ABSORB YOUR SYMBIOTE...EAT IT... AND THEY'LL EAT YOU WITH IT!
DOES THAT MEAN JEAN--
JEAN!
YOU CAN'T STOP US, MY TERRIFIED LITTLE FREEZE-POP.
THOSE SYMBIOTES OF YOURS ARE MEANT TO BE WITH US!
YOU'LL SEE SOON ENOUGH--
--AND SO WILL MY CREW!
GET THIS THING AWAY FROM ME!
GET IT A--

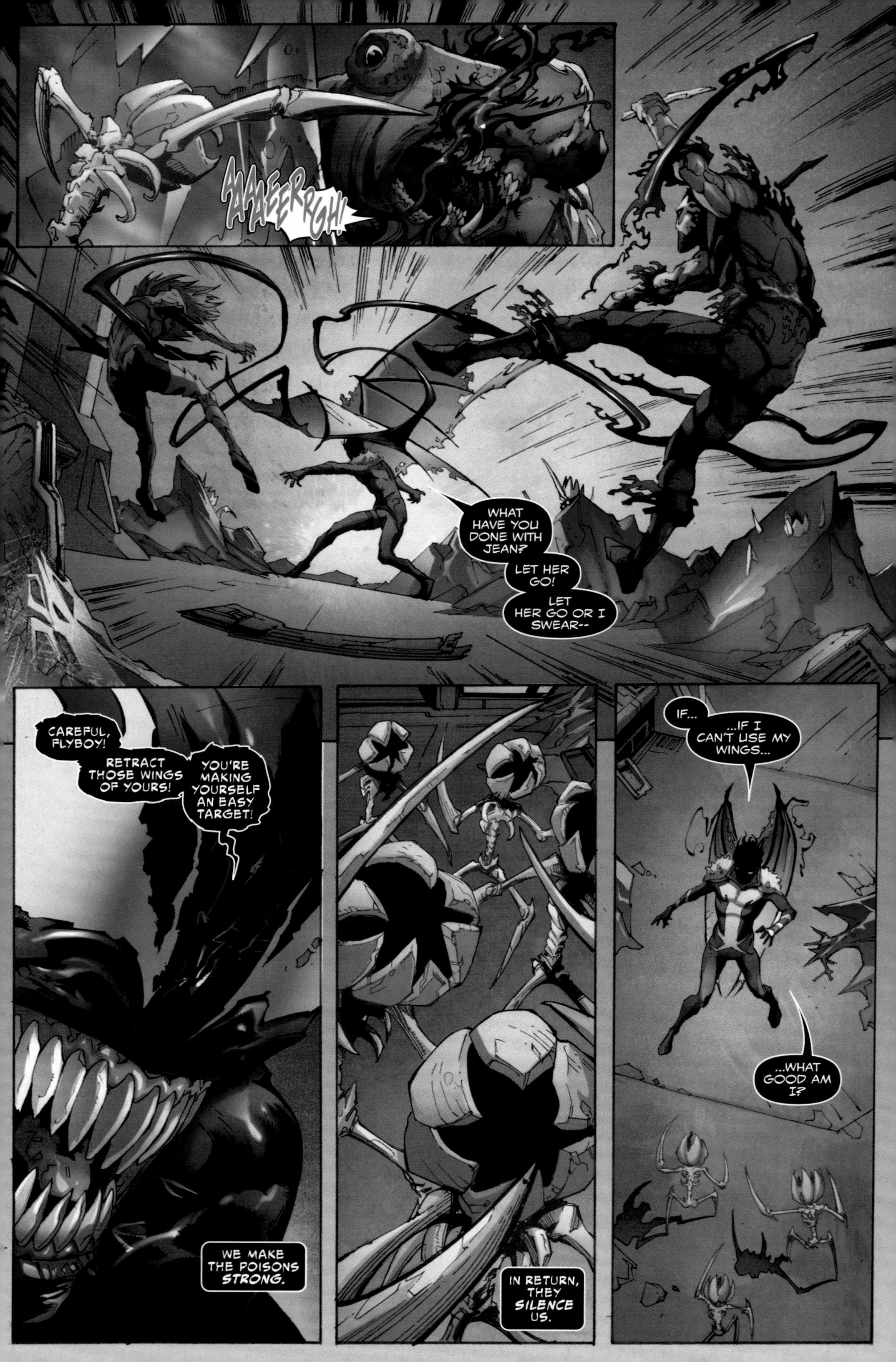
AAAAEERRGH!
WHAT HAVE YOU DONE WITH JEAN?
LET HER GO!
LET HER GO OR I SWEAR--
CAREFUL, FLYBOY!
RETRACT THOSE WINGS OF YOURS!
YOU'RE MAKING YOURSELF AN EASY TARGET!
WE MAKE THE POISONS STRONG.
IN RETURN, THEY SILENCE US.
IF...
...IF I CAN'T USE MY WINGS...
...WHAT GOOD AM I?

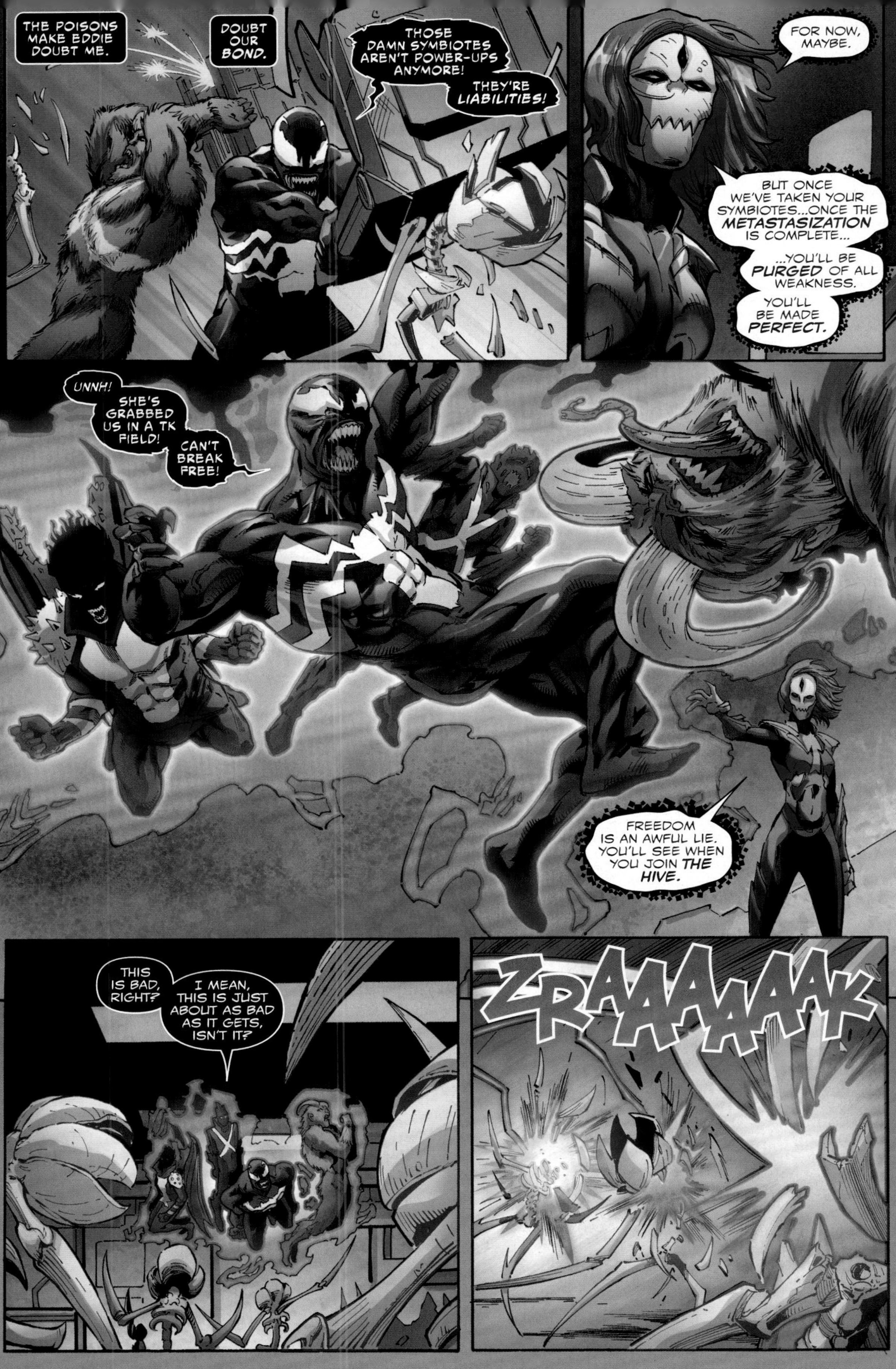

THE POISONS MAKE EDDIE DOUBT ME.
DOUBT OUR BOND.
THOSE DAMN SYMBIOTES AREN'T POWER-UPS ANYMORE!
THEY'RE LIABILITIES!
FOR NOW, MAYBE.
BUT ONCE WE'VE TAKEN YOUR SYMBIOTES...ONCE THE METASTASIZATION IS COMPLETE...
...YOU'LL BE PURGED OF ALL WEAKNESS.
YOU'LL BE MADE PERFECT.
UNNH!
SHE'S GRABBED US IN A TK FIELD!
CAN'T BREAK FREE!
FREEDOM IS AN AWFUL LIE. YOU'LL SEE WHEN YOU JOIN THE HIVE.
THIS IS BAD, RIGHT?
I MEAN, THIS IS JUST ABOUT AS BAD AS IT GETS, ISN'T IT?
ZRAAAAAAK

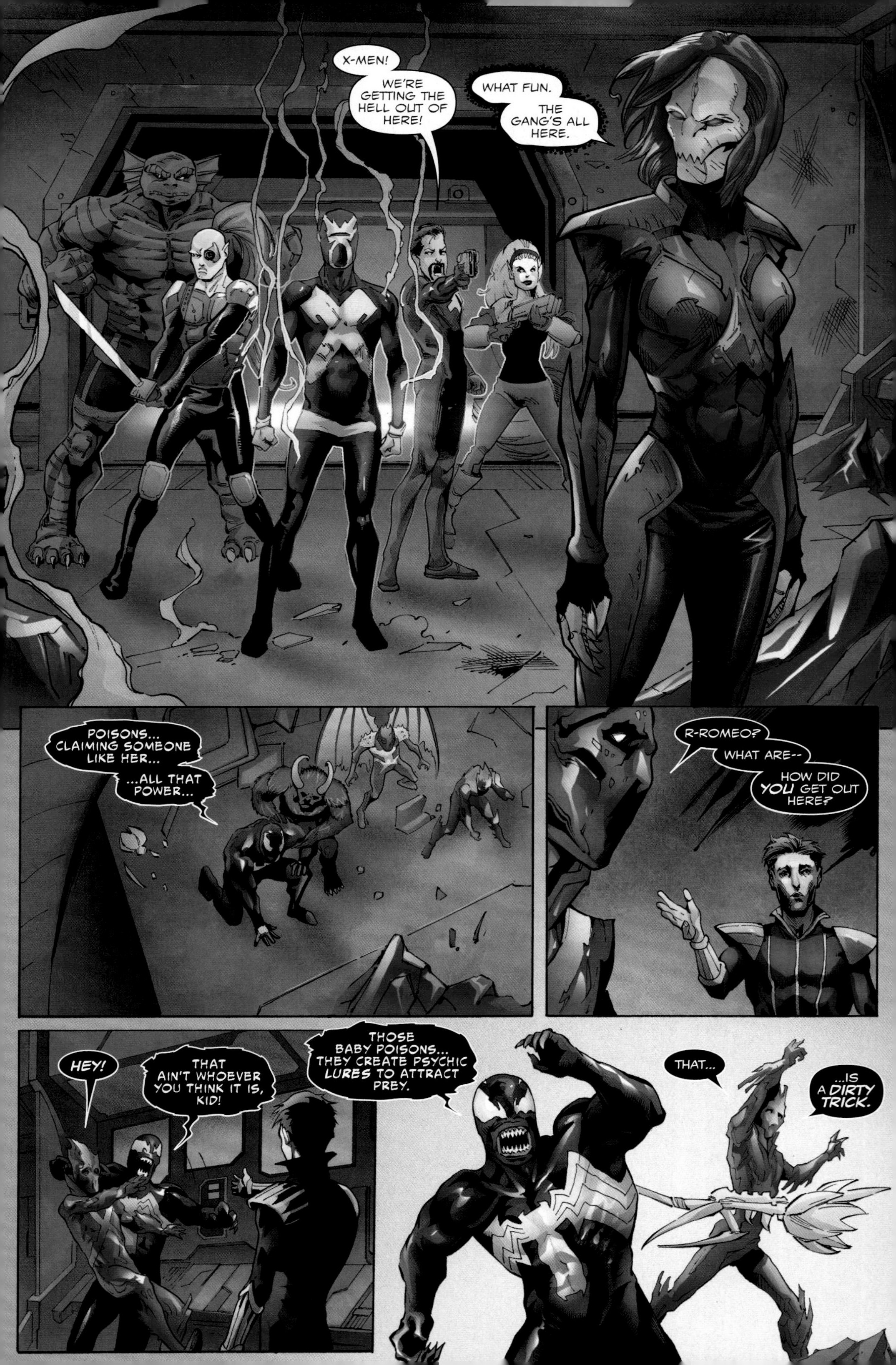
X-MEN!
WE'RE GETTING THE HELL OUT OF HERE!
WHAT FUN.
THE GANG'S ALL HERE.
POISONS... CLAIMING SOMEONE LIKE HER...
...ALL THAT POWER...
R-ROMEO?
WHAT ARE--
HOW DID YOU GET OUT HERE?
HEY!
THAT AIN'T WHOEVER YOU THINK IT IS, KID!
THOSE BABY POISONS... THEY CREATE PSYCHIC LURES TO ATTRACT PREY.
THAT...
...IS A DIRTY TRICK.

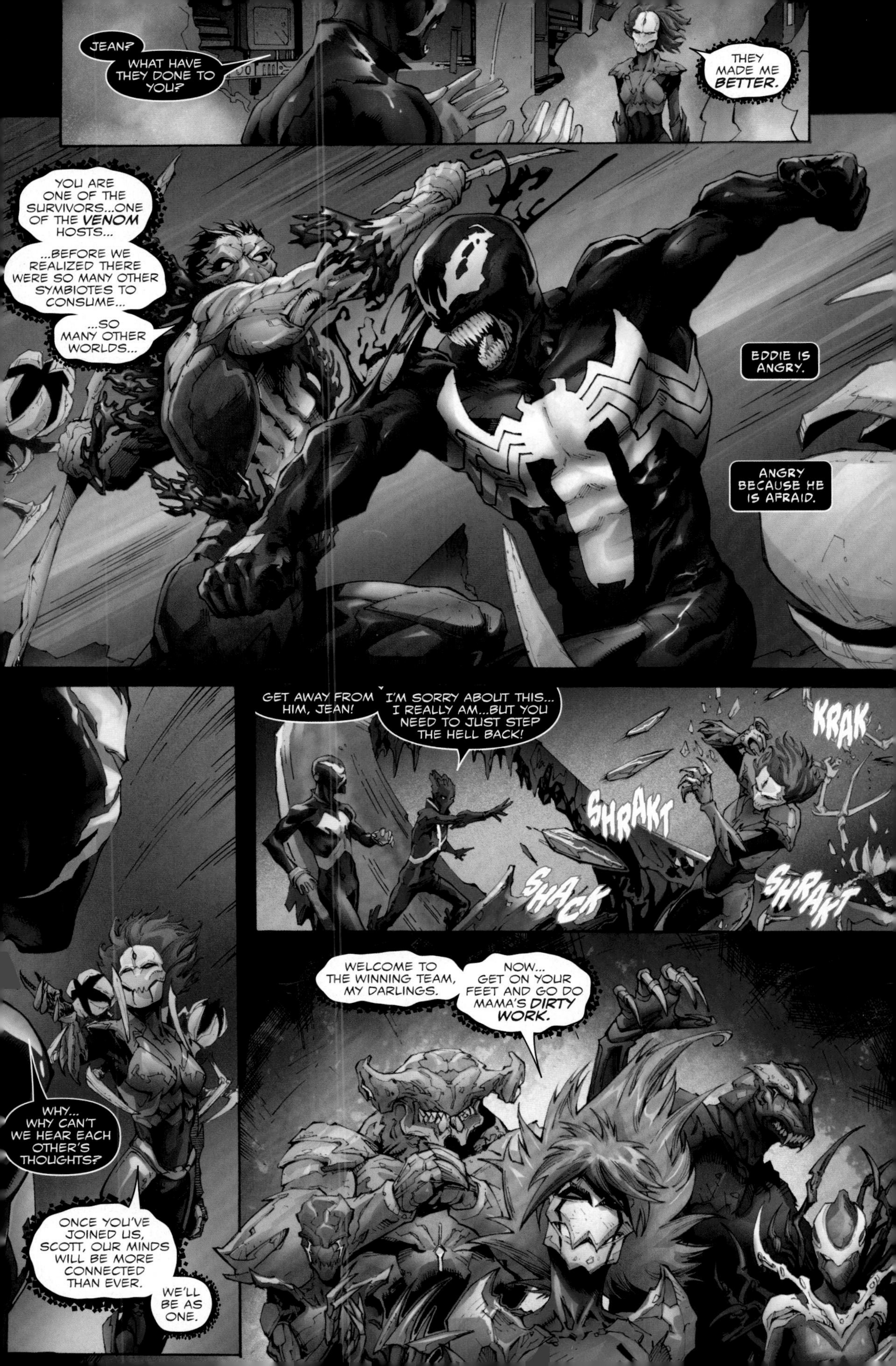
JEAN?
WHAT HAVE THEY DONE TO YOU?
THEY MADE ME BETTER.
YOU ARE ONE OF THE SURVIVORS...ONE OF THE VENOM HOSTS...
...BEFORE WE REALIZED THERE WERE SO MANY OTHER SYMBIOTES TO CONSUME...
...SO MANY OTHER WORLDS...
EDDIE IS ANGRY.
ANGRY BECAUSE HE IS AFRAID.
GET AWAY FROM HIM, JEAN!
I'M SORRY ABOUT THIS... I REALLY AM...BUT YOU NEED TO JUST STEP THE HELL BACK!
KRAK
SHRAKT
SHACK
SHRAKT
WHY... WHY CAN'T WE HEAR EACH OTHER'S THOUGHTS?
ONCE YOU'VE JOINED US, SCOTT, OUR MINDS WILL BE MORE CONNECTED THAN EVER.
WE'LL BE AS ONE.
WELCOME TO THE WINNING TEAM, MY DARLINGS.
NOW... GET ON YOUR FEET AND GO DO MAMA'S DIRTY WORK.

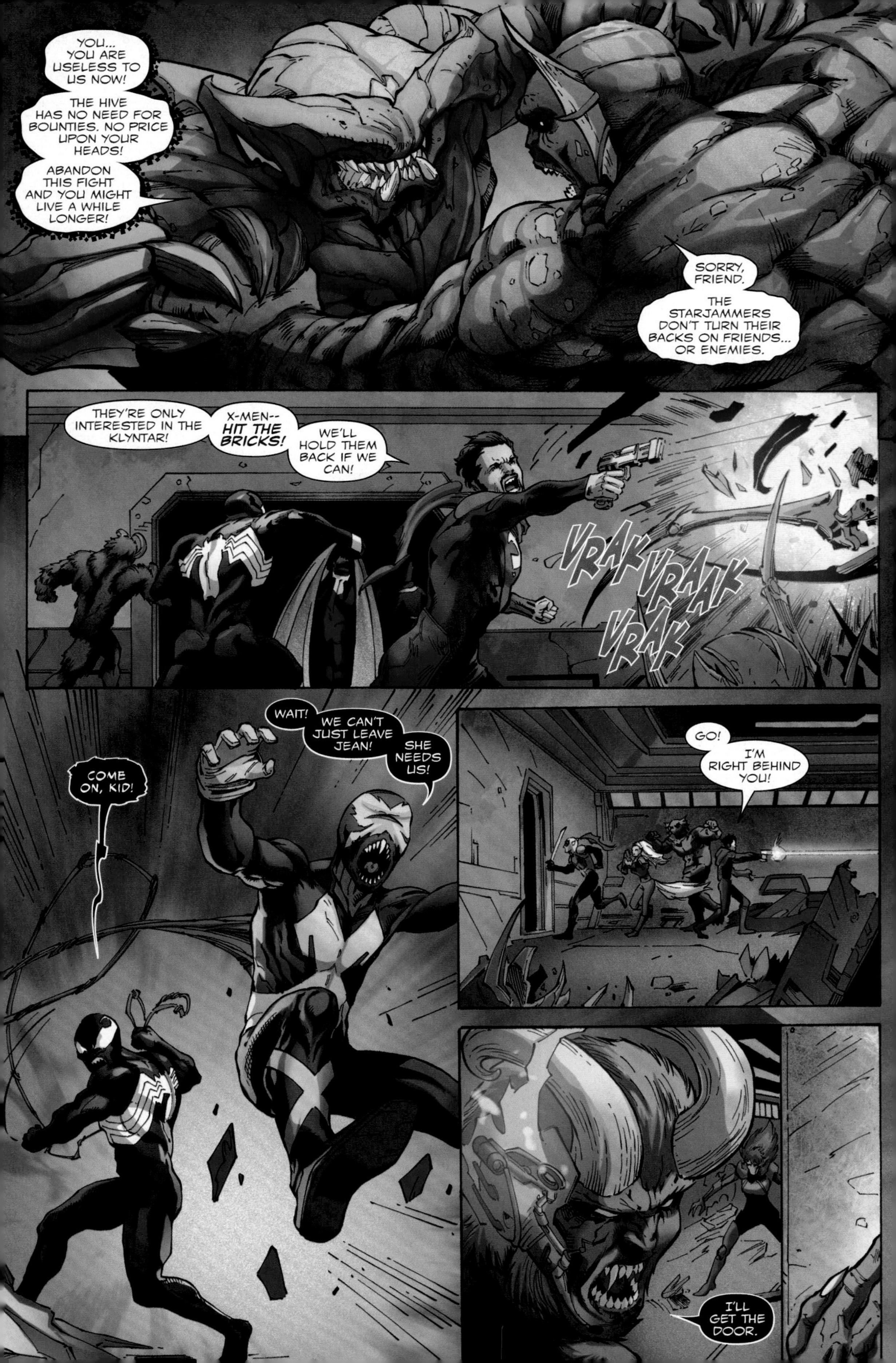
YOU... YOU ARE USELESS TO US NOW!
THE HIVE HAS NO NEED FOR BOUNTIES. NO PRICE UPON YOUR HEADS!
ABANDON THIS FIGHT AND YOU MIGHT LIVE A WHILE LONGER!
SORRY, FRIEND.
THE STARJAMMERS DON'T TURN THEIR BACKS ON FRIENDS... OR ENEMIES.
THEY'RE ONLY INTERESTED IN THE KLYNTAR!
X-MEN-- HIT THE BRICKS!
WE'LL HOLD THEM BACK IF WE CAN!
VRAK VRAAK VRAK
COME ON, KID!
WAIT!
WE CAN'T JUST LEAVE JEAN!
SHE NEEDS US!
GO!
I'M RIGHT BEHIND YOU!
I'LL GET THE DOOR.

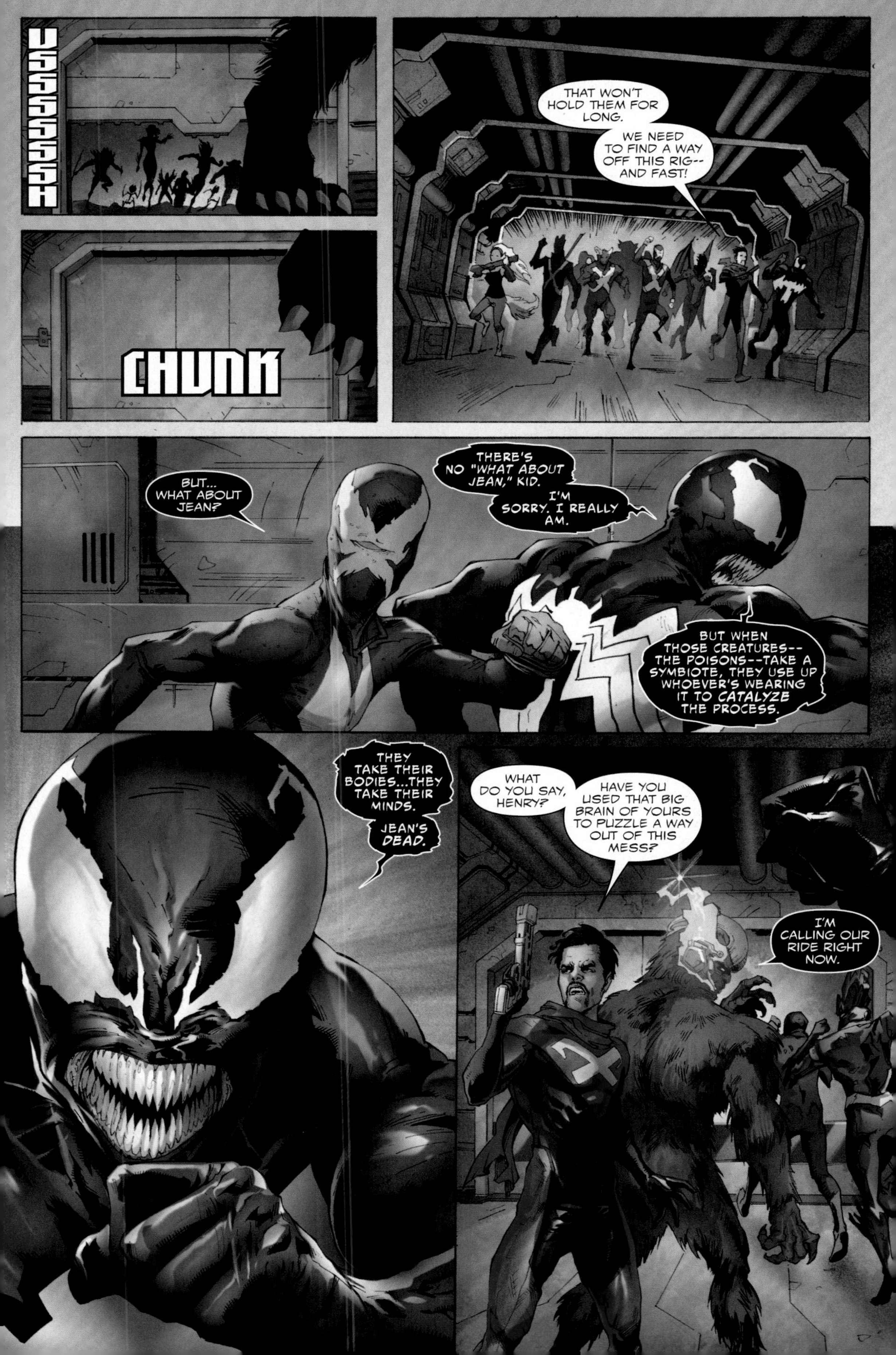
VSSSSSSH
CHUNK
THAT WON'T HOLD THEM FOR LONG.
WE NEED TO FIND A WAY OFF THIS RIG-- AND FAST!
BUT... WHAT ABOUT JEAN?
THERE'S NO "WHAT ABOUT JEAN," KID.
I'M SORRY. I REALLY AM.
BUT WHEN THOSE CREATURES-- THE POISONS--TAKE A SYMBIOTE, THEY USE UP WHOEVER'S WEARING IT TO CATALYZE THE PROCESS.
THEY TAKE THEIR BODIES...THEY TAKE THEIR MINDS.
JEAN'S DEAD.
WHAT DO YOU SAY, HENRY?
HAVE YOU USED THAT BIG BRAIN OF YOURS TO PUZZLE A WAY OUT OF THIS MESS?
I'M CALLING OUR RIDE RIGHT NOW.

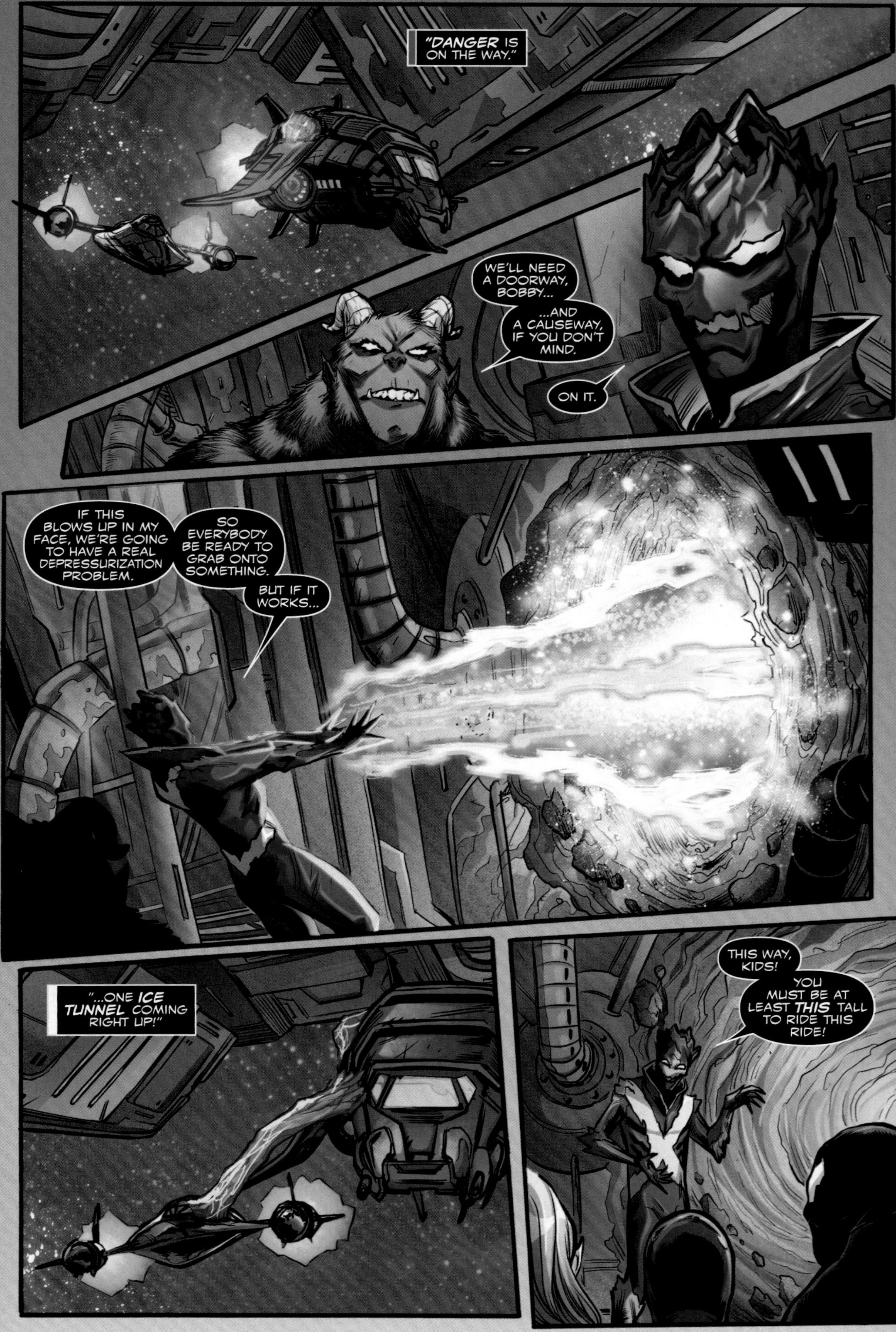
"DANGER IS ON THE WAY."
WE'LL NEED A DOORWAY, BOBBY...
...AND A CAUSEWAY, IF YOU DON'T MIND.
ON IT.
IF THIS BLOWS UP IN MY FACE, WE'RE GOING TO HAVE A REAL DEPRESSURIZATION PROBLEM.
SO EVERYBODY BE READY TO GRAB ONTO SOMETHING.
BUT IF IT WORKS...
"...ONE ICE TUNNEL COMING RIGHT UP!"
THIS WAY, KIDS!
YOU MUST BE AT LEAST THIS TALL TO RIDE THIS RIDE!

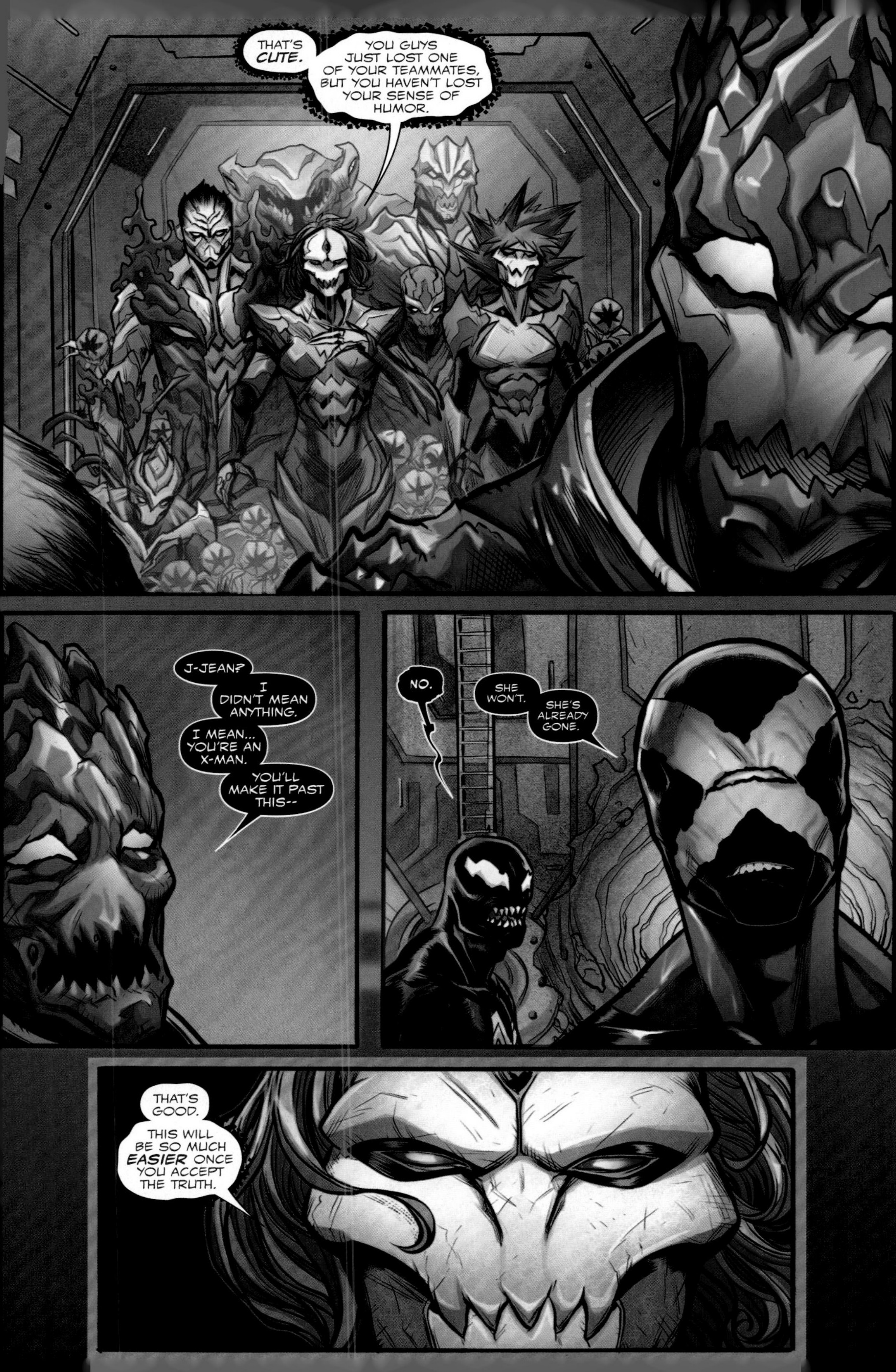
THAT'S CUTE.
YOU GUYS JUST LOST ONE OF YOUR TEAMMATES, BUT YOU HAVEN'T LOST YOUR SENSE OF HUMOR.
J-JEAN?
I DIDN'T MEAN ANYTHING.
I MEAN... YOU'RE AN X-MAN.
YOU'LL MAKE IT PAST THIS--
NO.
SHE WON'T.
SHE'S ALREADY GONE.
THAT'S GOOD.
THIS WILL BE SO MUCH EASIER ONCE YOU ACCEPT THE TRUTH.

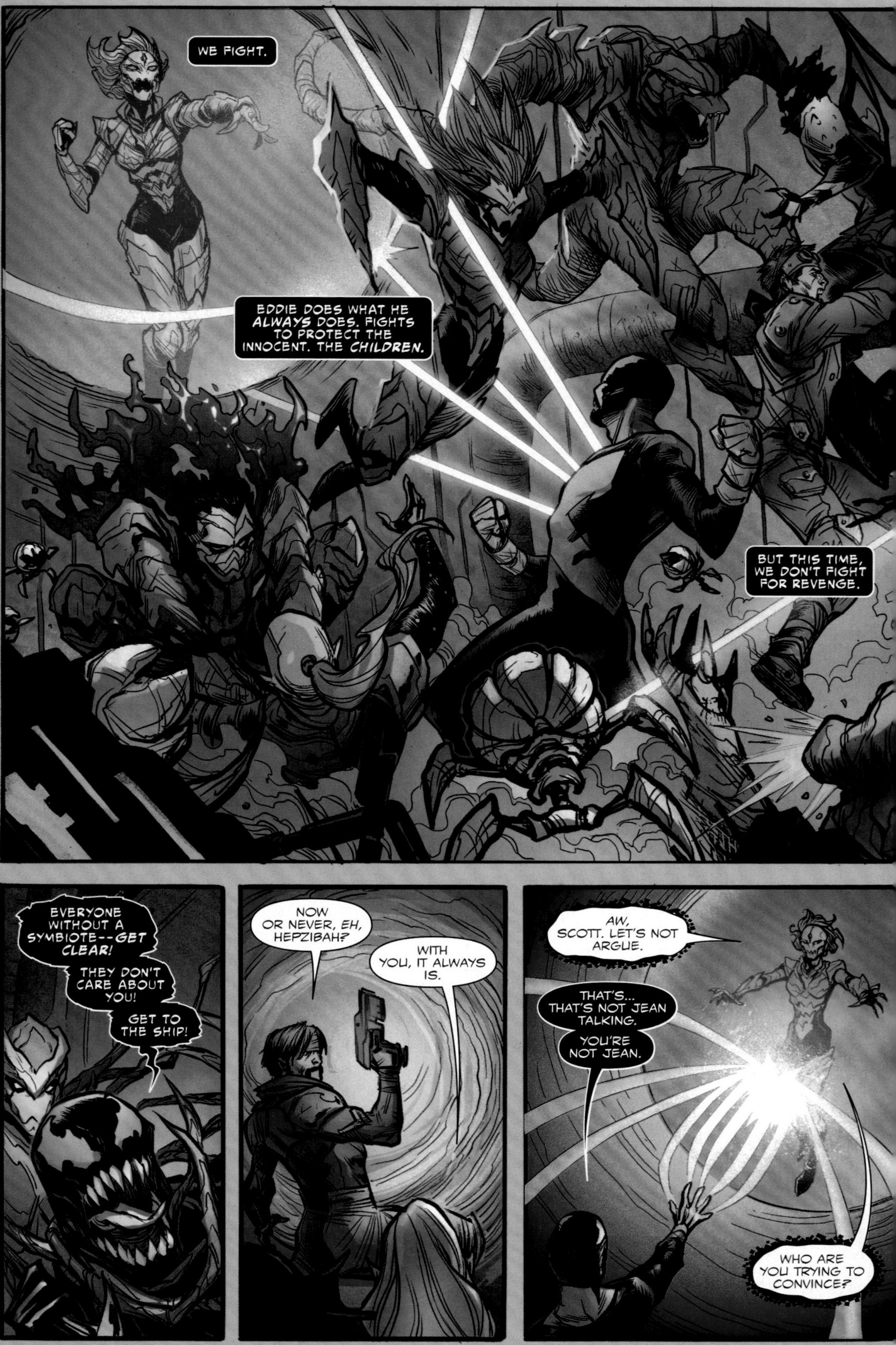
WE FIGHT.
EDDIE DOES WHAT HE ALWAYS DOES. FIGHTS TO PROTECT THE INNOCENT. THE CHILDREN.
BUT THIS TIME, WE DON'T FIGHT FOR REVENGE.
EVERYONE WITHOUT A SYMBIOTE--GET CLEAR!
THEY DON'T CARE ABOUT YOU!
GET TO THE SHIP!
NOW OR NEVER, EH, HEPZIBAH?
WITH YOU, IT ALWAYS IS.
AW, SCOTT. LET'S NOT ARGUE.
THAT'S... THAT'S NOT JEAN TALKING.
YOU'RE NOT JEAN.
WHO ARE YOU TRYING TO CONVINCE?

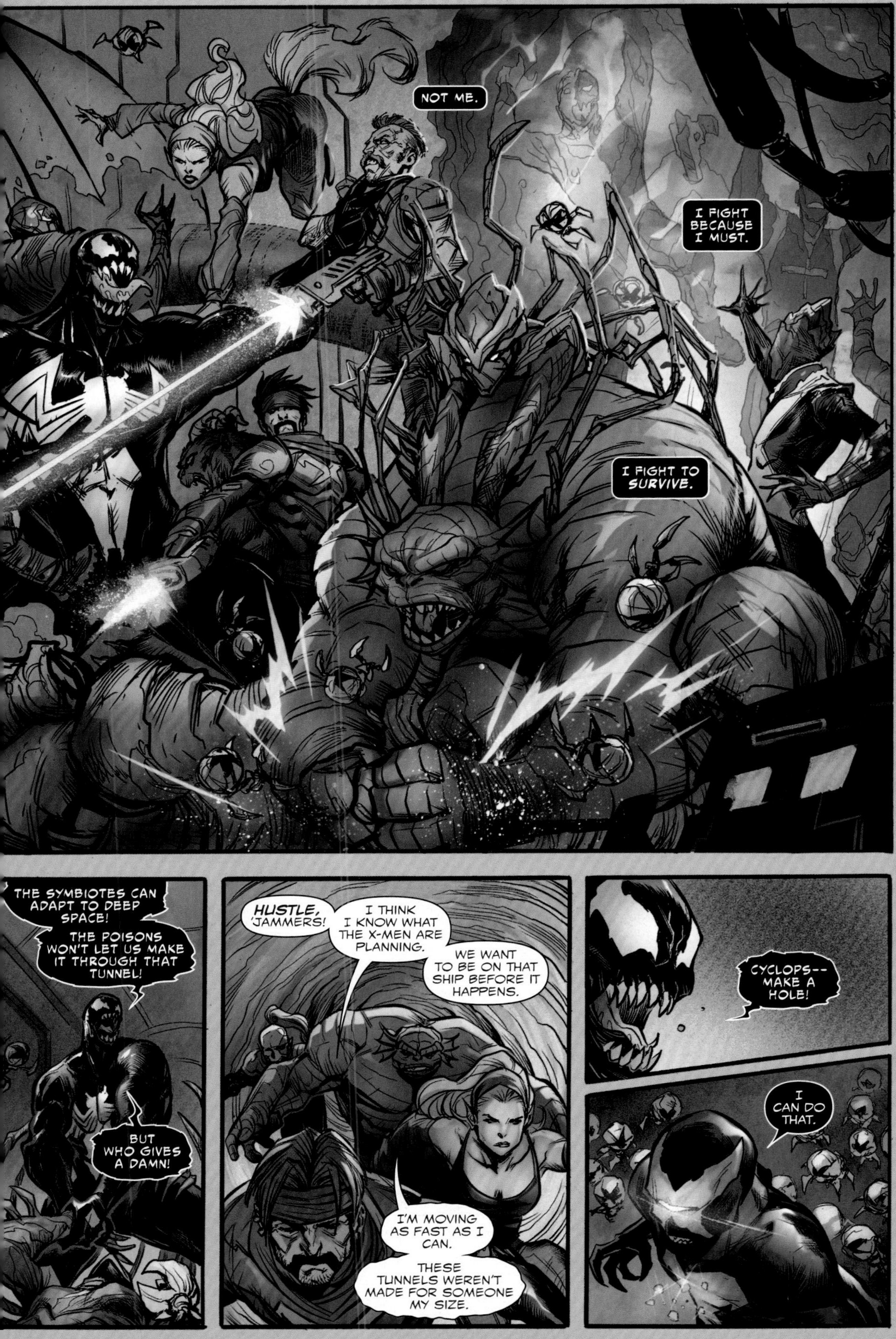
NOT ME.
I FIGHT BECAUSE I MUST.
I FIGHT TO SURVIVE.
THE SYMBIOTES CAN ADAPT TO DEEP SPACE!
THE POISONS WON'T LET US MAKE IT THROUGH THAT TUNNEL!
BUT WHO GIVES A DAMN!
HUSTLE, 'JAMMERS!
I THINK I KNOW WHAT THE X-MEN ARE PLANNING.
WE WANT TO BE ON THAT SHIP BEFORE IT HAPPENS.
I'M MOVING AS FAST AS I CAN.
THESE TUNNELS WEREN'T MADE FOR SOMEONE MY SIZE.
CYCLOPS-- MAKE A HOLE!
I CAN DO THAT.

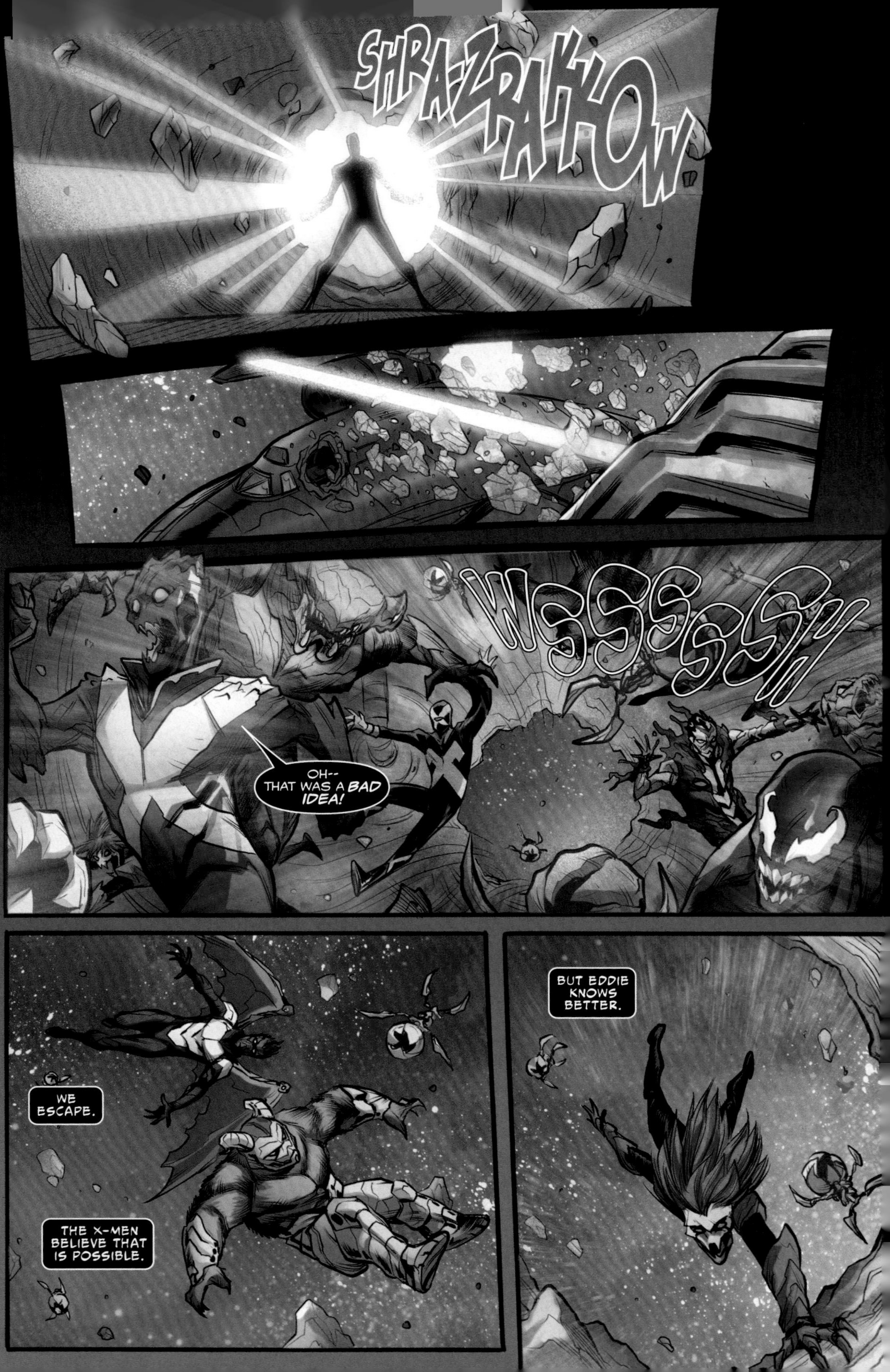
SHRA-ZRAKKOW
WSSSSSH
OH-- THAT WAS A BAD IDEA!
WE ESCAPE.
THE X-MEN BELIEVE THAT IS POSSIBLE.
BUT EDDIE KNOWS BETTER.

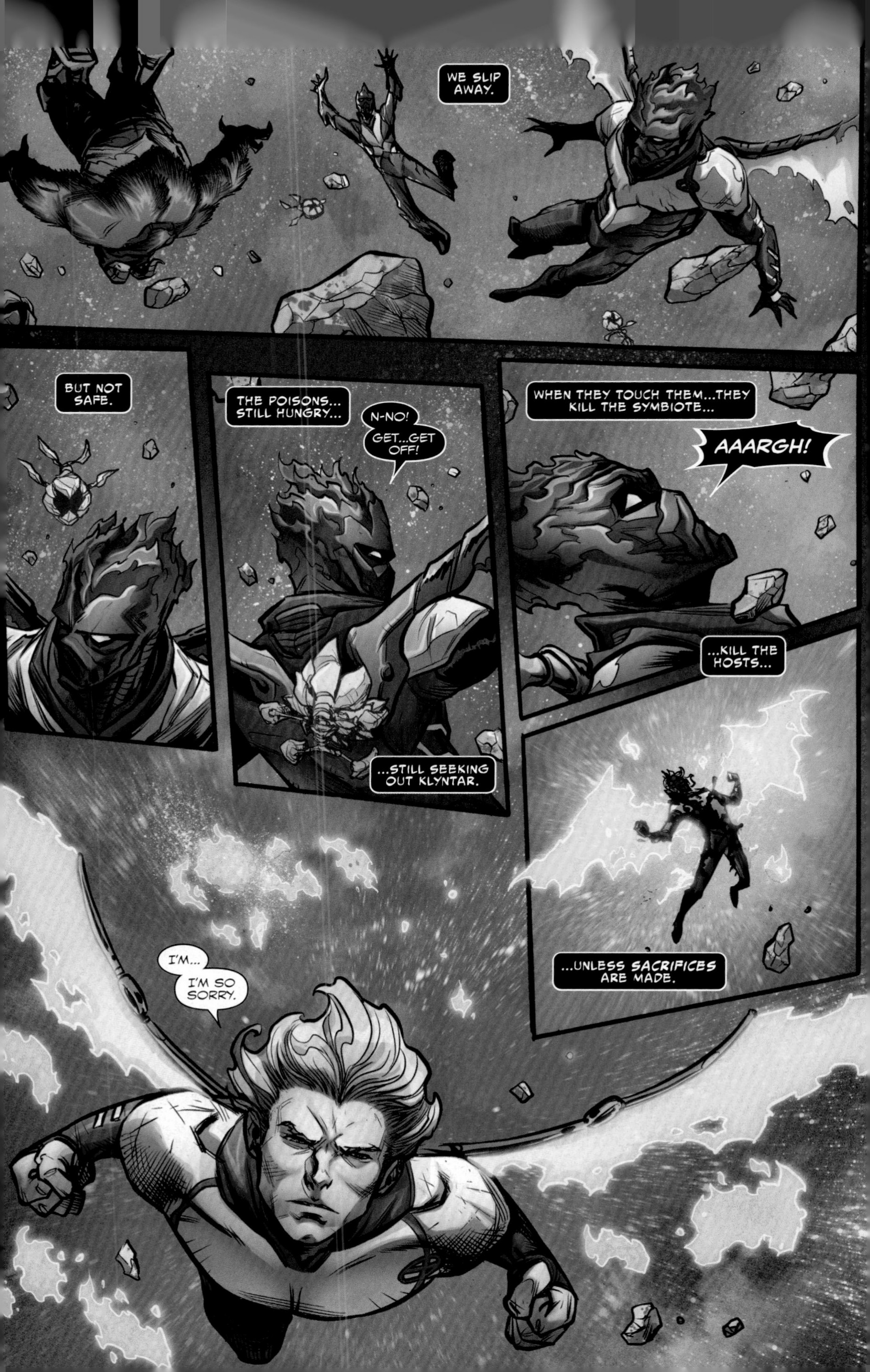
WE SLIP AWAY.
BUT NOT SAFE.
THE POISONS... STILL HUNGRY...
N-NO! GET...GET OFF!
...STILL SEEKING OUT KLYNTAR.
WHEN THEY TOUCH THEM...THEY KILL THE SYMBIOTE...
AAARGH!
...KILL THE HOSTS...
...UNLESS SACRIFICES ARE MADE.
I'M... I'M SO SORRY.

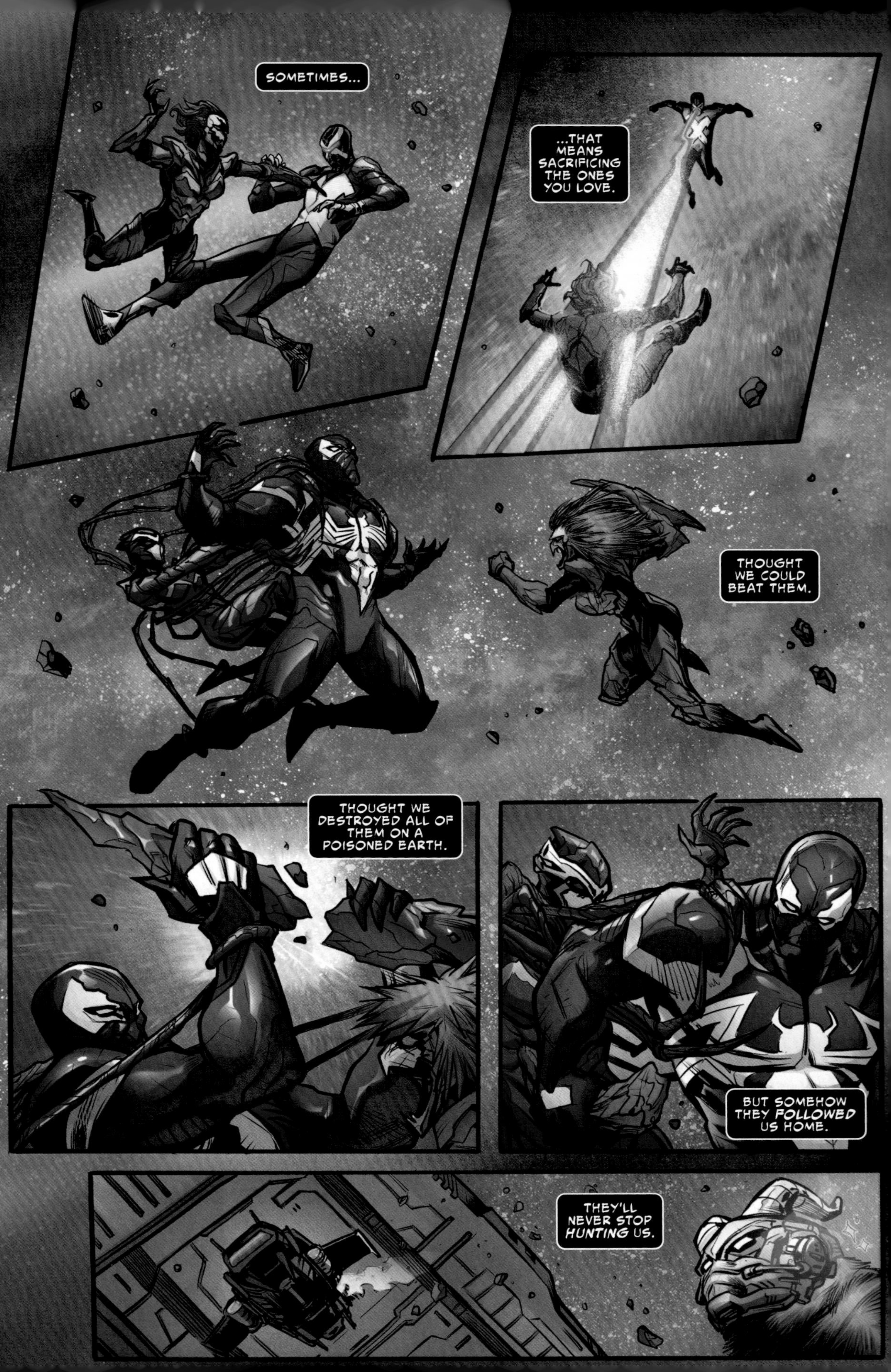
SOMETIMES...
...THAT MEANS SACRIFICING THE ONES YOU LOVE.
THOUGHT WE COULD BEAT THEM.
THOUGHT WE DESTROYED ALL OF THEM ON A POISONED EARTH.
BUT SOMEHOW THEY *FOLLOWED* US HOME.
THEY'LL NEVER STOP *HUNTING* US.

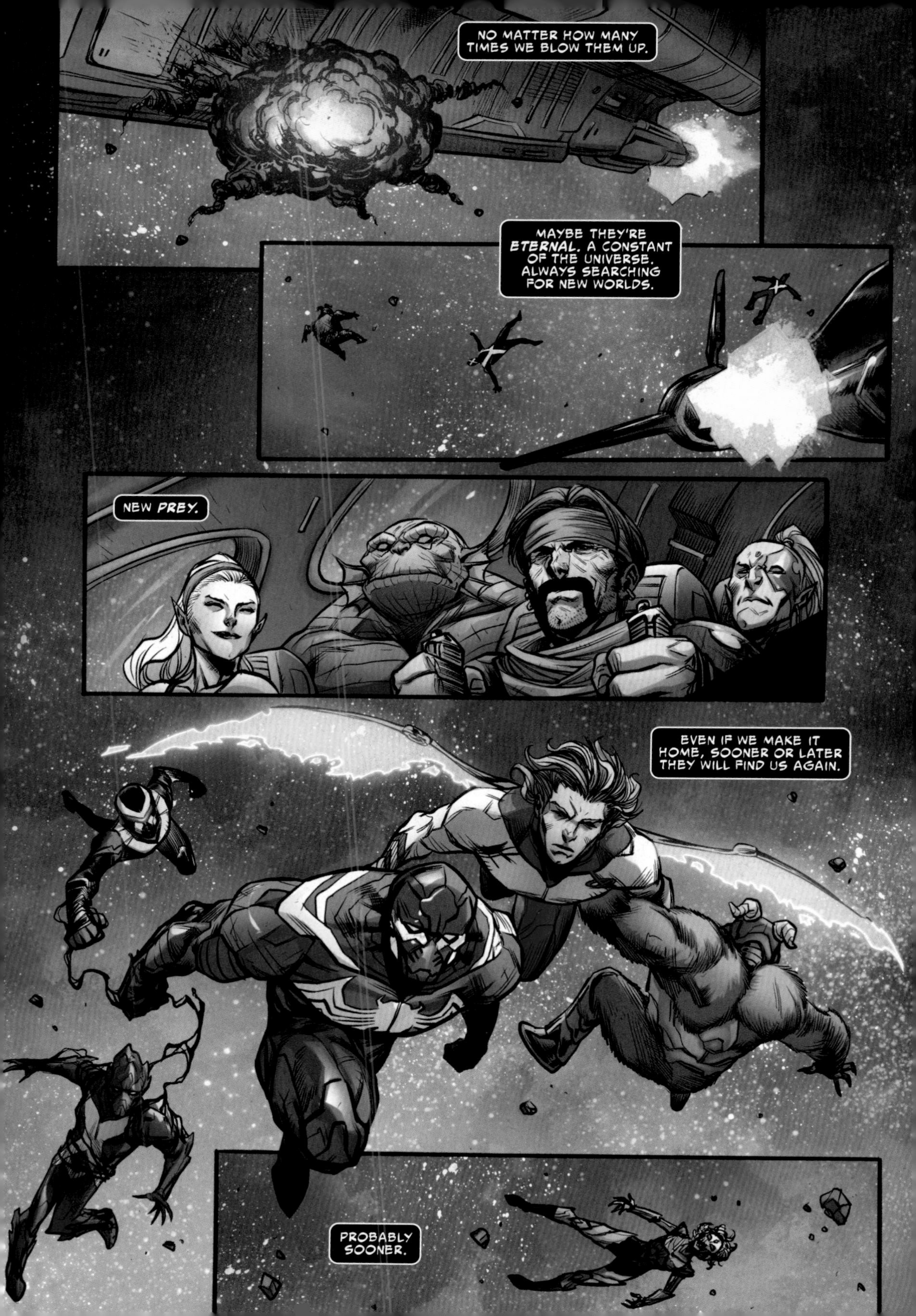
NO MATTER HOW MANY TIMES WE BLOW THEM UP.
MAYBE THEY'RE *ETERNAL.* A CONSTANT OF THE UNIVERSE. ALWAYS SEARCHING FOR NEW WORLDS.
NEW *PREY.*
EVEN IF WE MAKE IT HOME, SOONER OR LATER THEY WILL FIND US AGAIN.
PROBABLY SOONER.

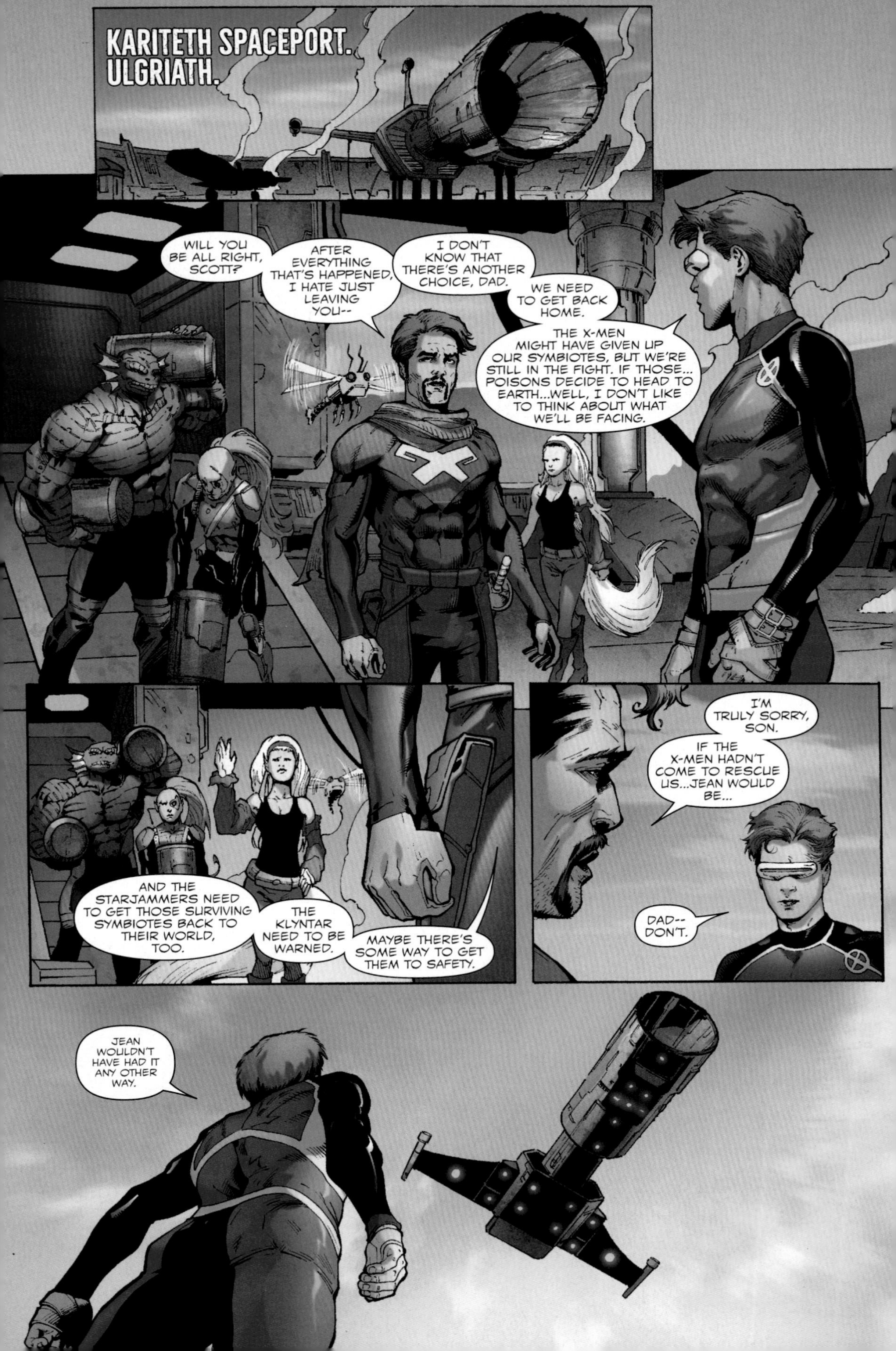
KARITETH SPACEPORT. ULGRIATH.
WILL YOU BE ALL RIGHT, SCOTT?
AFTER EVERYTHING THAT'S HAPPENED, I HATE JUST LEAVING YOU--
I DON'T KNOW THAT THERE'S ANOTHER CHOICE, DAD.
WE NEED TO GET BACK HOME.
THE X-MEN MIGHT HAVE GIVEN UP OUR SYMBIOTES, BUT WE'RE STILL IN THE FIGHT. IF THOSE... POISONS DECIDE TO HEAD TO EARTH...WELL, I DON'T LIKE TO THINK ABOUT WHAT WE'LL BE FACING.
AND THE STARJAMMERS NEED TO GET THOSE SURVIVING SYMBIOTES BACK TO THEIR WORLD, TOO.
THE KLYNTAR NEED TO BE WARNED.
MAYBE THERE'S SOME WAY TO GET THEM TO SAFETY.
I'M TRULY SORRY, SON.
IF THE X-MEN HADN'T COME TO RESCUE US...JEAN WOULD BE...
DAD-- DON'T.
JEAN WOULDN'T HAVE HAD IT ANY OTHER WAY.

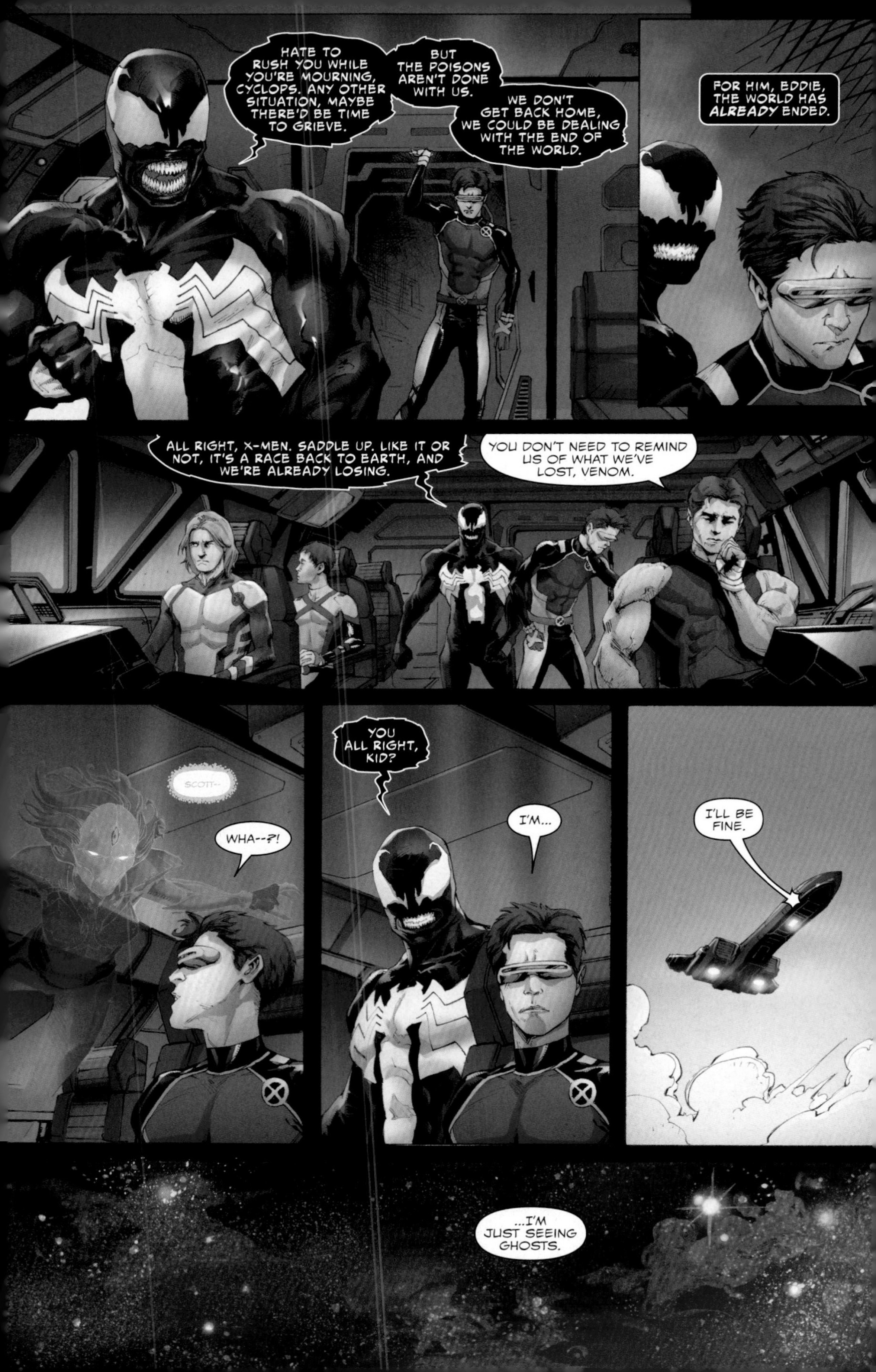
HATE TO RUSH YOU WHILE YOU'RE MOURNING, CYCLOPS. ANY OTHER SITUATION, MAYBE THERE'D BE TIME TO GRIEVE.
BUT THE POISONS AREN'T DONE WITH US.
WE DON'T GET BACK HOME, WE COULD BE DEALING WITH THE END OF THE WORLD.
FOR HIM, EDDIE, THE WORLD HAS ALREADY ENDED.
ALL RIGHT, X-MEN. SADDLE UP. LIKE IT OR NOT, IT'S A RACE BACK TO EARTH, AND WE'RE ALREADY LOSING.
YOU DON'T NEED TO REMIND US OF WHAT WE'VE LOST, VENOM.
SCOTT--
WHA--?!
YOU ALL RIGHT, KID?
I'M...
I'LL BE FINE.
...I'M JUST SEEING GHOSTS.

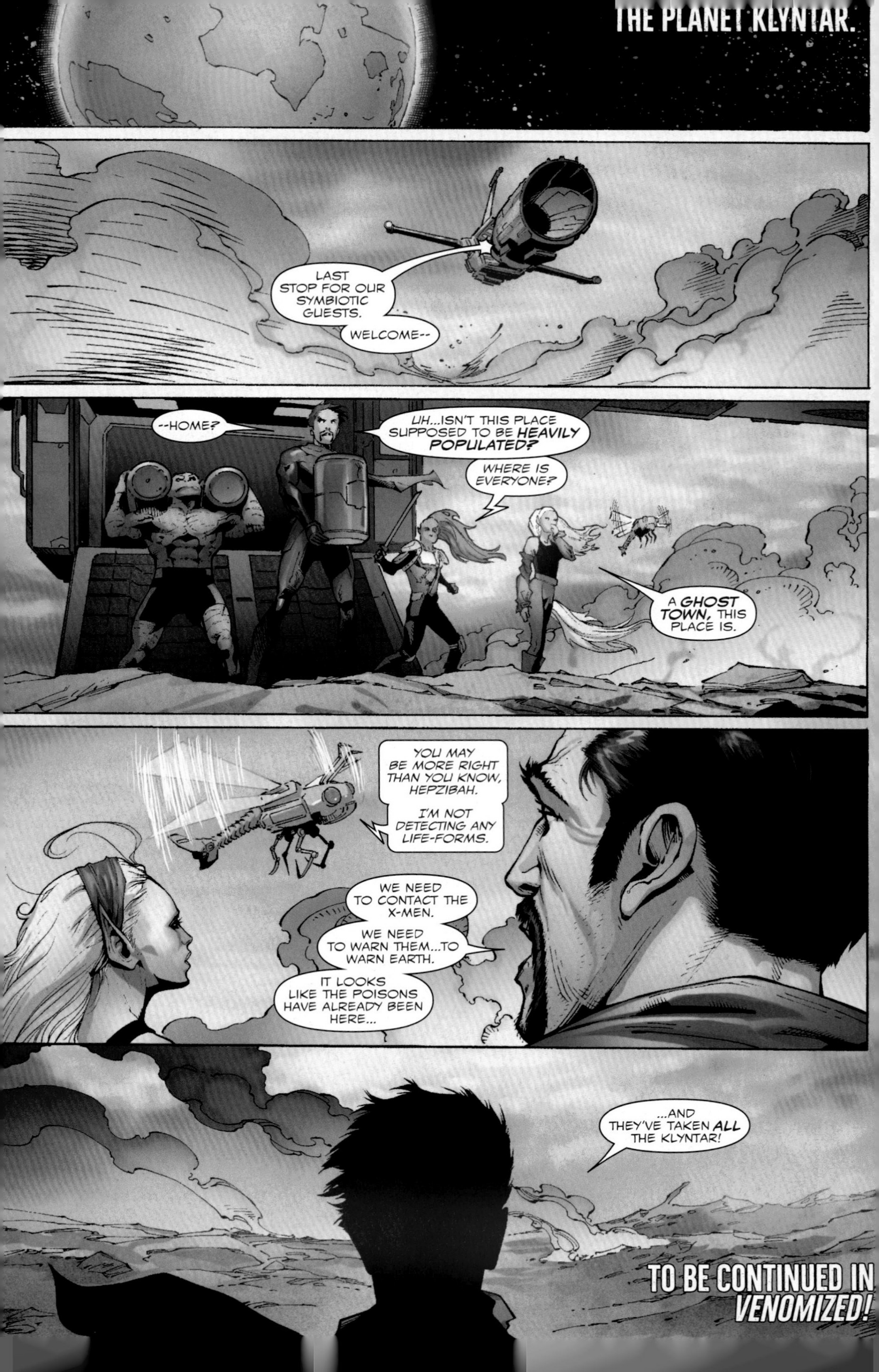
THE PLANET KLYNTAR.
LAST STOP FOR OUR SYMBIOTIC GUESTS.
WELCOME--
--HOME?
UH...ISN'T THIS PLACE SUPPOSED TO BE HEAVILY POPULATED?
WHERE IS EVERYONE?
A GHOST TOWN, THIS PLACE IS.
YOU MAY BE MORE RIGHT THAN YOU KNOW, HEPZIBAH.
I'M NOT DETECTING ANY LIFE-FORMS.
WE NEED TO CONTACT THE X-MEN.
WE NEED TO WARN THEM...TO WARN EARTH.
IT LOOKS LIKE THE POISONS HAVE ALREADY BEEN HERE...
...AND THEY'VE TAKEN ALL THE KLYNTAR!
TO BE CONTINUED IN VENOMIZED!

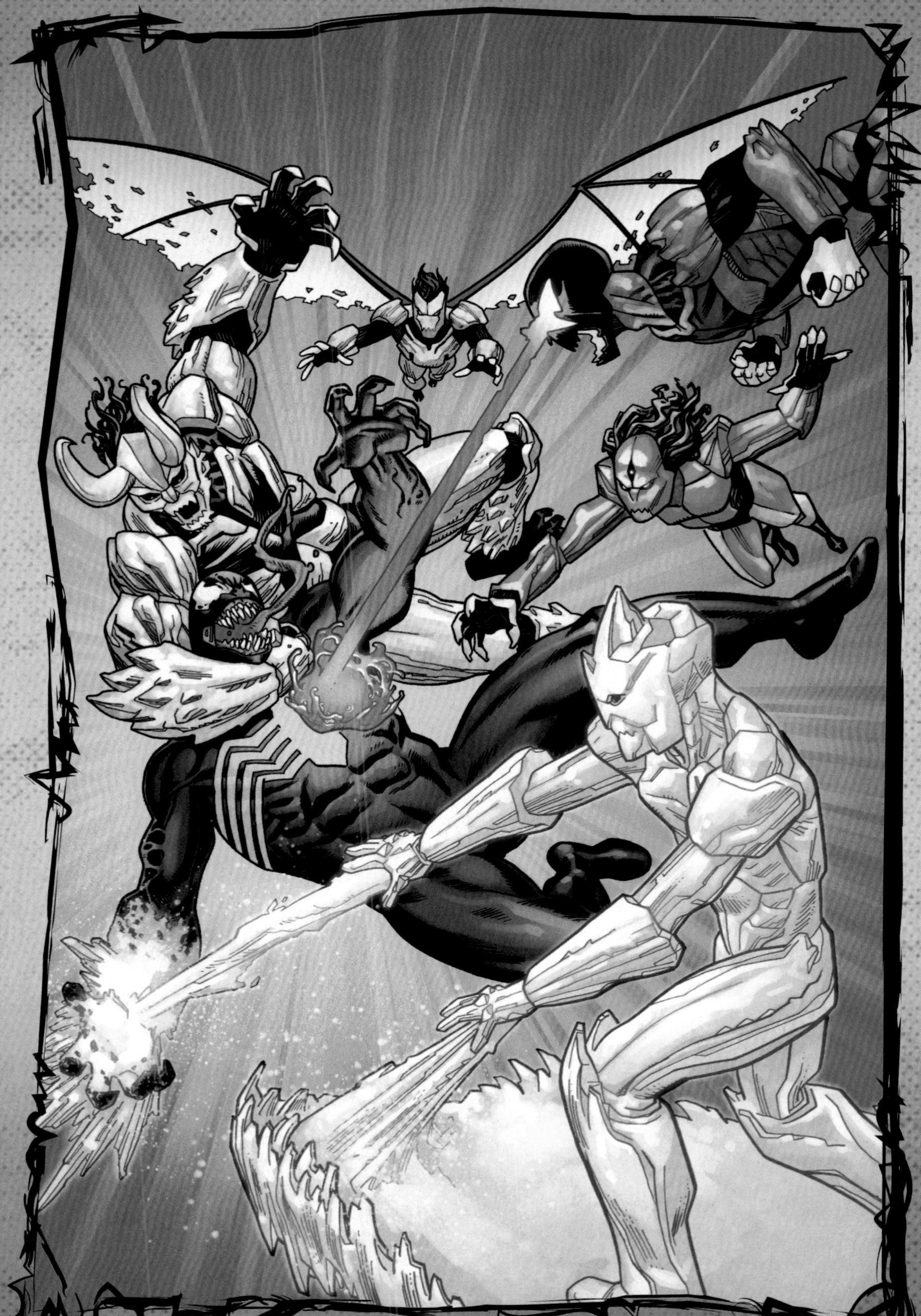

X-MEN BLUE ANNUAL #1 VARIANT
BY ***MIKE HAWTHORNE*** & ***GURU-eFX***

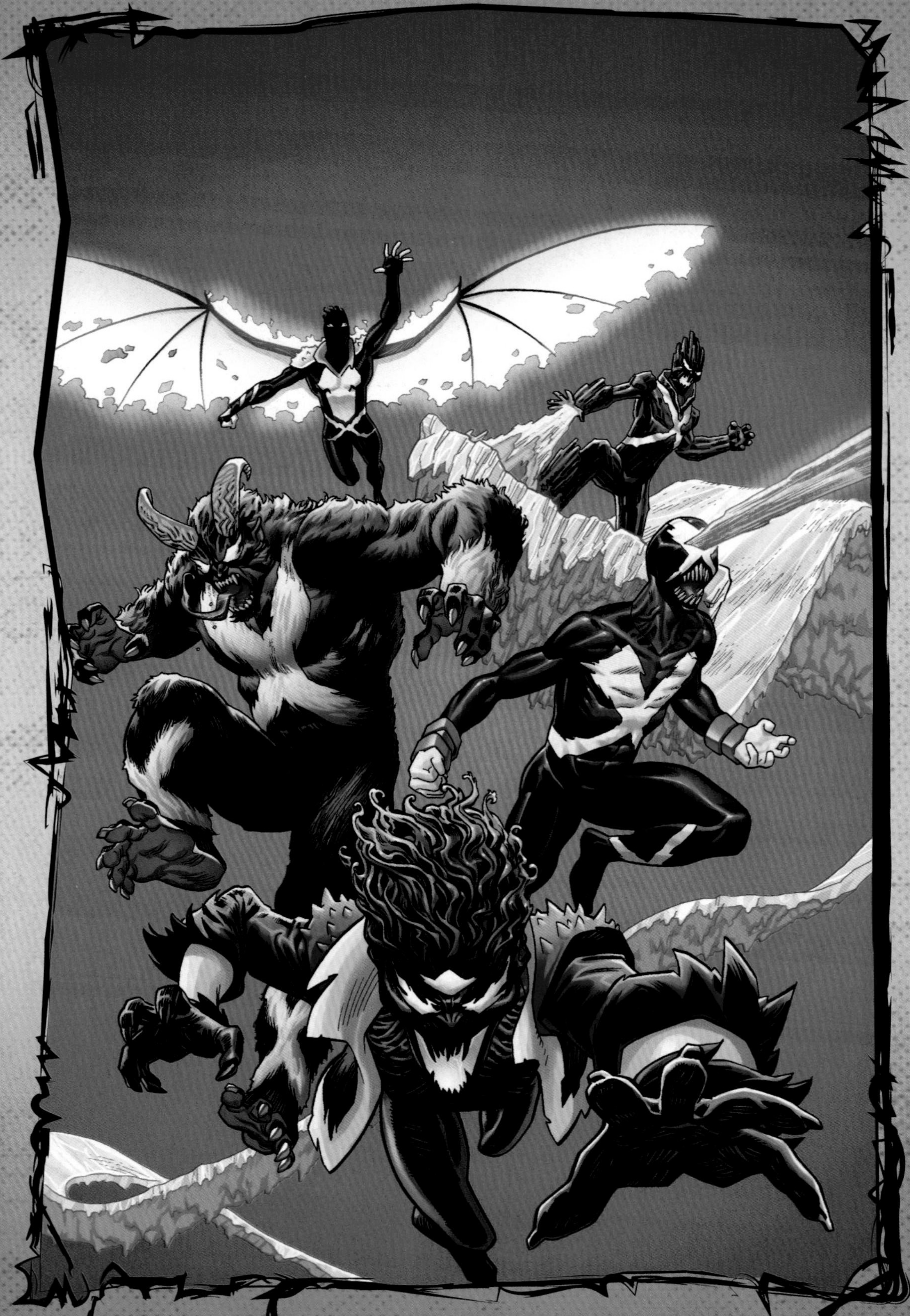

X-MEN BLUE ANNUAL#1 VARIANT
BY **_MIKE HAWTHORNE_** & **_NOLAN WOODARD_**

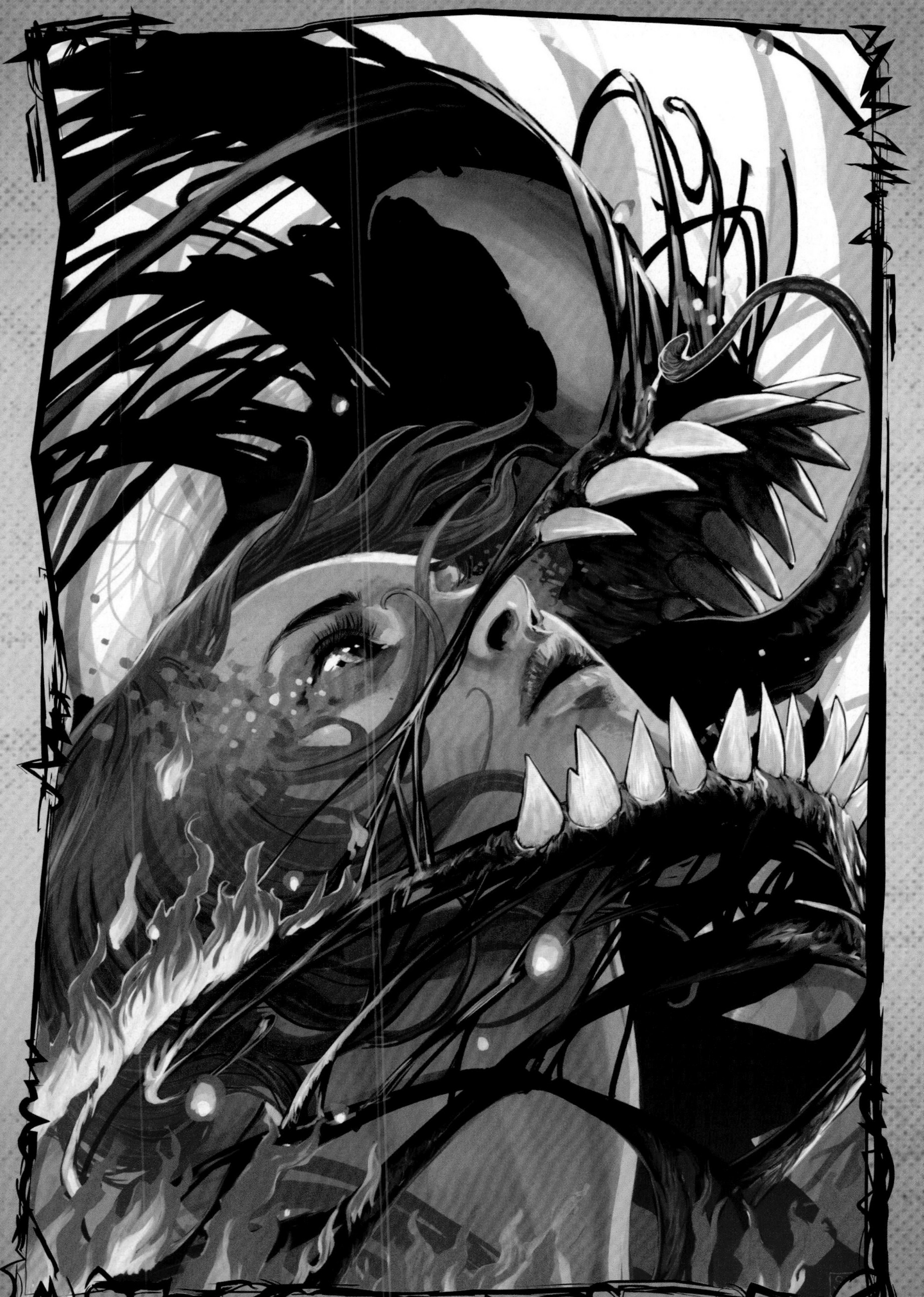

X-MEN BLUE #22 VARIANT BY **STEPHANIE HANS**

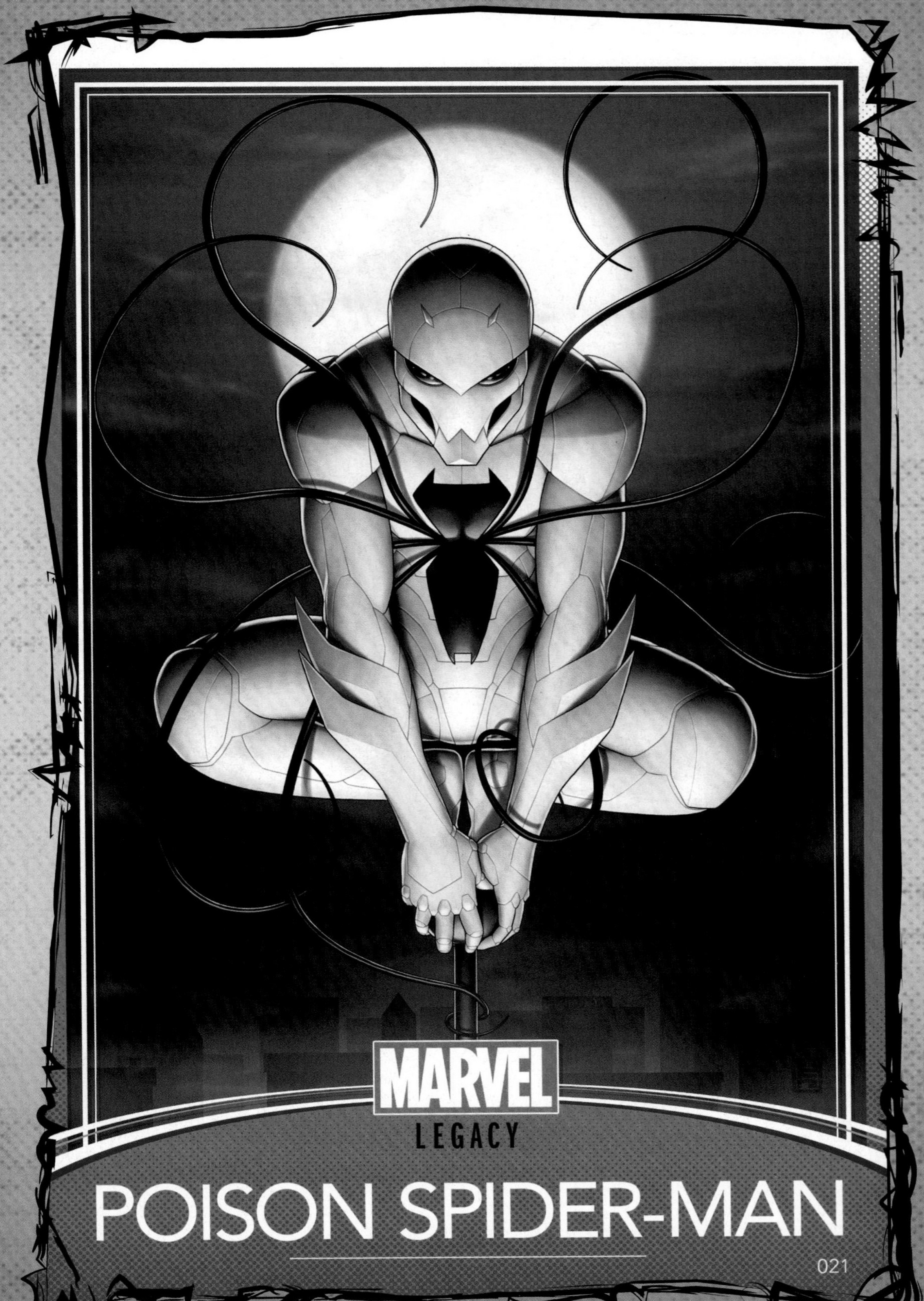
MARVEL
LEGACY
POISON SPIDER-MAN
021

X-MEN BLUE #21 TRADING CARD VARIANT
BY *JOHN TYLER CHRISTOPHER*

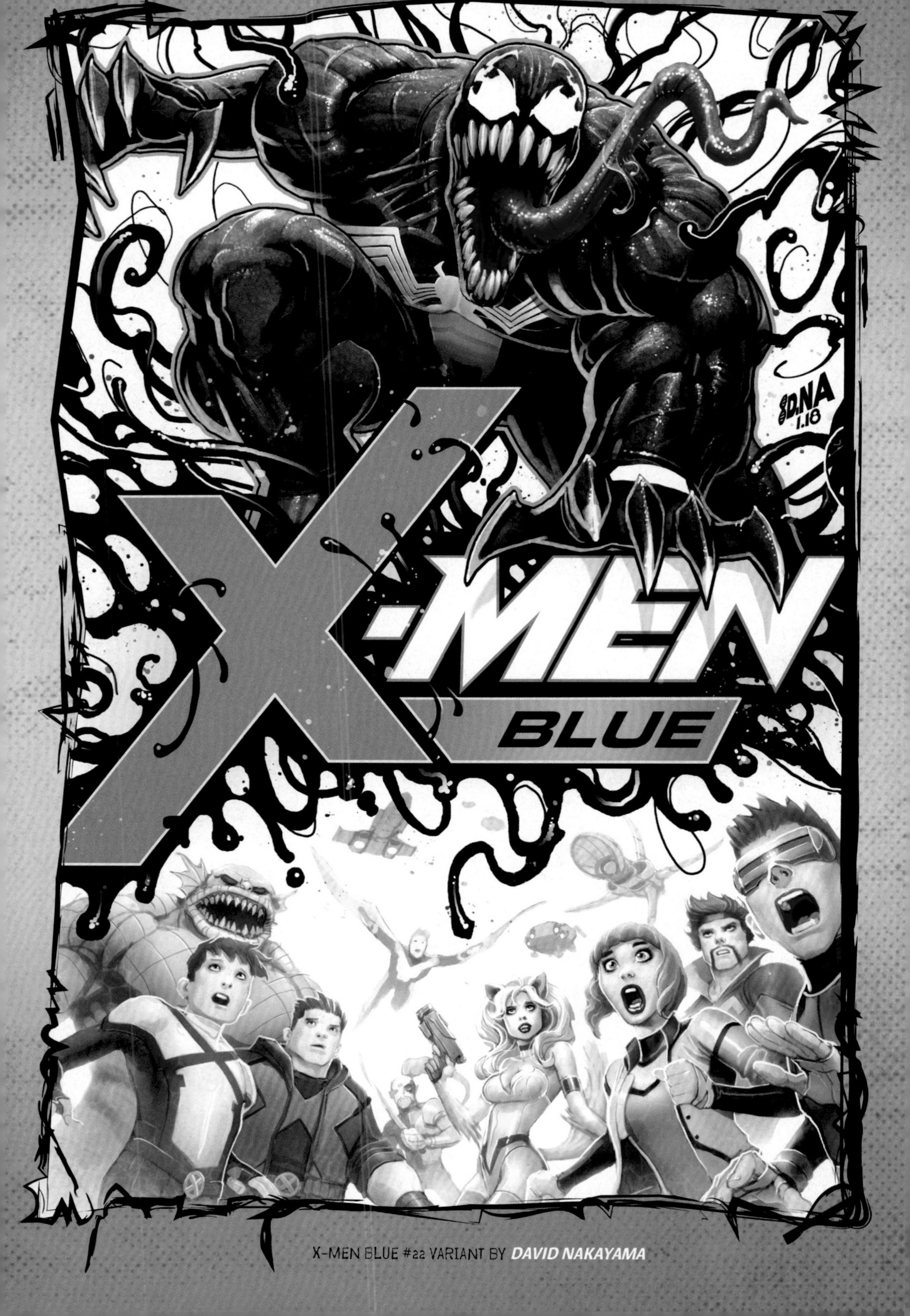
D.NA
1.18
X-MEN
BLUE

X-MEN BLUE #22 VARIANT BY ***DAVID NAKAYAMA***

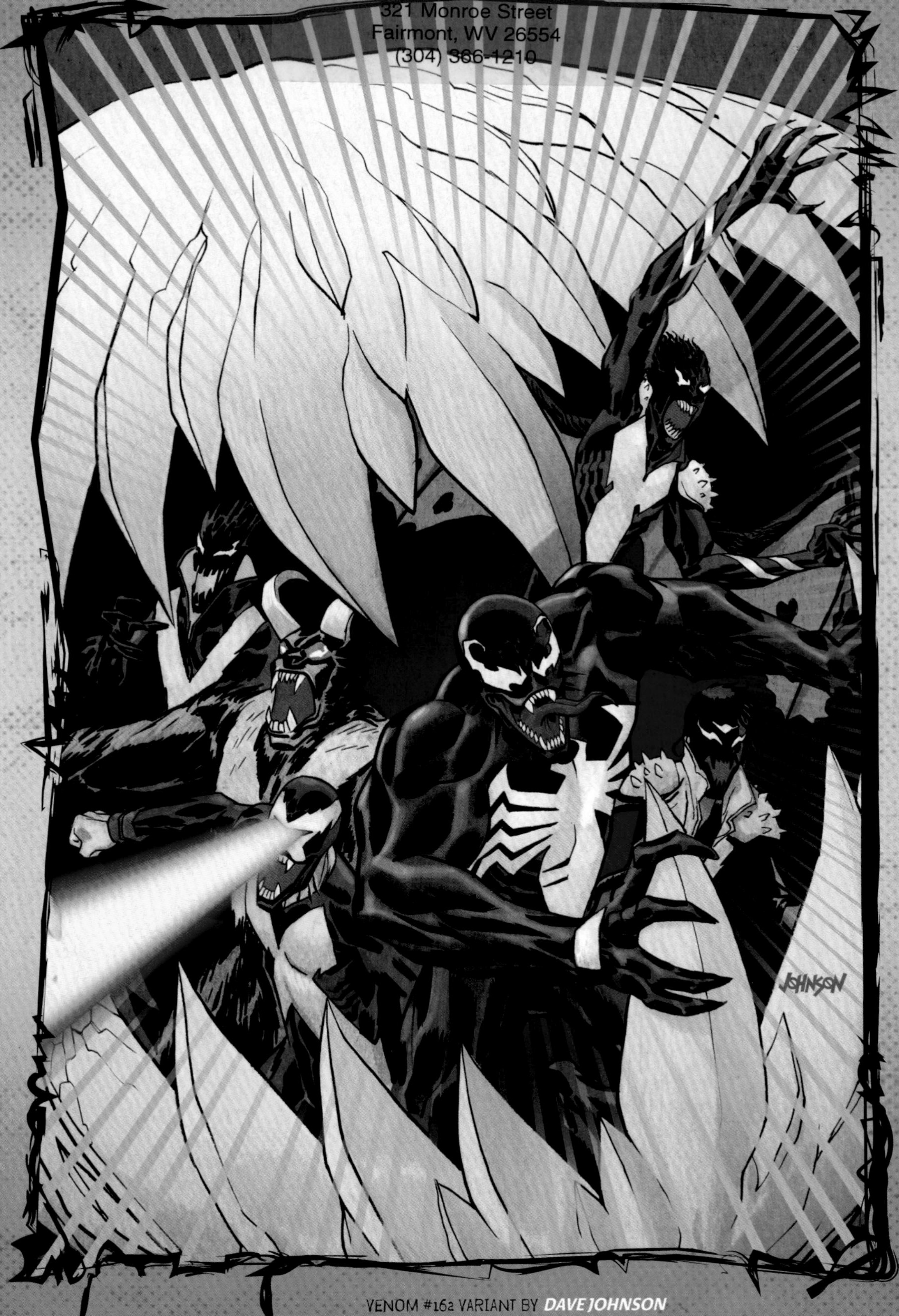
JOHNSON

VENOM #162 VARIANT BY ***DAVE JOHNSON***